Discover Economics

Discover Economics

Graham Teager

PITMAN PUBLISHING
128 Long Acre, London WC2E 9AN

First published in Great Britain 1985
Reprinted 1987

British Library Cataloguing in Publication Data

Teager, Graham
   Discover economics.
   1. Economics—Examinations, questions, etc.
   I. Title
   330'.076   HB171.5

Typeset and printed in Great Britain at The Bath Press, Avon

ISBN 0 273 02061 7

Contents

Acknowledgments

The authors and publishers would like to thank the following for permission to reproduce copyright material:

Andrew Aarons

Bairstow Eves
Barclays Bank
British Caledonian Airways Ltd
British Insurance Association
British Petroleum plc
British Railways Board
British Standards Institute
Building Societies Association

Controller of Her Majesty's Stationery Office
Cooperative Development Agency
Cooperative Union Ltd

Daily Express
Daily Mail
Daily Star
Daventry District Council Planning Department
Department of Employment
Department of Trade and Industry

Engineering Careers Information Service
Everest Double Glazing
Essex County Council
European Parliament

Ford Motor Company Ltd

Granada Television
Grand Metropolitan plc
Guardian Newspaper

HMSO

Ilford Recorder

Knitting, Lace and Net Industry Training Board
LBC Radio
Lloyds Bank
Londis (Holdings) Ltd
Low Pay Unit
Mauritius Trade Delegation
National Union of Public Employees
National Westminster Bank plc
Observer
Polly Toynbee
Port of London Authority
Redbridge Area Health Authority
Richard Baxendale (Baxi Heating)
Road Haulage Association Ltd
Royal Mint
Sainsbury plc
Selfridges
South Wales Electricity Consultative Council
Surrey County Cricket Club
Tesco plc
The Bank of England
The CBI
The Central Electricity Board
The GLC
The Mail on Sunday
The Stock Exchange
The Transport and General Workers Union
The TUC
Tottenham Hotspur Football and Athletic Club

The author would also like to thank those colleagues who offered helpful advice, in particular, Steve Hodkinson, Deputy Director of 14–16 Economics Project.

1 The Economic Problem

CASE STUDY

Tottenham Hotspur Football and Athletic Company

The income of a football club depends mainly upon the sale of tickets for home matches. This will in turn depend upon the success of the club. If it does well in knockout competitions, like the Milk Cup (formerly the League Cup), the FA Cup and the various European Championships then it will play more home matches:

Tottenham Hotspur (Income/Number of Home Games)

Season ending	No of home games	Gross Income £'000
May 1981	57	2 464
May 1982	65	3 873
May 1983	54	3 566

Average Home League Attendances at White Hart Lane (Cap: 50 000)

Season Ending May	1979	1980	1981	1982	1983
Average League Gate	34 900	32 000	30 700	35 100	30 600

Note In 1981 and 1982 Tottenham Hotspur won the FA Cup. Therefore in 1982 not only did they take part in all rounds of that competition but also took part in the European Cup Winners' Cup as the previous years winners of the FA Cup.

Source Tottenham Hotspur prospectus October 1983

As the previous tables show it is not only how many games that are played which determine income but also how many people pay to watch those games. White Hart Lane, like so many other Football Clubs, does not always attract a full house to league matches. In 1983 the club made £168 000 trading profit but because transfer fees cost a net £617 000 it left a net loss of £449 000.

Clearly, the best way for the club to earn more income would be to attract more people to watch home matches. How could this be done? There are several ways:

a buy new players
b improve ground facilities
c advertise matches on radio and television

In recent years Tottenham like other clubs have tried all 3 of these suggestions and many more.

They have 31 registered professional players, 19 in the 'first team pool' of whom 12 have represented their country.

The Club's new West Stand built in 1982 cost £$5\frac{1}{4}$m and includes not only seating to watch the games but also bars, restaurants, banqueting

1

and conference accommodation, the players' changing rooms and club offices. This recent large expenditure partly explains the Club's debts which stood at £3.2m in September 1983.

Advertising matches is a fairly new idea at Tottenham. During the 1982–83 season some home matches were advertised on commercial radio. This experiment was taken further during the following season by the appointment of Saatchi and Saatchi, the famous advertising agency, which, with a budget of £100 000, has also produced television commercials.

It is perhaps too soon to evaluate the success of this venture; time will tell whether additional spending on advertising will help to fill the ground on Saturday afternoons.

The Tottenham Hotspur case study illustrates an important idea which is central to the study of economics. Tottenham are an important and rich football club. They do not, however, have unlimited funds. This requires their directors to make a **choice**—how to spend these funds. This year they chose to spend £100 000 on an advertising campaign. They could have spent this on additional playing staff, ground improvements, higher wages for the players or have paid off some of their debts. Once this decision was made those funds were committed to advertising and could not be spent upon anything else—ever!

People, businesses and governments are making such choices all the time.

Exercise

Between 1979 and 1983 Surrey County Cricket Club relaid 20 pitches at their ground, the Oval, Kennington. This for many people has meant better cricket viewing, since the wicket is now less unpredictable. It cost £12 000 and included the hire of digging equipment, lorries, extra staff, top soil and grass seed.

1 To what alternative uses could the Club have put this £12 000?

2 Why do you think the committee decided to improve the playing pitches?

Most people have found themselves in the position of wanting more than they can afford. Perhaps you have received money for a birthday present and found several ways you could spend it—the trouble is you can only spend the money in **one** way. You must make a **choice**.

Much of the world faces a similar dilemma. The resources of the world are limited. There are a fixed amount of minerals and chemicals, land and sea and they have been here for millions of years. Many resources have yet to be discovered but the total is limited. The population of the world is vast and growing quickly—6 350 million by the year 2000. These people all have **wants**—as the population grows so their wants increase (see Fig 1).

Economics is about just how we decide which of the ever growing wants of the world to satisfy. Also how best to use the limited resources avail-

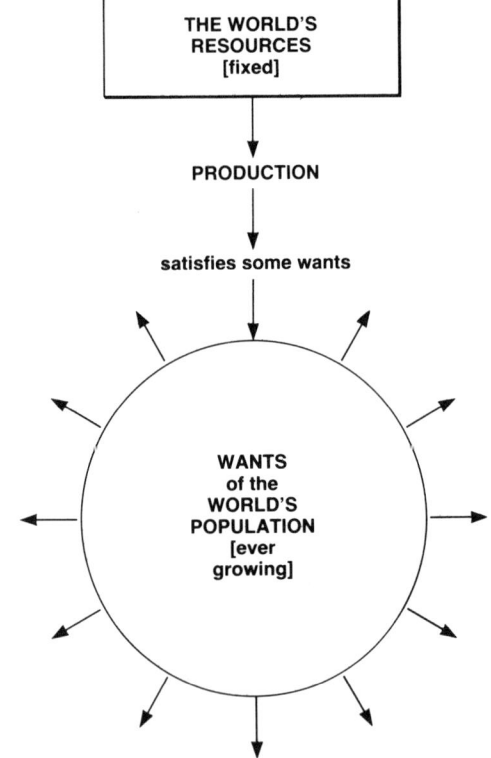

Fig 1 Scarcity—the economic problem

able to maximise production.

If we satisfy some wants we will not be able to satisfy others. This basic idea is called **opportunity cost**. If we use metal and wood to make guns we cannot use that same metal and wood to make a kidney machine. The opportunity cost is the lost alternative use of given resources.

Most of the goods and services that people want do not occur naturally so have to be manufactured or **produced**. Economics investigates how decisions about what to produce—which wants to satisfy—are made. Not all of these wants can be satisfied and for this reason economics has been called the 'gloomy science' or the 'science of scarcity'. Neither is correct. Economics can be fun, interesting and even exciting. The economist looks at the problem of scarcity and suggests how production can be made more efficient so that more wants can be satisfied. He helps businessmen and politicians make good decisions by looking at alternative uses of resources and comparing them in a systematic and logical way. The study of economics should help you make sensible choices in your life.

Wants and Needs

It is important to distinguish between **wants** and **needs**.

In order to survive we **need**:

1 **Air**
2 **Water**
3 **Food**
4 **Warmth/shelter**

These are listed in the order in which, if they were not supplied, people would cease to exist most quickly. If a person were denied **air** for example they would last for only a few seconds but they could survive for several days without food. Air is very important to a person's survival but it is free which at first appears strange. Air is one of the few basic human needs which is not scarce in most places on earth. It is free for people to use as they need and is called a **free good**.

If all the goods and services which people wanted were listed it would fill the rest of this book. It is certain that for many people most of their wants will never be satisfied and for some even basic needs are barely catered for.

Exercise

1 Where might **air** not be free?
2 Where might the other needs listed above be **free goods?**
3 Give **one** want which would be satisfied, in this country, for a person even if they could not afford to buy it.
4 Give **one** want which might not be satisfied for a person however rich they might be.
5 Give **one** further **free good**.

Opportunity Costs

Once the decision has been made to use some resources to satisfy one particular want, it cannot then be used to satisfy any further wants. If the wood from a tree is pulped to make paper then it cannot be used to manufacture furniture. If a teenager uses birthday money to buy a record then she cannot use it to have her hair styled. If a local council uses £1 million to build a sports centre that money cannot be used to build an old peoples' home. Economists call these lost alternatives the **opportunity costs** of using the resources. In the first case study the opportunity cost to Tottenham Hotspur of advertising might be a new player not signed.

It is a fact that the money required to provide adequate food, water, education, health and housing for everyone in the world has been estimated at £17 billion a year. It is a huge sum of money, about as much as the world spends on arms every two weeks.

Perhaps the economist would say that the opportunity cost of war and mistrust is malnutrition and poor housing.

Classifying Resources

The resources used in the production of goods and services are not all of the same type. They can be classified into **four** main types.

The assignment overleaf highlights these.

ASSIGNMENT

An unemployed school leaver discovers a new board game similar to chess but not quite so complicated. With the aid of her father she makes a prototype in her garden shed. To her surprise everyone likes it which leads her to think of starting her own business.

List all of the things she would need to start a small business to make and sell this game. It is mainly constructed from wood. (Do not put down money—which she would clearly need—only the resources she would need to buy.)

The resources listed in your answer to the assignment (the resources needed for production), ought to fall into 4 categories:

1 Natural resources
To produce anything you will need some land—to produce it on. This, however, is not the only resource included here. You will also need raw materials and minerals to produce most goods and perhaps geographical features, like the sea or rivers or even climatic conditions.

2 Human resources
Machines can do a great deal but we still need people to help produce goods and services—even if it is only to push buttons! Here we must include all contributions made by humans whether it be with their hands, as with a carpenter, or their minds, as with an accountant.

3 Man-made resources
Some goods called either **producer goods** or **capital goods** are made in order to help make other goods and services to satisfy certain wants. For example, factory buildings, machines and equipment. We do not want these to satisfy wants directly—nobody wants a fork-lift truck in the garage instead of a car—nor would you want to sit and watch a lathe instead of a television. We need to produce these capital goods in order to produce those goods we do want.

4 Enterprise/risk taking
This is a special type of human resource. To make anything you need natural, human and man-made resources. These resources will not come together to satisfy wants on their own. In our example you would have to decide to make the board game and bring together the necessary resources even if these were only the back garden, you, a friend, a rusty saw and a few pieces of wood. The people who bring together the resources necessary for production and start that production; even the person who decides to take these resources and make cars, plastic garden gnomes or kidney machines is called an **entrepreneur**. These people start or initiate production and in so doing they take a risk. It is their money and expertise that are put into the project and if the good or service sells well they will be rewarded with large profits.

If you look at Fig 2 you will see that it is much the same as Fig 1 only more complicated. At the top are the world's resources broken down into different types. To produce anything we need natural, human and man-made resources brought together by enterprise.

As you can see, the actual making of the good is called **production**. Not all goods are the same. In the diagram we distinguish between 3 types of output.

CONSUMER GOODS

These are all those products which satisfy wants. We can see them, touch them, buy them and take them home. Some we call **durable consumer goods** because they last a long time, eg washing machines, televisions and cars. Others only last a very short while and are called **non-durable consumer goods**, eg food, matches or a pint of beer.

SERVICES

Sometimes our wants are satisfied by someone doing something for us. We call these **services**. An example would be a visit to the dentist.

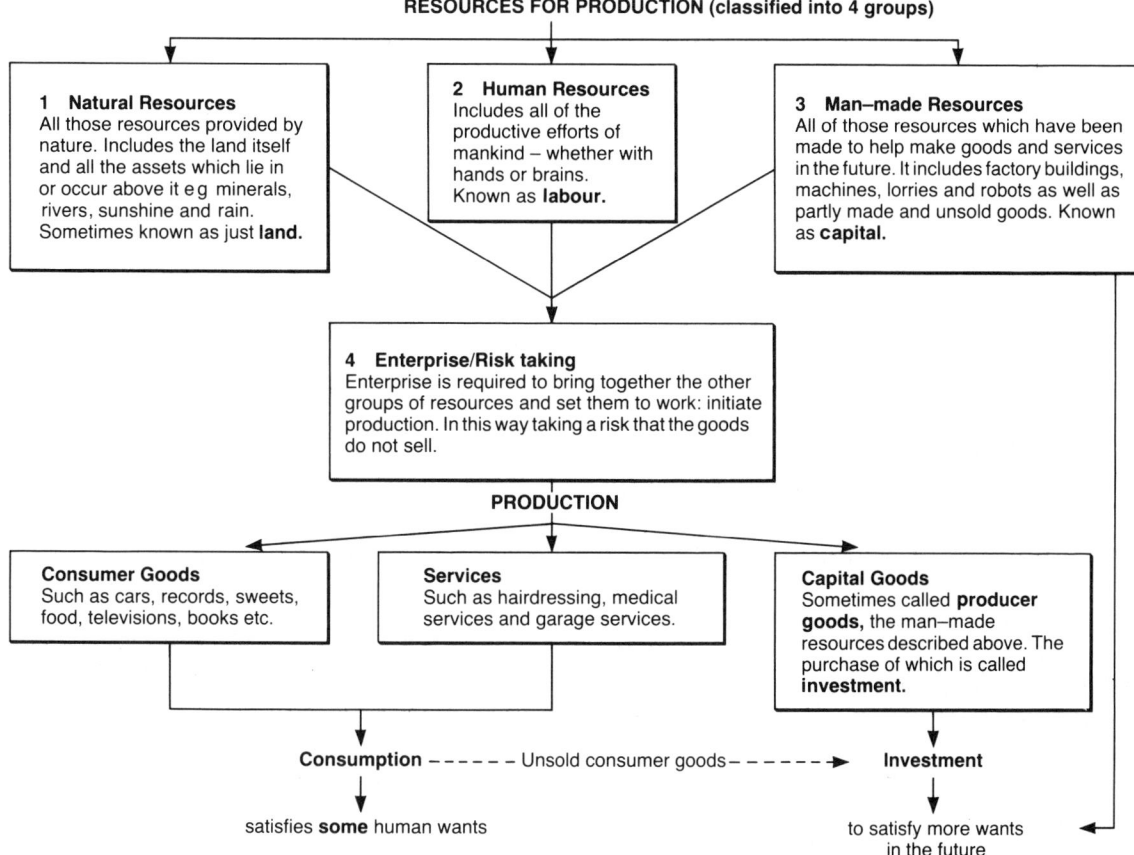

RESOURCES FOR PRODUCTION (classified into 4 groups)

1 Natural Resources
All those resources provided by
nature. Includes the land itself
and all the assets which lie in
or occur above it e g minerals,
rivers, sunshine and rain.
Sometimes known as just **land.**

2 Human Resources
Includes all of the
productive efforts of
mankind – whether with
hands or brains.
Known as **labour.**

3 Man–made Resources
All of those resources which have been
made to help make goods and services
in the future. It includes factory buildings,
machines, lorries and robots as well as
partly made and unsold goods. Known
as **capital.**

4 Enterprise/Risk taking
Enterprise is required to bring together the other
groups of resources and set them to work: initiate
production. In this way taking a risk that the goods
do not sell.

PRODUCTION

Consumer Goods
Such as cars, records, sweets,
food, televisions, books etc.

Services
Such as hairdressing, medical
services and garage services.

Capital Goods
Sometimes called **producer
goods,** the man–made
resources described above. The
purchase of which is called
investment.

Consumption – – – – – Unsold consumer goods – – – – – ➤ **Investment**

satisfies **some** human wants

to satisfy more wants
in the future

Fig 2 Process of production

CAPITAL GOODS

These are pieces of equipment wanted by a producer to help make consumer goods.

Exercise

The following is a list of factors of production, goods and services. For each one see whether you can say which it is:

An accountant
A sales representative's car
A packet of crisps
A haircut
A bricklayer
A ploughed field
A tractor

A bank manager
A garden shed
A child's bicycle
A postman's bicycle
A farmer's cow
A farmer's wife

In our list of goods we missed out 2 very important types of good.

1 The public good
Some goods are consumed by all of us at the same time. They are satisfying public wants. An example would be defence. The problem with such goods is that you cannot sell them to people. Imagine a door-to-door salesman selling defence. He knocks on your door. 'Excuse me Sir,' he says, 'Would you like to buy some defence—we have a very special offer today just £10 per head to defend the Falklands against the Argentine.'

Do you think he would sell very much? Of course not. What would he do if you did not buy any? The only way such goods can be provided is if the Government provides them. They still have to be paid for—by us—but the Government has the power to make us pay—we must pay our taxes!

2 Merit goods

Some goods are so important that the Government provides them for those who deserve them, not those who can afford them. We call these **merit goods**. You are enjoying one such merit good now—education. We all receive education, and in this country medical attention and basic housing from the Government if we have insufficient money to provide them for ourselves.

Types of Enterprise

As we have seen, things will only be produced and therefore wants satisfied if someone or a group of people collect together the necessary factors of production. Enterprise will differ from country to country. In some countries, for example, all enterprise is undertaken by the Government. Such economies are called **planned**. The nearest to this is Russia. In other countries all enterprise is undertaken by private individuals. This is called a **market economy**. In most countries, however, like our own we have a mixture—some enterprise is undertaken by the Government, for example, British Rail and some by private individuals like J Sainsbury plc. We call this a **mixed economy**.

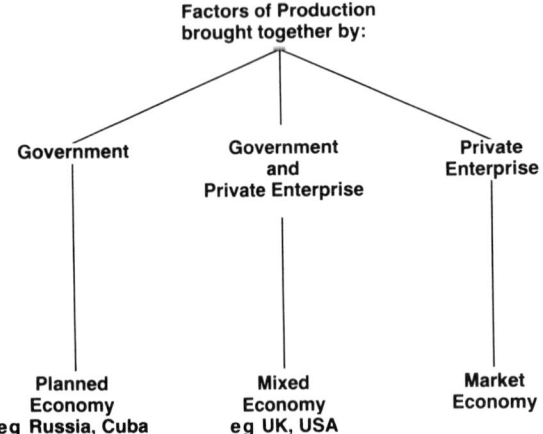

Fig 3 Economics systems

In the UK we have what is known as a **private** and **public sector**. The private sector includes all

enterprises which are owned and run by private individuals. If you look at Fig 4 you will notice that there are many different types of private sector enterprises. Each type has a different number of entrepreneurs and is organised differently. We shall learn about each type in Chapter 2.

The **public sector** includes all enterprise undertaken by the Government. This ranges from the provision of merit and public goods like education and defence to large nationalised industries like the Coal Board or British Rail. We shall learn about these in Chapter 3.

Sometimes the workers own their own factory collectively. They are both the labour and entrepreneurs. Also it is possible for the consumers to own their own shops and factories. These are both called cooperative enterprise and again we shall look at these in detail in a later chapter.

Note In economics ordinary words have precise meanings. Before going any further learn these 3:

a plant	is one factory or place of production
a firm	is any business unit, eg a company
an industry	is all the firms producing similar products

Example The Ford plant at Dagenham is part of the Ford Motor Company (firm), which in turn is part of the motorcar industry. List 2 examples from your area.

In this country the population supply labour, sometimes land and a few people enterprise to firms. This is not done for the fun of it but for the return or income received. We usually call the payment by businesses to their workers **wages** but this covers all payments to workers whether they be on a weekly wage or salary. People who own land and let others use it receive **rent** and people who take risks as entrepreneurs do so because they expect to make **profits**.

Those who work or supply some other resource for production receive an **income**. What do they do with this income? Much of it will be spent on goods and services. If you look at Fig 5 you will see a diagram of how this works. People supply the resources to businesses, all, that is except man-made resources, which, if you remember, are produced by businesses anyway.

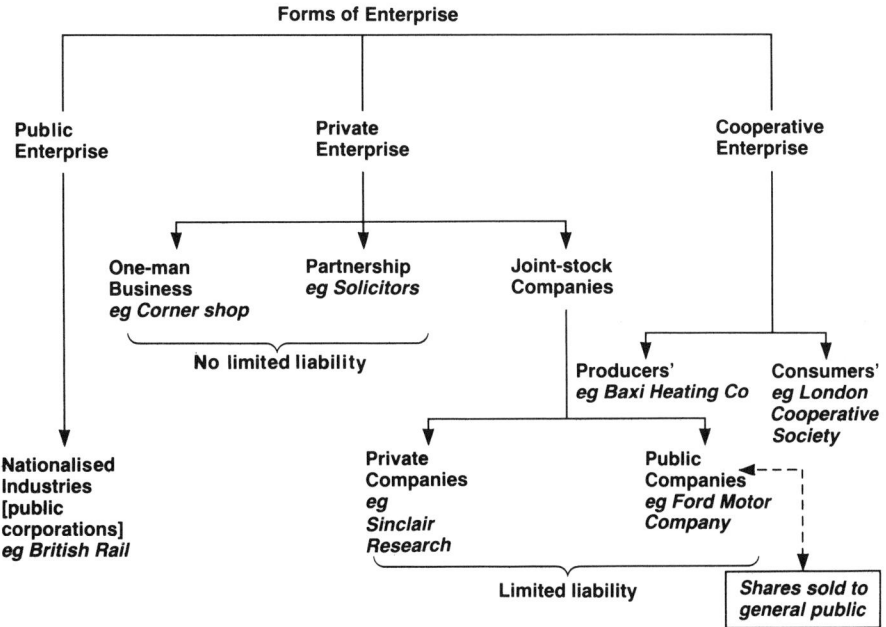

Fig 4

In return they are rewarded with money payments called factor payments. These are broken down into wages, profits and rent.

The people who now have money spend it on goods and services so that it becomes income for the businesses again. Money is constantly changing hands therefore from people to businesses and back to people.

To measure how much a country produces in

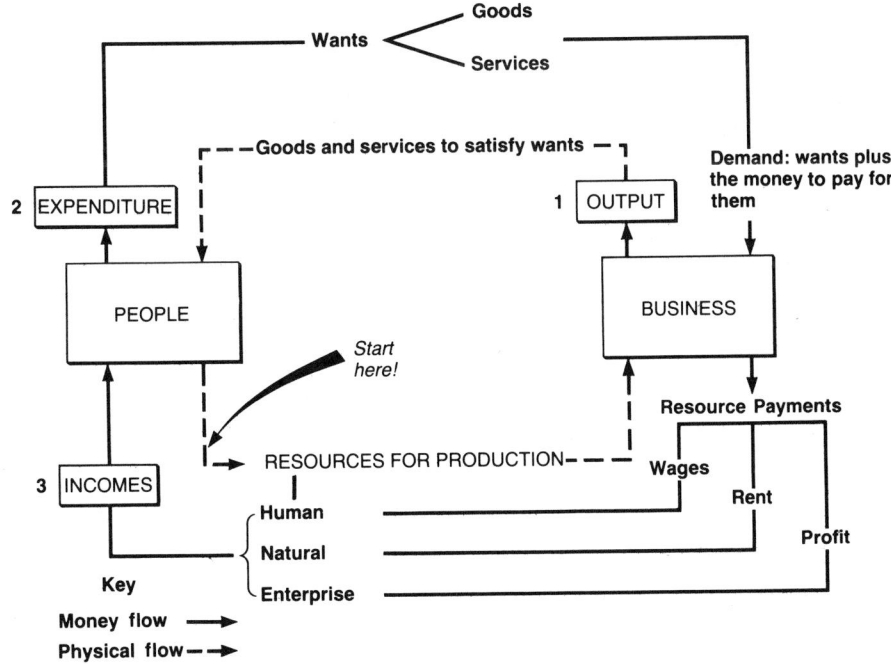

Fig 5 The circular flow of income

one year a Government can measure output (**1**). However, since output is bought they can also measure expenditure (**2**) and since this comes from income they can measure this (**3**). In fact the Government uses all 3 methods to measure how much is produced and the resulting figure is called **national income**—how much a country produces in any one year. This was £228.4 billion for the UK in 1982 or £4071 for every man, woman and child in the country. Dividing by the population is often undertaken in order to compare output in different countries:

Output per head	UK	France	West Germany	Italy	Japan	USA
US$ 1981	8886	10552	11076	6123	9606	12647

As can be seen there are considerable differences between western developed economies.

SUMMARY EXERCISE

1 Explain the difference between a **want** and a **need**.

2 Why is it that all of the World's **wants** cannot be satisfied?

3 Could all of the World's **needs** ever be satisfied?

4 Explain what economists mean by the term **opportunity cost** using as an example the steel used to produce a motorcar.

5 For each of the following list the type of resource:

Teacher	Washing machine
Lathe	(in laundry)
Lorry	Bricks
Machine operator	Washing machine
Nurse	(in private house)
Iron ore	Water

6 Give an example of a **public good**.

7 What is meant by the term **mixed economy?**

8 List any disadvantages that could occur whilst living in a **planned economy**.

9 List any advantages that could occur whilst living in a **planned economy**.

10 Define the term **national income**.

2 Private Sector Enterprise

To produce anything resources, human, man-made and natural, are needed. These are sometimes known as the **factors of production**. These resources are not in a form which will satisfy **wants** until they have been brought together and set to work. This is performed by the **entrepreneur**—in other words the person in control of the enterprise or business. The following case is about Jack Cohen, the founder of the famous Tesco chain of supermarkets and without a doubt an entrepreneur.

CASE STUDY

'Pile it high sell it cheap'

The story of Jack Cohen and his creation, Tesco, is so remarkable that Maurice Corina has written a book called *Pile it high sell it cheap* which gives the full account and facts behind his life.

When Jack Cohen left the flying corps after the First World War he had just £30. Although his family were not in favour he spent this money on tins of surplus war rations and sold them from a hand cart in the London street markets.

He continued to buy cheap goods and sell them in markets. It was hard work, getting up early to secure a good position and working until late.

The name Tesco was first used by Jack to name tea bought from importers by the chest and re-packed. One of the owners of the tea importing firm was called T E Stockwell. By taking his initials TES and adding the first two letters of his own surname Jack Cohen invented the brand name Tesco.

As years went by Jack started selling large quantities of goods to fellow stall holders—he acted as a middleman, or wholesaler, operating from a small warehouse. He used his talent to spot a good bargain, then fill his small warehouse with cheap goods he could re-sell to the London street traders. For example, in 1930 he bought 87 000 cases of 'Snowflake milk' at 10 shillings per case (50p)—which he sold at 12–14 shillings per case (60–70p). The milk was a condensed variety which had proved difficult to sell for the importers, Amalgamated Dairies. Jack was soon buying 500 cases a week.

As time went by it became obvious Jack was capable of selling far more stock and, therefore, making far more profit if he had a greater number of outlets. In 1930 he opened a shop in a covered arcade in Tooting with a partner, Sam Freeman. The next year he opened a second shop in partnership with a nephew in Chatham and a third was built in partnership with Michael Kaye. (This last venture blossomed into Pricerite Ltd which became a private company in 1934 and a public company in 1963, Jack Cohen having sold his 50% stake in 1956.) More shops followed in Becontree and Edgware.

In 1932–33 he formed 2 private companies, Tesco and J E Cohen & Co Ltd (the first for retailing, the second wholesaling). Both businesses grew and by 1938 had a turnover (value of goods sold) of £2 million and 100 shops.

Jack Cohen now moved into production buying farm land to grow his own vegetables and fruit. Many Tesco brands already existed including the now famous original tea.

Visits to America convinced Jack that self-service supermarkets were the future for retailing and soon after the Second World War he experimented in one shop. However, it failed.

In 1947 all his different companies were brought together in one holding company—Tesco Stores (Holding) Ltd. In December 1947 the company became a public company with 250 000 shares sold at 75p each. (A public company sells shares to the public who then own a tiny part of the company. They receive their share of the profits and have the right to vote at annual meetings to elect the directors to run the company.)

In the first full year of trading this new public company made enough profit to pay each shareholder a 20% return on the price of their shares. This influx of money resulted in larger stores and the introduction of American style self-service stores which proved successful. Further sales of

shares allowed the company to expand quickly during the 50s and 60s. Less profitable smaller groceries were bought and unlikely sites such as churches and cinemas were converted into supermarkets. By 1983 Tesco ran 500 stores (80 of them superstores—see Fig 6) and employed 40 000 people—quite a jump from a barrow and £30!

Fig 6

Not only did Jack Cohen pioneer self-service supermarkets, he also took part in the campaign to remove **resale price maintenance** (RPM). Under this practice a manufacturer could tell a retailer the price at which he wanted his products sold. Tesco could buy in bulk and sell at lower prices. Jack Cohen's whole philosophy was to pile his goods high and sell them cheap. In this way he might not make much profit upon each item but he sold so many this did not matter. RPM prevented him from operating like this. In 1964 after a long campaign RPM was banned and Tesco were able to drop the prices on many lines, for example a 20% reduction in the price of Gillette razor blades.

The story of Tesco is of particular interest for, as the student's summary table shows (see opposite), it has passed through most of the forms of business which have been developed in the UK private sector.

hand-cart he had formed a business. In such a case there is one entrepreneur who takes all of the risk, makes all the decisions and takes all the profits.

Types of Businesses

ONE-MAN BUSINESSES

A one-man business is very easy to form. When Jack Cohen bought his first £30 of stock and

Constraints

Money   The one-man business has very limited sources of finance—his own savings and any loans he might be able to negotiate from banks or even friends.

Exercise

Complete this summary chart of the growth of Tesco
by filling in the gaps, using the case study.

The Growth of Tesco

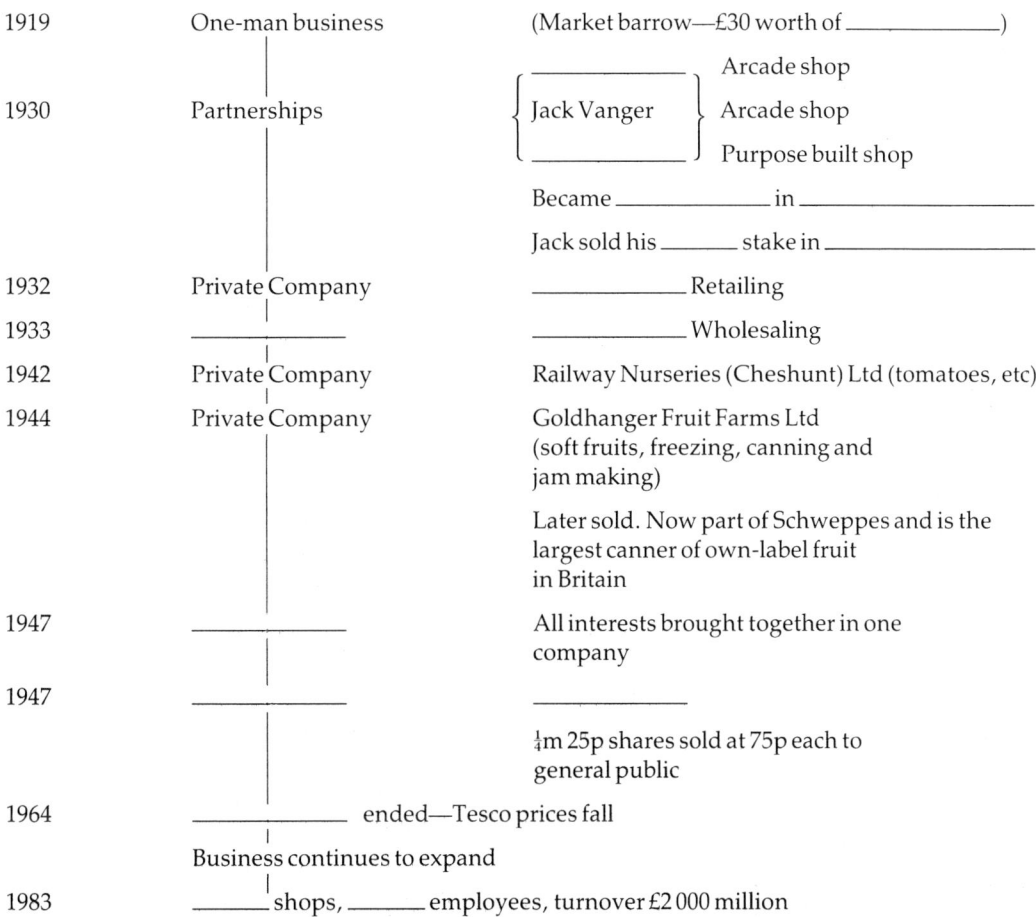

1919	One-man business	(Market barrow—£30 worth of _____)
		_____ ⎫ Arcade shop
1930	Partnerships	{ Jack Vanger } Arcade shop
		_____ ⎭ Purpose built shop
		Became _____ in _____
		Jack sold his _____ stake in _____
1932	Private Company	_____ Retailing
1933	_____	_____ Wholesaling
1942	Private Company	Railway Nurseries (Cheshunt) Ltd (tomatoes, etc)
1944	Private Company	Goldhanger Fruit Farms Ltd (soft fruits, freezing, canning and jam making)
		Later sold. Now part of Schweppes and is the largest canner of own-label fruit in Britain
1947	_____	All interests brought together in one company
1947	_____	_____
		¼m 25p shares sold at 75p each to general public
1964	_____ ended—Tesco prices fall
	Business continues to expand
1983	_____ shops, _____ employees, turnover £2 000 million

1 Jack Cohen was an entrepreneur. Using the case
study explain fully the term **entrepreneur**.
2 Using the case study give one example of each of
the following resources or factors of production used
by Jack in his early street trading days:

a Capital
b Labour
c Land

3 How did Jack compete against other entrepreneurs
and what made him so successful?
4 When Jack took on partners in 1930 and again
when the company became public in 1947 he gained
more money to expand his operations—but what did
he lose?
5 Some one-man businesses do not expand as Jack
Cohen's market stall did but prefer to remain small.
Why do you think this is so?

Skill Although a talented man, Jack Cohen needed the selling skills of his partners when he expanded his business. A brilliant craftsman may be a poor salesman and this could hold back the business.

Benefits

Independence Some people like to work for themselves, to make their own decisions and, therefore, like to run a one-man business. Some plumbers or shopkeepers who are their own bosses could earn far more money working for someone else but prefer to work for themselves. They also have an incentive or reason to work hard since all the profits are their own!

PARTNERSHIP

To overcome some of the constraints of a one-man business people can join together to take an equal share in the running and ownership of a business. They are called partners and the business a **partnership**. Jack Cohen took on partners who had experience as salesmen to run shops. Other people take on partners to share the costs of the business. Many professional people, such as opticians, solicitors and estate agents, are partners. Two or more professionals can share accommodation and secretarial help, split the costs of telephones, premises, heating bills etc. They can also specialise in one aspect of their profession. The **Partnership Act (1890)** limits the number of partners to 20 (although the Department of Trade and Industry can now permit more).

Constraints

Money Although additional funds are available from partners money for expansion is still limited and borrowing from a bank the only other source.

Liability The business and the partners are in law seen as being the same. This means that if the business makes a loss and owes money the property and the wealth of the partners would be used to settle these debts. The partners are said to have **unlimited liability**. They are collectively liable for any debts the business might have. This is also true for a one-man business.

Benefits

Additional money Extra partners mean money for expansion.

Additional skill New partners might bring fresh ideas or skills to the business.

Control Although a one-man business has total control a partner has a great deal of say in the running of the business. On some issues, such as the introduction of a new partner, there must be a unanimous decision by all existing partners.

Costs

Loss of control Every partner has the right to take decisions and enter into agreements on behalf of the other partners. The one-man business who forms a partnership therefore will face this cost. It is an opportunity cost—the cost of increasing the money available for expansion or expertise is a loss of personal control and independence.

The **Limited Partnership Act 1907** made it possible for some partners to be known as **limited partners** who would only contribute money to the business and not play any part in the running of it. The advantage to the limited partner is that they gain **limited liability** and, unlike the ordinary partner, if the business fell into debt would only be liable to lose the money they had originally put into the business. Their own personal wealth could not be touched. This would encourage people with savings to put them into a partnership. They are sometimes known as **sleeping partners**.

The Company

The constraint shared by the 2 forms of business discussed previously is the lack of funds for investment. Over time a company evolved into a business owned by a number of people who might or might not take an active role in the running of the business. Each would own only part or a share of the business and would receive part or a share of its profits which would be paid in the form of a dividend. To encourage people to purchase shares in a business Acts of Parliament during the mid-nineteenth century gave such shareholders limited liability (they could not be asked to sell their own property to pay the debts of the company). A company is seen in law to be separate from its owners. There are 2 main types of company controlled by the Companies Act 1948 as amended in 1967 and 1976. All companies must register certain facts with the Registrar of Companies and follow certain rules.

PRIVATE LIMITED COMPANY

Such a company is often a small family affair although very popular. Before the Companies Act 1980 changed the law the private limited company was restricted to 50 shareholders. The Act abolished this constraint, and private limited companies are no longer restricted in terms of growth. They cannot, however, advertise shares to the general public.

Benefits

Limited liability   Every shareholder has limited liability which certainly makes buying such shares an attractive proposition.

Continuity   A company can exist for ever. It does not die with the shareholders, the ownership simply passes from one person to another.

Costs

Loss of control   When an entrepreneur sells shares it is no longer his company. He may keep the majority of shares himself and since voting is on the basis of the number of shares each shareholder owns he could retain control. He would lose independence but gain limited liability and funds for expansion.

PUBLIC LIMITED COMPANY

These are the forms of business which have produced the massive international companies.(See Fig 7 overleaf.)

Benefits

Unlimited source of funds   A public company can have as many shareholders as needed. This can often be several thousand and means that vast sums of money for expansion can be raised. Shares can be advertised to the general public and anyone can buy them. If a shareholder wishes to sell his part ownership of the firm he can do so in the special market place which has developed for this purpose called **The Stock Exchange**.

Limited Liability   As with a private company all shareholders have limited liability.

Costs

Gulf between owners and managers   Public Companies are owned by so many shareholders it is impossible for them all to have a say in the decision making of the firm. They elect Directors therefore to control the firm. A small shareholder is at a disadvantage since votes are allocated on the basis of one vote per share. Institutions such as pension funds and insurance companies often own vast quantities of shares and can out-vote the small shareholder. The cost of unlimited funds is that control becomes remote from the ownership.

Shares

RAISING CAPITAL IN A PUBLIC COMPANY

A public company will need additional funds if it wishes to expand. Indeed, as we saw from our case study, this is often the reason for changing from a private company to a public company.

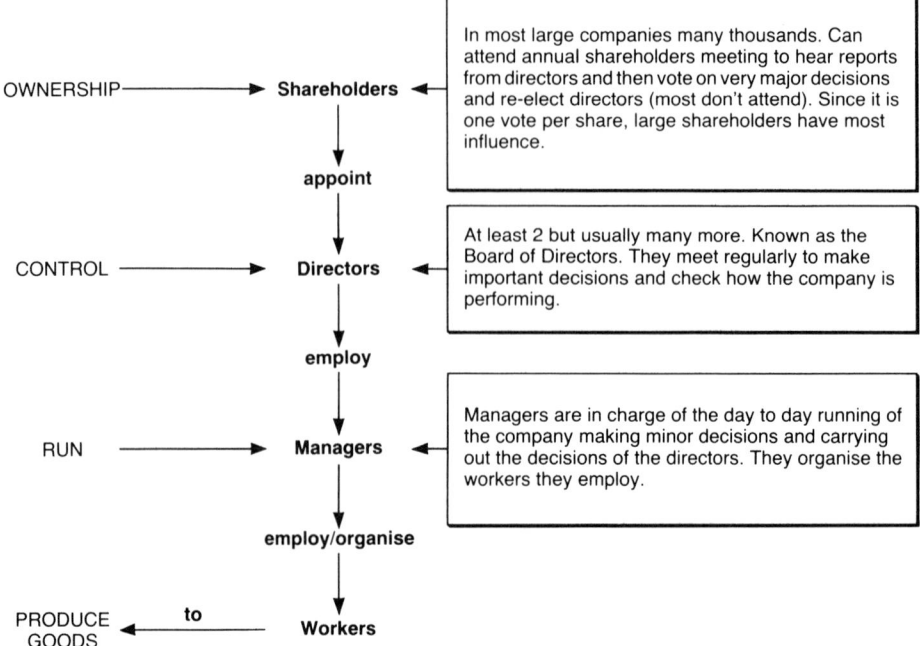

Fig 7 Public joint stock company

If it is performing well a public company may well keep back some of last year's profits and use this money for expansion—**retained profits**. It can always borrow money either from a bank or from the public. Such loans are often called **stock** or **debentures**. A firm will borrow a certain amount from a person at a fixed rate of interest for a fixed length of time. They are given a certificate and twice a year receive interest. At the end of the set period of time the loan is repaid. If the person who lent the money wants it back before the time is up they can sell it to somebody else.

The public company has no limit upon the number of shares or shareholders it can have, so another way of raising money for expansion is to sell more shares. This can be done in several ways. The most usual way is to advertise in quality newspapers that there are shares on offer—**an offer for sale**. People who are interested answer the advertisement and send a cheque for all or part of the cost and later will receive their share certificate.

An alternative method is called a **rights issue**. Here existing shareholders are given the chance to buy more shares. If they do not wish to buy them the remainder will be offered to the general public.

Illustrated on page 16 is the front cover of the Offer for Sale of shares in J Sainsbury in 1973. Look at it carefully.

Selling shares for the first time is called **issuing** and it is a very complicated business. It is important to get the price of the shares just right. If the price is too high people will not buy them, too low and you will not make as much money as you could. For this reason companies often pay for the help of a special bank to do it for them. Such banks are called **merchant banks**

Before shares in public companies can be bought and sold on the Stock Exchange permission must be obtained from the Stock Exchange Council which will need to look at the books of the company over the last 5 years. In this way potential investors are protected from bogus companies selling shares and then disappearing with the money.

Look carefully at the Sainsbury Offer for Sale and answer the questions.

Examples of Public Companies

Company	Number of Shareholders*	Turnover† £m	Capital Value £m
British Petroleum	268 150	30 624	16 614
ICI	421 146	6 581	5 294
Grand Metropolitan	98 503	3 221	2 264
Unilever	72 906	4 935	2 377

* 1983   † 1981

Summary of forms of Private Sector Enterprise

Form of Business Enterprise	Ownership and Control	Advantages	Disadvantages	Capital Source
One-man Business (small shop)	One-man	a Personal control b Easy to start c Easy to make decisions d Incentive to work	a Limited skill b Limited capital c Unlimited liability	a Personal savings b Loans from friends and banks c Ploughed back profits
Partnership (professions)	2–20 partners	d Same as to c above e Additional capital f Additional skill	d Same as to c above e Each partner responsible for the acts of the other partners	a Partners' savings b Loans from banks c Ploughed back profits
Private Company (small family firm)	2+ shareholders + 1 director	a Limited liability b Continuity	a Corporation tax b Shares cannot be offered to public c Capital still limited	a Shareholders' capital b Private placing c Loans from banks d Ploughed back profits
Public Company (large national companies)	7+ shareholders + 2 directors	a As above b Additional capital as shares can be sold to the public	a As above b Publication of accounts c Gulf between management and shareholders	a Stock Exchange placing b Offer for sale c Public issue d Rights issue e Ploughed back profits

A copy of this Offer for Sale, having attached thereto the documents specified below, has been delivered to the Registrar of Companies for registration. Application has been made to the Council of The Stock Exchange for the ordinary share capital of the Company to be admitted to the Official List. This Offer for Sale contains particulars given in compliance with the Regulations of the Council of The Stock Exchange for the purpose of giving information to the public with regard to the Company. The Directors collectively and individually accept full responsibility for the accuracy of the information given and confirm, having made all reasonable enquiries, that to the best of their knowledge and belief there are no other facts the omission of which would make any statement herein misleading.

The Application List for the Ordinary Shares now offered for sale will open at 10 a.m. on Thursday 12th July, 1973 and will close at any time thereafter.

J Sainsbury Limited

(Incorporated under the Companies Acts 1908 to 1917: registered in England No. 185,647)

Offer for Sale

by

S. G. Warburg & Co. Ltd.

of

10,000,000 Ordinary Shares of 25p each

at

145p per share

payable in full on application

The Ordinary Shares now offered for sale rank in full for all dividends hereafter declared or paid on the ordinary share capital of the Company.

Share Capital

	Issued and fully paid or to be fully paid
Authorised	

£25,000,000 in 100,000,000 Ordinary Shares of 25p each £20,174,751

The Company has outstanding £1,499,995 7 per cent. Irredeemable Unsecured Loan Stock. A subsidiary has outstanding £2,749,942 6½ per cent. First Mortgage Debenture Stock 1988/93, £2,887,547 7½ per cent. First Mortgage Debenture Stock 1987/92 (of which £2,000,000 is held by the Company) and £1,500,000 8 per cent. Guaranteed Unsecured Loan Stock, guaranteed by the Company. The Company has guaranteed the bank indebtedness of associated companies to a maximum principal amount of £6,651,200 (of which £2,617,172 was outstanding at the close of business on 22nd June, 1973). At the same date, there were also outstanding other guarantees by the Company to an aggregate principal amount not exceeding £295,000. Save as aforesaid and except for inter-company liabilities between the Company and its subsidiaries ("the Group"), no company in the Group had outstanding at that date any loan capital, mortgages or charges, borrowings or indebtedness in the nature of borrowing, including bank overdrafts, liabilities under acceptances (other than normal trade bills) or acceptance credits, hire purchase commitments or (other than in the ordinary course of business) guarantees or other material contingent liabilities.

Exercise

1 Who are the merchant bankers employed by Sainsbury to sell these shares?
2 What is the **face** or **nominal value** of the shares on offer?
3 What price are people asked to pay for each share?
4 Why is the price of each share so much higher than its face value?
5 When do the shareholders have to pay for their shares?
6 If J Sainsbury sold all of the shares on offer how much capital would be raised?
7 What would they do with this money do you think?
8 Why would people wish to buy shares in such a firm?

The Stock Exchange

THE ROLE OF THE STOCK EXCHANGE

When a private company turns into a public company it is fully investigated by the Stock Exchange Council. Most people have heard of the Stock Exchange, but what does it do? When a public company wishes to sell shares it will advertise them in a newspaper or offer them to existing shareholders. Why do we need a Stock Exchange?

It is unlikely that people would be so happy to buy shares if they were not sure they could sell them again without too much difficulty. The Stock Exchange makes this possible. It is a market place for second-hand stocks and shares. When people sell shares they sell them to someone else who wants to own part of that public company for a while. Public companies can last for ever so that people who buy shares in them need some way of getting back their money.

Note When shares are sold at any other time than the **first** time the company receives no money, only the ownership of the firm changes. For this reason the company must be told of the transfer so that they know where to send the dividends. This is done on a **stock transfer form** (see right).

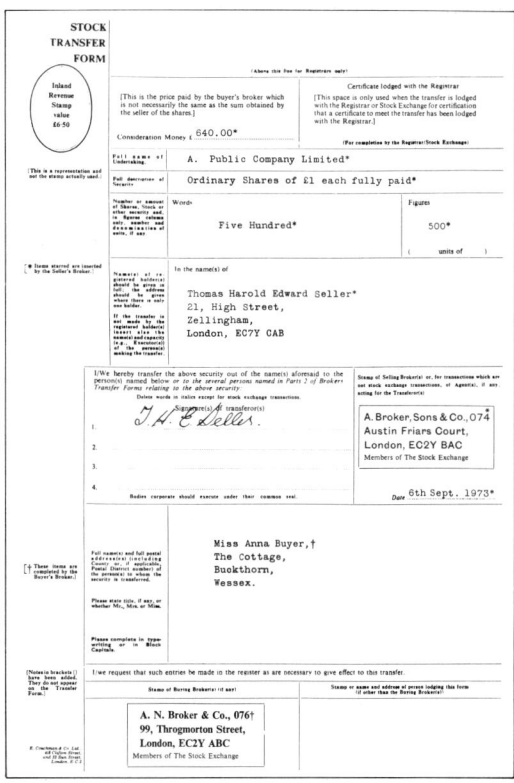

On 27 October 1986 The Stock Exchange implemented a large number of changes in the way in which shares are bought and sold. These changes, introduced on one day, were known as 'Big Bang'. At the heart of the change is new technology. All 'deals' to buy or sell shares are now recorded on a computerised dealing system called **SEAQ (Stock Exchange Automated Quotations)**. Members of The Stock Exchange are now known as **Broker/Dealers**. They can be individuals or represent large financial institutions (corporate members). Some of the Broker/Dealers are also **Market Makers**—that is they will undertake to buy or sell certain types of shares on a continuous basis. Market Makers 'advertise' the prices at which they are willing to buy or sell certain shares via TOPIC, The Stock Exchange videotext information system. All Broker/Dealers have this information as do financial institutions and wealthy investors. The SEAQ system sorts the Market Maker's prices so that the cheapest is at the top of each page. For most leading shares there are about 16 Market Makers in competition. If a Broker/Dealer wishes to buy from or sell to a Market Maker he will either telephone him or visit him in person, as they can operate from the floor of The Stock Exchange or their own dealing rooms. Deals are fed into the SEAQ system within 5 minutes so that the information is up-to-date. Investors can deal with any Broker/Dealer whether or not they are a Market Maker. The constantly up-dated data, available to all, gives investors total information and since all deals are recorded on the computer it is hoped that there now is greater protection for the investor.

Fig 8 The new Stock Exchange

CASE STUDY

How The Stock Exchange works

A retired couple sold their house and moved to a smaller cottage near the sea. They were left with £10 000 to spend or save. Since the man had worked for BP for many years he decided to buy shares in his old company with his spare £10 000.

They had never purchased shares before so they went to their Building Society who offered a share service. The Building Society contacted

BOUGHT	BY ORDER OF	BARGAIN NUMBER	BARGAIN DATE & TAX PT.
		23(W)	24th Nov. 1982

Miss A. BUYER
38 High Street
ANYTOWN   AN6 5QT

A Public Company Ltd. £1 Ordinary Shares

AMOUNT	PRICE	CONSIDERATION		
500	£1.28	£640.00		
		TRANSFER STAMP	13.00	N
	1.65% on £640.00	CONTRACT STAMP	0.30	N
		COMMISSION	10.56	T
		V.A.T. 15%	1.58	

E.&O.E.	FOR SETTLEMENT	6th December 1982	TOTAL £	665.44

E. Couchman & Co. Ltd.

A. N. BROKER & CO.
99 THROGMORTON STREET · LONDON EC2X ABC
LONDON · CHICAGO · SYDNEY · HONG KONG

TELEPHONE:	TELEX:	V.A.T. REGISTRATION
01-588 2365 (20 lines)	44259	NUMBER: 242 0024

PARTNERS
T. H. WOOD   S. G. CORK
A. B. JONES   S. H. THUMB
C. D. SMITH   A. K. WOOD
K. A. WIER   B. G. OAK
T. D. CHILD   R. N. SWEEPER

CONSULTANT
T. C. BOOTH

A. N. BROKER & CO.

CONTRACT
STAMP
£0·30

MEMBERS OF THE STOCK EXCHANGE
Subject to the rules and regulations including temporary regulations of The Stock Exchange
For Capital Gains and V.A.T. purposes this contract note should be retained
An asterisk means commission is shared with yourselves a member of the staff or an agent
V.A.T. Symbols;   T = Taxable;   E = Exempt.   N = Outside the scope

a Broker/Dealer who consulted a SEAQ screen. With such a well-known company many Market Makers dealt in these shares but the lowest selling price is at the top of the screen. (If selling the highest purchase price is shown.) The Broker/Dealer contacted the Market Maker selected by telephone. (It can be done in person on the floor of The Stock Exchange as it once had to be.) The deal was agreed by word of mouth but then entered into SEAQ, displayed and recorded. The investors knew they had paid the lowest possible price. Within a couple of days they received a contract note which gave full details of the amount owed and when it had to be paid. This invoice included not only the price of the shares but also 'Commission' (the amount charged by the Broker/Dealer) and various Government taxes. BP was sent a stock transfer form to tell them of the change in ownership and in due course, after they had paid the balance due, our retired couple received their share certificate (opposite).

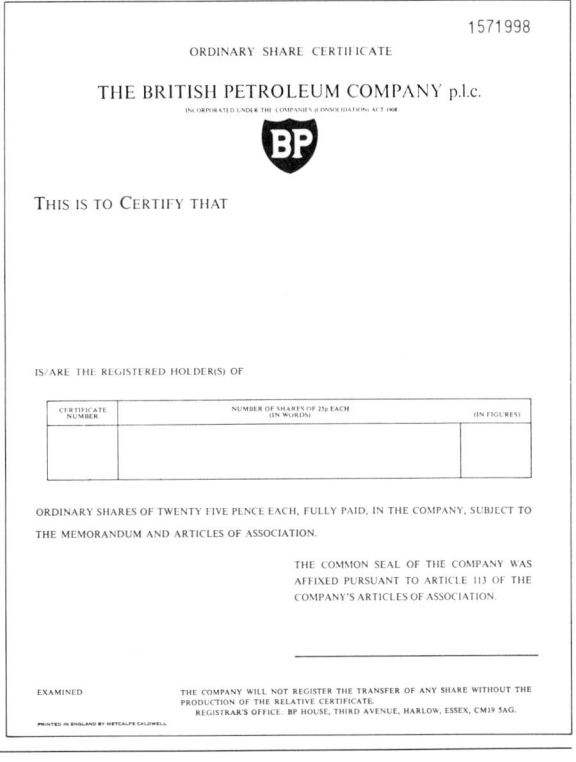

SPECULATION

Figure 9 shows that the Stock Exchange year is divided into 20 two week accounts and 4 three week accounts. This means that any transaction which takes place during an account does not have to be settled until the account day which is always one week after the close of the account. So if we take the account underlined and you were to purchase shares on 1 June you would not have to pay for them until 22 June. It would also mean that if you sold shares on 1 June you would not have to give them to the purchaser until 22 June nor would you receive the money until then.

Stock Exchange Account Days 1981

First Day of Dealings	Option Declaration Day	Last Day of Dealings	Account Day
Dec 8 1980	Dec 22 a	Dec 23 b	Jan 5*
Dec 24 c	Jan 8	Jan 9	Jan 19
Jan 12	Jan 22	Jan 23	Feb 2
Jan 26	Feb 5	Feb 6	Feb 16
Feb 9	Feb 26	Feb 27	Mar 9*
Mar 2	Mar 12	Mar 13	Mar 23
Mar 16	Mar 26	Mar 27	Apr 6
Mar 30	Apr 8 c	Apr 9 d	Apr 21 b
Apr 10 e	Apr 29 c	Apr 30 d	May 11*
May 1 e	May 14	May 15	May 26 b
May 18	May 28	May 29	Jun 8
Jun 1	Jun 11	Jun 12	Jun 22*
Jun 15	Jun 25	Jun 26	Jul 6
Jun 29	Jul 9	Jul 10	Jul 20
Jul 13	Jul 23	Jul 24	Aug 3
Jul 27	Aug 6	Aug 7	Aug 17
Aug 10	Aug 26 c	Aug 27 d	Sep 7*
Aug 28 e	Sep 10	Sep 11	Sep 21
Sep 14	Sep 24	Sep 25	Oct 5
Sep 28	Oct 8	Oct 9	Oct 19
Oct 12	Oct 22	Oct 23	Nov 2
Oct 26	Nov 5	Nov 6	Nov 16
Nov 9	Nov 19	Nov 20	Nov 30
Nov 23	Dec 3	Dec 4	Dec 14

* = 3-Week Account
a Monday   b Tuesday   c Wednesday
d Thursday   e Friday

Fig 9

This arrangement allows people to **speculate**. They can guess which way share prices are going to move and buy and sell the same shares within the one account. If they guess correctly they can make a lot of money. To help illustrate this Fig 9 shows some of the share prices for the first and last days of the account underlined. Remember, if you were a speculator you would only know the first days prices! Page 21 shows the prices for oil and gas shares for the two dates. Three shares are underlined. The first is the Century Oil Group Ltd.

On 1 June 10p shares in this company were sold for 76p. Even if there were no shares to sell some could still be sold on 1 June allowing enough to be bought to cover the sale later in the account. This is called **selling short**. It works because the share certificates do not have to be produced until 22 June. So if 100 000 Century Oil shares were sold on 1 June you would receive £76 000 on 22 June but would have to present the purchaser with the shares on that day as well— and you have not got any. By 12 June the price of Century Oil shares has fallen to 70p each so 100 000 shares will only cost you £70 000 and you will not have to pay until 22 June which is when you are paid £76 000. You will also now have 100 000 Century Oil shares to hand over to the original purchaser. This will leave you with a capital gain of £6 000. Some of this goes to the stockbroker who charges a fee or commission which in this case reduces your gain to £5 767.50 upon which you would be taxed at a special rate.

This commission is how the broker makes his living and is charged at different rates depending upon how large the deal is and how important the customer is.

If you look at the third share underlined, Ranger Oil, you will see that unlike Century Oil share price its price rose during our account. To make money here the speculator would have to buy at the beginning of the account and sell at the end. If say, he were to buy 10 000 at the beginning of the account he would owe the broker on the 22 June £58 000. If he then sells at the end of the account he would be paid £63 000, a gain of £5 000 from which would be deducted commission and tax.

When prices are rising as in this second case it is sometimes called a **bull** market and such speculators are known as **bulls**. When prices are falling as in the first example it is said to be a **bear** market and such speculators are said to be **bears**.

Exercise

1 Using the second share underlined, LASMO, show in detail how you could make £2 750 gain (before tax and commission).

1 June, 1981

OIL AND GAS

Dividends Paid		Stock	Price	Last xd	Div Net	C'yr	Y'ld Gr's	P/E
Jan.	July	Do. 8% Pf. £1	64	24.12	5.6%	1435	12.5	—
Jan.	July	Burmah £1	147	1.5	6.5	q2.2	6.3	(8.3)
Jan.	July	Carless Capel 10p	136	8.12	12.5	4.1	2.6	12.9
Jan.	Aug.	Century 10p	76	8.12	h2.25	5.5	4.2	4.6
—		Ceres Res. C$5.00	150	—	—	—	—	—
—		Charterhall 5p	67	3·67	—	—	—	—
—		Charterhouse Pet.	81	10.4	1.0	3.8	1.8	21.3
	July	Cie Fr. Petroles B.	£12½	7·77	Q54%	Φ	19.0	Φ
—		Jessel Trust 5p	20½	—	—	—	—	—
Oct.	June	KCA	182xd	18.5	5.25	1.2	4.1	(26.1)
—		LASMO	580	—	—	—	—	19.5
Feb.	Aug.	LASMO 14% 1981–83	£99½	26.1	Q14%	—	14.1	—
Apr.	Oct.	LASMO "Ops" 10p	962	30.3	71.19	—	10.6	—
—		Magellan Pet.	470	—	—	—	—	—
—		Magnet Metals 10c	20	10.12	—	—	—	—
—		‡‡Marinex Pet. 10p	132	—	—	—	—	Φ
—		††Penine Res.	48	—	—	—	—	—
—		•Pict. Petroleum	280	—	—	—	—	—
	June	Premier Cons. 5p	68	—	—	—	—	—
—		Ranger Oil	580	—	—	—	—	—
May	Oct.	Royal Dutch Fl.10	£16¼xd	18.5	Q68½%	3.9	7.8	3.3

12 June, 1981

OIL AND GAS

Dividends Paid		Stock	Price	Last xd	Div Net	C'yr	Y'ld Gr's	P/E
Nov.	May	Brit. Petroleum	352	16.3	20.25	3.4	8.2	4.0
Jan.	July	Do. 8% Pf. £1	61	24.12	5.6%	1435	13.1	—
		Brunswick Oil NL	13	—	—	—	—	—
Jan.	July	Burmah £1	141	1.5	6.5	q2.2	6.6	(8.0)
Jan.	July	Carless Capel 10p	120	8.12	2.75	Φ	3.3	Φ
Jan.	Aug.	Century 10p	70	8.12	2.8	Φ	5.9	Φ
—		Ceres Res. C$5.00	155	—	—	—	—	—
—		Charterhall 5p	60	3·67	—	—	—	—
—		Charterhouse Pet.	75	10.4	1.0	3.8	1.9	19.7
	July	Cie Fr. Petroles B.	£12	1.7	Q54%	Φ	19.6	Φ
—		Jessel Trust 5p	23½	—	—	—	—	—
Oct.	June	KCA	160	18.5	5.25	1.2	4.7	(23.0)
—		LASMO	525	—	—	—	—	17.6
Feb.	Aug.	LASMO 14% 1981–83	£99½	26.1	Q14%	—	14.1	—
Apr.	Oct.	LASMO "Ops" 10p	900	30.3	71.19	—	11.3	—
—		Magellan Pet.	510	—	—	—	—	—
—		Magnet Metals 10c	17	10.12	—	—	—	—
—		‡‡Marinex Pet. 10p	120	—	—	—	—	Φ
—		††Penine Res.	42	—	—	—	—	—
—		•Pict. Pet. £1	235	—	—	—	—	—
—		Premiers Cons. 5p	65	—	—	Φ	—	Φ
—		Ranger Oil	630	—	—	—	—	—
May	Oct.	Royal Dutch Fl.10	£16⅛	18.5	Q68½%	3.9	7.9	3.3

Share prices

2 Look at the mining shares. Give the names of shares where bulls and bears could have made a gain. (One of each.)

3 Using the table of Stock Exchange Account days on page 20 write down when the four 3 week account days are. Why do you think these are so timed?

4 Speculators who buy new issues of shares in order to sell them quickly for a gain are called **stags**.

Put this into everyday language: '. . . stags (who are really a form of bull) profited handsomely from an issue of Penguins.'

(*Taken from page 33 Guide to the British Economy, Donaldson Peter, Penguin, 1965.*)

The Size and Growth of Companies

There are about 600 000 companies in the United Kingdom, most of them are private (about 99%) and the vast majority of them are small.

There are several ways of studying size. We shall look at 2 ways. The bar graph opposite shows just how many small firms existed in British manufacturing industry in 1979. Nearly three quarters (72%) of all manufacturing firms employed less than 20 people whereas just 563 firms ($\frac{1}{2}$%) employed over 1 500 people and together one third of all manufacturing employees.

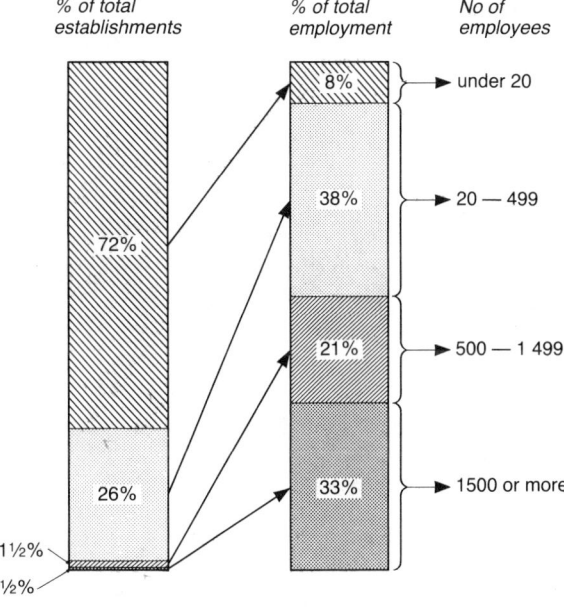

Size of firms in manufacturing industry (1979)

Manufacturing: Size Distribution of Establishments

Number of employees	Number of establishments	% of total establishments	% of total employment
under 20	76 888	71.6	7.6
20 to 499	28 164	26.2	38.4
500 to 1 499	1 778	1.7	21.2
1 500 or more	563	0.5	32.9

Fig 10 Source: Report on the Census of Production 1979

Figure 10 shows only manufacturing firms. If it were to include services like shops and garages do you think that it would be any different?

A second way is to look at the value of a company's assets. Figure 11 shows that of the new companies formed in 1981 well over half had a recorded capital value of less than £100.

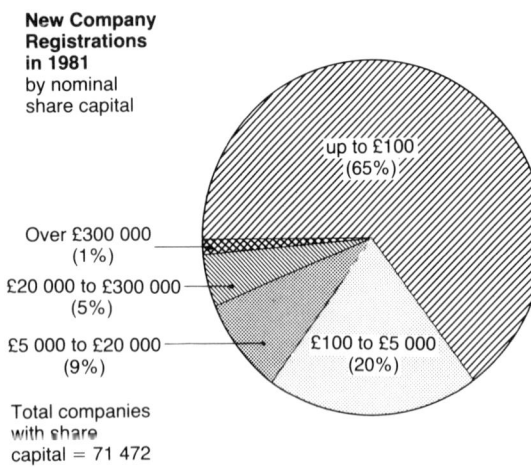

New Company Registrations in 1981 by nominal share capital

up to £100 (65%)

Over £300 000 (1%)

£20 000 to £300 000 (5%)

£5 000 to £20 000 (9%)

£100 to £5 000 (20%)

Total companies with share capital = 71 472

Fig 11 New Company registrations 1981, Source: Barclays Bank Review, February 1983

ECONOMIES OF SCALE

Have you noticed that things are cheaper if a giant size is bought? This is particularly so when buying for the freezer.

This can also be true for a business and is one of the reasons why it is often possible for a large company to produce goods more cheaply than a smaller company. The firm can make savings by producing on a large scale, in other words **economies of scale**. Not only is it cheaper to buy in bulk, but it is also cheaper to sell. Think of trans-port costs. A 10 ton lorry will not cost twice as much as a 5 ton lorry to buy or run; it will still only need one driver. The same goes for machinery inside the factory. Bigger, faster machinery may need the same number of workers as smaller, slower machinery and will not cost proportionately much more. The firm might use the same management team. If a firm doubles its output it will not need twice as many accountants. Sometimes it becomes worthwhile for a large company to re-use waste materials and actually save money.

This being the case, why have we so many small companies in the UK?

There are many reasons but there are 3 which stand out:

1 Lack of finance. Firms would often grow but cannot raise the necessary finance.
2 Firms do not start large, they start small and grow. In 1919 Jack Cohen had one small market stall and stock of £30. We saw how his company developed into a multi-million pound operation. For every firm which grows there might be hundreds which stay small or even close down.
3 Some goods have such a small market they only need a small firm to satisfy all of the demand. For example, it would be rather silly to mass produce ballet shoes in a large factory.

Can you think of any other reasons?

THE GROWTH OF FIRMS

As shown in the case study, Tesco grew in several ways. At first profits were ploughed back into the business to buy more stock and new openings to sell. Then money was borrowed to open shops. When the firm became a company shares were sold in order to open new shops.

Also Tesco expanded by buying the shares of less successful retailing companies. This is called a **takeover**. For example, in 1956 Tesco bought a controlling interest (over 50% of the shares) in a company called Williamsons Ltd which ran 70 shops. Later in 1957 Tesco bought all of the remaining shares by giving Williamsons Ltd shareholders Tesco shares and so Williamsons Ltd became part of Tesco which now owned 185 shops. This is called **integration**. It can take several forms. The example just given is called **horizontal integration** because it involves 2 firms in the *same* industry at the *same* stage of production, in this case retailing groceries.

Tesco ⟵————————⟶ **Williamson**

Horizontal integration

Sometimes, when companies merge a new company is formed and the name tells us of the merger:

National Provincial Bank + Westminster Bank = National Westminster Bank plc

A third example can be taken from the UK motor industry. (See below.)

A firm can grow in other directions. As we saw earlier in 1942 Jack Cohen bought a nursery in Cheshunt to supply tomatoes to his shops. Here integration was in another direction. Although in the same industry they were not at the same stage of production. Growing the tomatoes was the stage before distributing and selling them. For this reason such integration is known as **backward vertical**.

Railway Nurseries

Tesco Stores Ltd

Backward vertical integration

Vertical integration can be forwards, eg a brewery taking over a pub. Can you think of any other examples?

Sometimes a firm will move into a completely new field by taking over a firm in a different industry altogether. This is called **diversification** and has led to some huge companies producing all sorts of products.

As you can see overleaf a firm like Grand Metropolitan Ltd has many different operations. Every brand name or company name you see in the 'street' are in fact one company. Can you think why a company would expand in this way?

SUMMARY EXERCISE

1 Give **one** example of each of the following types of businesses from your local area: *a* a one-man business and *b* a partnership.
2 A one-man business can increase the funds available for expansion by taking one or more

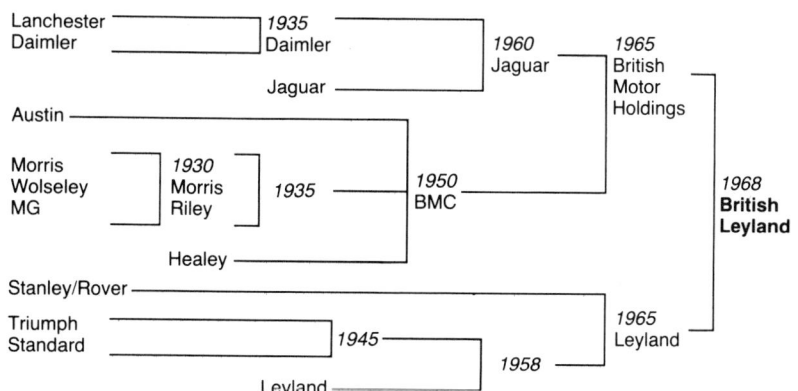

Contraction of the UK Motor Industry

partners. List **two** further advantages taking partners would give.

3 Give **one** reason for the legal requirement of companies to register with the Registrar of Companies.

4 State **two** differences between private and public companies.

5 What is a **rights issue of shares?** Why do companies make use of such issues?

6 Give **one** way in which companies protect potential purchasers of stocks and shares.

7 What percentage of manufacturing businesses in this country employ less than 20 people? Give **one** reason why so many businesses remain small.

8 Give **one** advantage to the UK from the existence of so many small businesses.

9 List three examples of **horizontal integration** between firms. Give **one** reason for such expansion.

10 What is an **economy of scale?** How do *you* benefit from such economies?

ASSIGNMENT

1 Read the first case study on Tottenham Hotspur again (see p 1). In October 1983 the Club went 'public'; that is became a public limited company. 3 800 000 25p shares were sold at £1.00 per share.

a Why do you think Spurs went public?
b Explain why a 25p share sold at £1.00.
c Find out how much a 25p Spurs' share would cost today. Were these shares a 'good buy' in October 1983?
d Give one disadvantage to the board of Tottenham Hotspur of becoming public.
e Do you think people would buy shares in Spurs for different reasons than they would buy Tesco shares? If so what would these different reasons be?

2 A distant relative, Mr Elwin Griffiths, has been made redundant. He was a coal miner for many years and has received £10 000 redundancy pay. Together with his life savings and the sale of his cottage he can raise £20 000 towards buying and opening a small shop. He is well thought of by his bank manager.

Taking into account what you have learnt in this chapter would you advise Elwin to open a shop or not? Remember to consider:

a What competition might he face?
b What problems might he run into?
c What would the advantages be?
d What are the **alternative** uses for his savings?

3 The Public Sector

Many of the goods and services needed to satisfy the wants of people in the UK are produced either directly or indirectly by the Government. On our behalf the Government has, over a period of time, either taken over (nationalised) private sector industries or started whole industries which today produce goods and services for the country. These are called **public corporations** and form part of the **public sector**.

CASE STUDY
The Nationalisation of Electricity

1 HISTORY

Electricity was originally generated and supplied by a large number of small private sector companies (400 by 1900). Since there were no controls several different electrical systems emerged some AC others DC and all using different voltages. In these early days this did not cause too many problems as electricity was new and experimental and it was not possible to transmit over a large area. Many rural areas were without electricity in any form. This was soon to change with the discovery of how to conduct electricity all over the country. It was now possible to have one large company, but Parliament decided it ought to be owned by the public!

In 1926 the Central Electricity Board was created by an Act of Parliament. It was a **public corporation**; this meant that it was run by a Board, not unlike a Board of Directors in a public or private company, only in this case the members were appointed by the Government on behalf of the whole country. The task of the Central Electricity Board was to build a National Grid to supply electricity all over the country. Only a Government run organisation would have the resources to construct such a network or the authority to build pylons or bury cables throughout the land. The new Board owned all of the generating plants. Each had covered a small area and it was found that all could produce more electricity than was ever required—spare capacity. By closing down smaller inefficient generators the Board was able to reduce the spare capacity between 1930–1938 from 80% to just 15% and therefore cut the cost of producing electricity by 24%. One company with fewer generators distributing electricity all over the country was cheaper and less wasteful.

Selling the electricity was left in the hands of local private sector companies. This meant that some rural areas were left without electricity as it was too expensive to lay cables and no profit could be made. It also left the country with different voltages and prices in different regions of the country.

In 1947 this distribution side of the industry was **nationalised**. An Act of Parliament forced the shareholders of the 560 separate companies to exchange their shares for Government securities. Twelve Area Boards were appointed by the Government.

AREA ELECTRICITY BOARDS

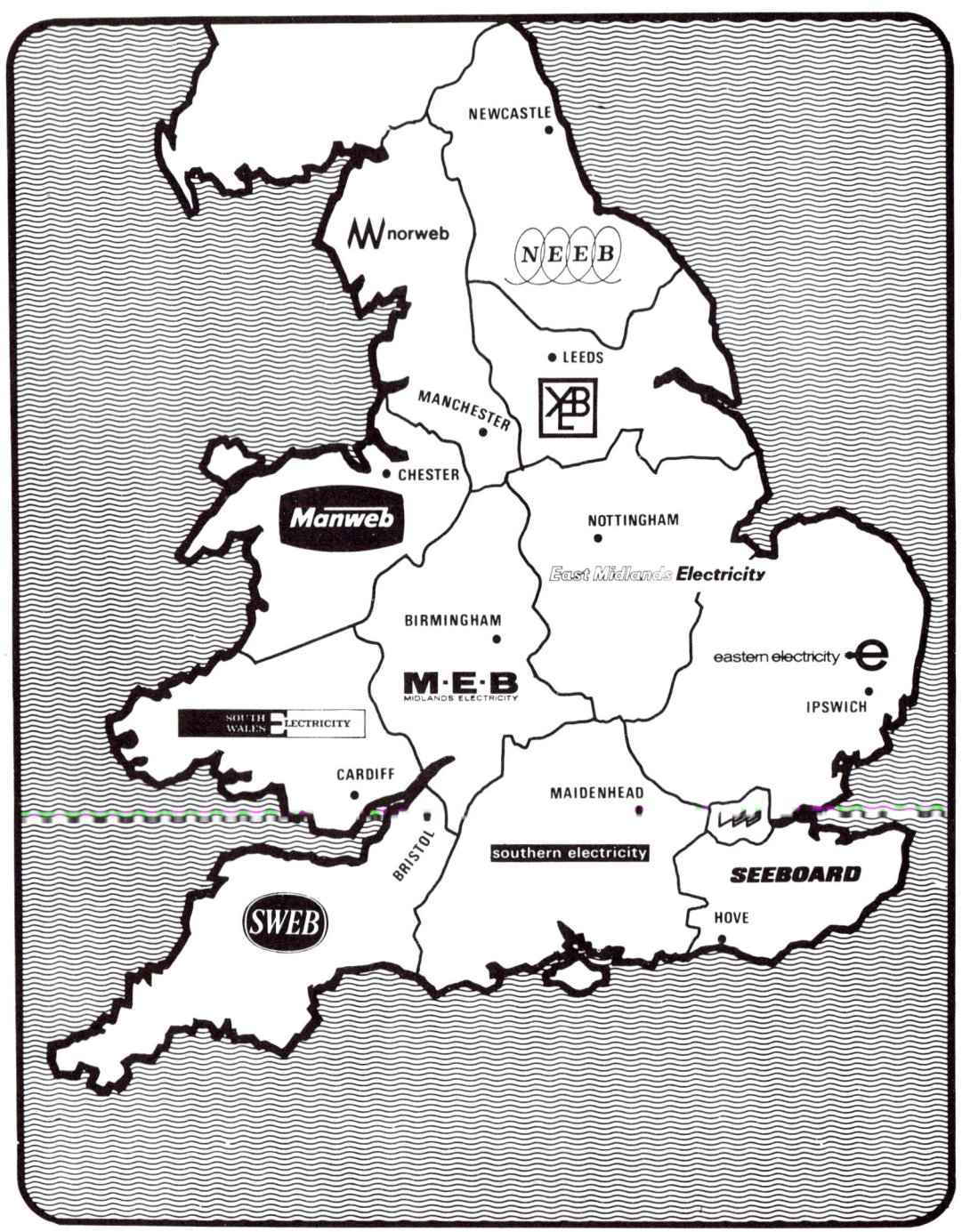

THE BOARDS' HEADQUARTERS ARE LOCATED IN THE TOWNS SHOWN

All of the country could now enjoy a standard electricity supply.

2 THE ORGANISATION OF THE ELECTRICITY INDUSTRY TODAY

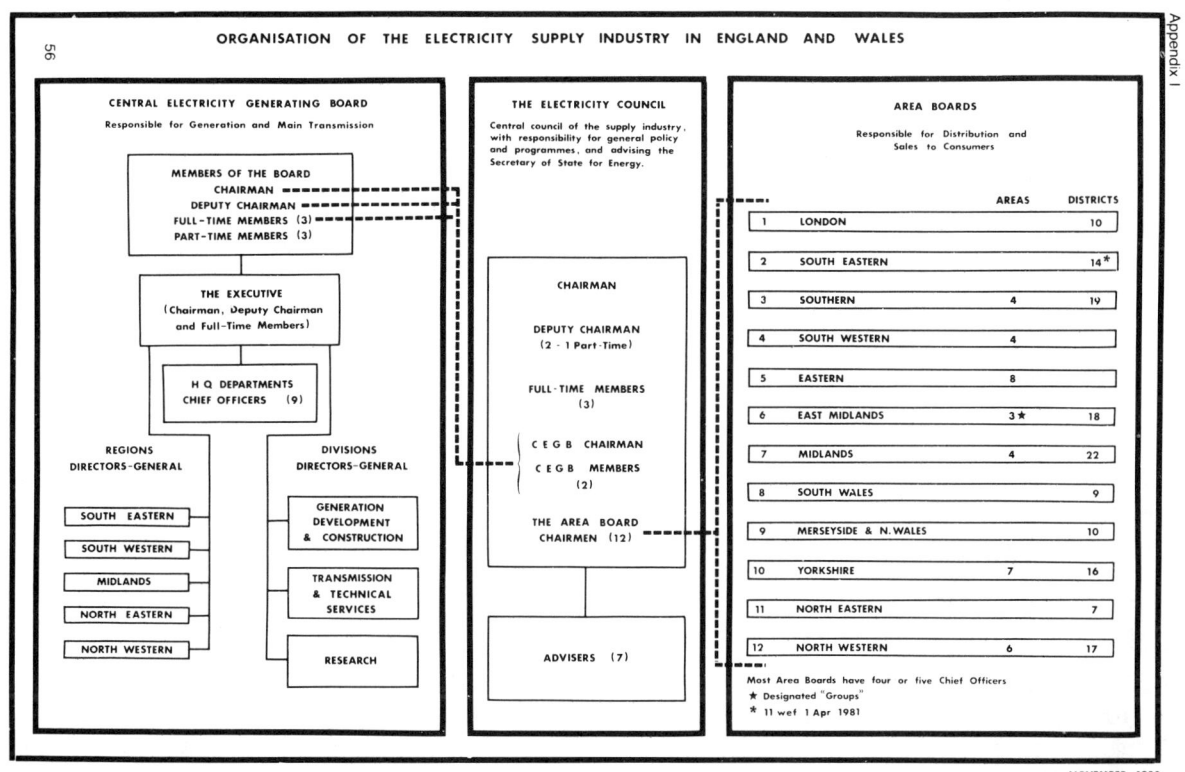

ORGANISATION OF THE ELECTRICITY SUPPLY INDUSTRY IN ENGLAND AND WALES

CENTRAL ELECTRICITY GENERATING BOARD
Responsible for Generation and Main Transmission

MEMBERS OF THE BOARD
CHAIRMAN
DEPUTY CHAIRMAN
FULL-TIME MEMBERS (3)
PART-TIME MEMBERS (3)

THE EXECUTIVE
(Chairman, Deputy Chairman and Full-Time Members)

H Q DEPARTMENTS
CHIEF OFFICERS   (9)

REGIONS
DIRECTORS-GENERAL

SOUTH EASTERN
SOUTH WESTERN
MIDLANDS
NORTH EASTERN
NORTH WESTERN

DIVISIONS
DIRECTORS-GENERAL

GENERATION DEVELOPMENT & CONSTRUCTION

TRANSMISSION & TECHNICAL SERVICES

RESEARCH

THE ELECTRICITY COUNCIL
Central council of the supply industry, with responsibility for general policy and programmes, and advising the Secretary of State for Energy.

CHAIRMAN

DEPUTY CHAIRMAN
(2 - 1 Part-Time)

FULL-TIME MEMBERS (3)

C E G B CHAIRMAN
C E G B MEMBERS (2)

THE AREA BOARD CHAIRMEN (12)

ADVISERS (7)

AREA BOARDS
Responsible for Distribution and Sales to Consumers

		AREAS	DISTRICTS
1	LONDON		10
2	SOUTH EASTERN		14*
3	SOUTHERN	4	19
4	SOUTH WESTERN	4	
5	EASTERN	8	
6	EAST MIDLANDS	3★	18
7	MIDLANDS	4	22
8	SOUTH WALES		9
9	MERSEYSIDE & N.WALES		10
10	YORKSHIRE	7	16
11	NORTH EASTERN		7
12	NORTH WESTERN	6	17

Most Area Boards have four or five Chief Officers
★ Designated "Groups"
* 11 wef 1 Apr 1981

NOVEMBER 1980

Appendix I

56

There are today still 2 tiers in the organisation of the electricity industry:

a **Central Electricity Generating Board** Responsible for generating and transmitting electricity.

b **Area Boards** These 12 bodies are responsible for selling the electricity to the public and for certain electrical appliances.

To coordinate the activities of these 2 sections there is the **Electricity Council** which, as shown in the chart, has members drawn from both sections and all the Area Boards. The Board of the Electricity Council decides upon general policy concerning the industry and such important issues as finance and research are discussed. The Council is the body which reports to the Government and Parliament when asked.

Electricity is an example of a **natural monopoly**. A monopoly exists when there is only one firm in an industry. The consumer only has one choice—to buy electricity from the Electricity Board or do without it! This monopoly is state owned and was created by nationalisation. Electricity was already a monopoly in local areas however, people did not have a choice. It is expensive to connect a house or factory to the main supply and once connected one 'lump' of electricity is much like another. It would be ridiculous to have 24 sockets in a kitchen—all the same but with 6 from one company and 6 from another and so on. For this reason electricity would always be a monopoly and if not controlled by the Government a private firm would be able to charge any price it wanted. Electricity was nationalised so that it could operate 'in the public interest', that is in such a way that would be best for the people of the country. It would be little use if the public had no say in the running of these public corporations.

3 THE 'PUBLIC INTEREST' IN THE ELECTRICITY INDUSTRY

In a public corporation there are no shareholders. The business belongs to the country but it is left up to Parliament to look after our interests in 3 main ways:

a The Government will make sure that each nationalised industry is operating along the lines it wishes. If it is not the minister responsible for that industry, in this case the Secretary of State for Energy, can issue a directive to the Board with which they must conform.

b Parliament appoints committees, with MPs and Lords from all parties, to consider different topics in detail and report back to the whole Parliament. One such committee reports on the nationalised industries from time to time, looks in depth at the electricity industry and reports to Parliament. Other select committees sometimes turn their gaze upon electricity. For example in 1979–80 the Energy Select Committee considered nuclear power stations and in 1980 a Lords' Select Committee on Science and Technology looked at electric vehicles.

c Members of Parliament can ask questions on behalf of their constituents either in writing or orally, during question time, of any minister. If a member of the public had a serious complaint about the electricity they could write to their MP

who could ask the Secretary of State for Energy about the problem. Asking such a question can sometimes help to get the Board moving in the right direction.

The Act of Parliament which nationalised the electricity industry provided for far greater consumer participation than this however. Each Area Board has a 'Consultative Council'. This Council is appointed by the Secretary of State in consultation with the National Consumer Council. The 20–30 members of the Council are consulted by the Board on policy matters such as price increases and are also able to deal with complaints from electricity users. In the year 1980–81 the 12 Consultative Councils dealt with 21 000 consumer complaints of which 60% concerned bills. The Chairperson of each Consultative Council is also automatically a member of the Area Board. Each Consultative Council produces also an annual report. The 1982–83 report of the South Wales Board showed they received a total of 2 780 enquiries and complaints of which 349, the largest single group, concerned bills. This report concluded:

> Although meters on very rare occasions are found to be faulty, high electricity bills can usually be explained by people's pattern of consumption. Detailed investigation of complaints about excessive bills often indicates that the consumer underestimates his use of appliances.

If an independent test finds the meter faulty the customer will have his bill reduced. Although most complaints appear to be customer error it is comforting to know that they are investigated and that a body exists to look after minor complaints from the consumer.

In 1977 a National Consumers' Council was established for the electricity industry comprising all the Area Board Consultative Council Chairpersons. The aim was to form a national consumers' voice on matters to do with the electricity industry.

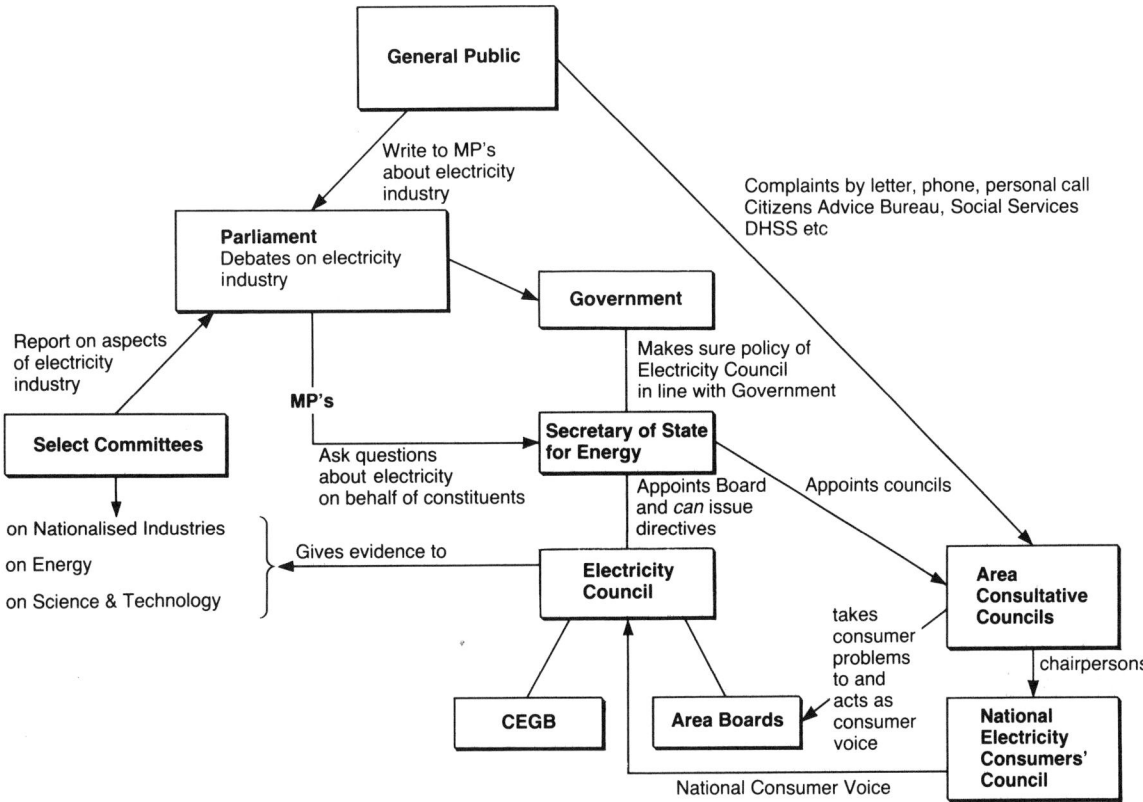

Fig 12 Public accountability of electricity industry

Exercise

1 In 1926 the Government established the Central Electricity Board. What evidence is there that this made the supply of electricity more efficient?

2 Nationalisation in 1947 meant that one standard voltage was used all over the country, and one standard price charged. What advantages would this have for the consumer?

3 Explain why electricity is said to be a 'natural monopoly'.

4 State which of the following industries you would consider to be most likely to produce natural monopolies and why:

a gas *d* water supply
b motor cars *e* banks
c railways

5 The electricity industry was controlled for the public interest by nationalisation. Give one other way in which the public interest might have been protected without this ultimate control being taken.

ASSIGNMENT

Your parents receive an electricity bill which is four times greater than any bill they had received for that time of the year over the last few years. They come to the conclusion that the meter must be faulty but the local Electricity Board do not agree. Outline the steps they should take to try to get the bill reduced. Find out the name and address of your Board's Consultative Council.

During the period 1945–51 many private sector industries were taken into public ownership, eg Coal Mining (1946), Railways (1947), Gas (1948), Iron and Steel (1949).

In common with other European countries the public sector has grown. For example, in 1973

$11\frac{1}{2}$% of French, German and Italian output was from the public sector—in the UK it was $10\frac{1}{2}$%.

For these and further nationalisation measures the main arguments used were **political**. For example, members of the Labour Party might argue that profits made by entrepreneurs in the private sector are morally wrong and that they should go to the Government to provide services for the poor. Members of the Conservative party, on the other hand, might argue that people ought to have a choice of goods and services and that others have the right to become entrepreneurs and produce those goods and services. We can, however, argue on pure **economic** grounds. Some would say that a nationalised industry can be coordinated, save money on wasted advertising and competition and be much more efficient. Others would argue that the nationalised industries are so large that they become inefficient and because they do not have to make a profit like private sector companies the managers do not care or try so hard. Although the political arguments are a question of opinion the economic arguments should be a question of fact but this is not so. Can you see why? We cannot compare a nationalised coal industry in this country with a private sector coal industry and see which is best since we only have a nationalised coal industry!

Let us compare a public corporation with a public company, say the Electricity Board with Tesco Ltd.

Copy out the table below filling in the blanks:

	Public Corporation	Public Company
Owned by		Shareholders
Controlled by	Board, appointed by Government Minister	
Run by		Professional Managers
Profit/surplus goes to	Government to spend on our behalf	
Losses		

Government Involvement other than Nationalisation

INDIVIDUAL FIRMS

The Government can take over individual firms or have a controlling interest in a company if they buy up shares. For example, during the First World War the Government bought a large share in British Petroleum (BP). Rolls Royce and British Leyland were bought more recently to prevent them from becoming bankrupt and sacking all or some of their workers.

LOCAL AUTHORITIES

Some local authorities run their own businesses. Most will charge for swimming pools and golf courses but this does not cover the full cost. We can consider these to be **services** and we shall look at these later. Hull, however, runs its own telephone service and Birmingham its own savings bank.

PUBLIC ENTERPRISE/PUBLIC SECTOR

In Chapter 1 we saw that everyone should enjoy some services such as education and health services. These we call **merit goods**. Other goods such as defence can only be provided by the Government. These we call **public goods**. The **public sector** includes not only the public corporations but also the Government departments and local authorities which provide these various goods and services. We pay for these through the different taxes which are collected by the Government. This does not mean that you cannot go to the private sector for such services as health care and education, but you do not have to since the Government will provide them for you. These are not enterprises as such like the public corporations since they do not charge for their service, but are however, part of the public sector.

Note Some of our public corporations were never part of the private sector, they could not therefore be nationalised. They were in fact formed by the Government. For example, the Post Office and BBC.

DENATIONALISATION AND PRIVATISATION

We saw earlier that many of the arguments for nationalisation are political. When there is a change in Government attitudes to public ownership can change. Iron and Steel, for example, was nationalised in 1949, **denationalised** (sold back to the private sector) in 1953 and then renationalised (brought back into public ownership) in 1969.

The present Government has undertaken a programme of **privatisation** (selling parts of a nationalised industry to the private sector). It has already sold Britoil, Cable and Wireless and British Aerospace as well as some of the public shareholding in BP. This raised £1.7 billion. It is hoped, by the Government, that it will be able to raise a further £11 billion over the next 5 years as it sells off such giant public corporations as British Telecom, British Airways and British Leyland (as well as many more).

SUMMARY EXERCISE

1 The public sector can be described as those parts of the economy which are controlled by the Government. This includes:

a Public Corporations
b Central Government Services
c Local Government Services

Give 2 examples of each.
2 Define the term **nationalisation**
3 Give one political argument **in favour** of nationalisation.
4 Give one political argument **against** nationalisation.
5 How do Governments pay for the services they provide?
6 Give **one similarity** between the organisation of a public corporation and a public company.
7 Give one **difference** between the organisation of a public corporation and a public company.
8 Give one economic argument **in favour** of increased nationalisation.
9 Give one economic argument **against** increased nationalisation.
10 Define the term privatisation and give an example.

ASSIGNMENT

You are an MP during the 1945–1951 Parliament. Today is the final debate on the nationalisation of electricity. Decide whether you are in favour or against and using the case study and the arguments set out below write a speech you hope to make.

Arguments For the Nationalisation of Electricity

- It would be possible to coordinate the whole industry.
- It is a very important industry and should be in Government control.
- It is a 'natural monopoly' and should be run in the public interest.
- No wasted competition and advertising.
- Would be far more efficient.
- Any profit should go to the Government.

Arguments Against the Nationalisation of Electricity

- It would lead to too much 'red tape'.
- People should have freedom of choice.
- Making a profit would make it efficient.
- Too large would lead to poor labour relations and strikes.
- It will have to be subsidised.
- Not fair on original owners.

4 Cooperative Enterprise

Cooperative enterprise can take very many forms.

WORKER   Business owned and controlled by its workers

HOUSING   Homes run and owned by tenants collectively

COMMUNITY   Groups from a community joining together to run recreational facilities etc

RETAIL   Shops owned and run by their customers

We shall be looking at 2 in detail—the worker and retail cooperative.

The worker cooperative

This is a business where all the workers are part owners. This means that they not only undertake to work for the firm, but also share in the important decisions which have to be made and of course share in the profits.

CASE STUDY

Richard Baxendale & Sons Ltd (Baxi Heating)

Richard Baxendale & Sons Ltd was founded over 100 years ago in Preston and until 1983 was a private company owned mainly by the Baxendale family. The company manufactures domestic heating equipment—you may well have one of their products in your fireplace at home. Richard Baxendale, who founded the firm in 1866, did not then know that his name would be given to a type of grate. In those days it was a small iron foundry supplying other firms with metal parts to order. The turning point came in 1935 when Richard's son, John invented a new type of grate—the Baxi Burnall. These grates are still very popular and the Baxi Burnall, today often fitted with a back boiler and pump to heat radiators, sells about 15 000 a year or 80% of the market. During the 1960s people started to change over to gas central heating which they found cheaper and more convenient. The Baxendale company was the first to

realise that most houses have very small kitchens allowing little room for a gas boiler.

Using the experience they had built up over the years they were able to develop a gas boiler that fitted into the old fireplace, heated the water and radiators and also looked good in the room with a normal gas fire at the front. The idea caught on and is still very popular—the *Baxi Bermuda*.

By 1973, 4 out of every 10 gas heating systems were powered by this system. Since then the company has developed wall boilers, very useful in flats and smaller houses and more recently floor standing boilers and wall mounted gas space heaters. This small family company grew by producing new products the customer wanted until in 1982 it employed 900 people and made an annual profit of nearly £6m.

The firm remained a **private company**—owned by the family. There were differences detectable however. In 1963 a system of 'worker participation' was introduced. This meant that the workers elected representatives who, along with members of the management and a trade union representative, formed a 'works council' where problems, ideas, production targets etc could be discussed.

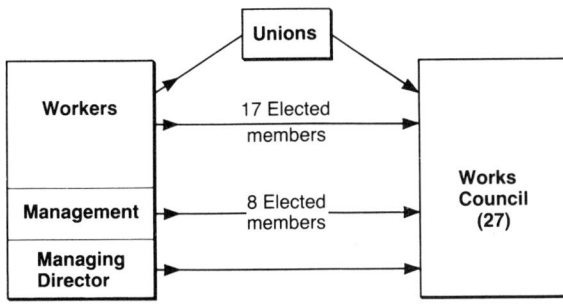

Baxi heating works council 1963–83

This system was introduced for several reasons:

- To make jobs more interesting.
- To give workers a say in important decisions.
- To help spread important information.

In 1965 a next step was to introduce a limited profit sharing scheme. Under this scheme any workers who had worked for more than 12 months would receive a cash bonus if profits were higher than a specified amount. The final change came in 1983 when the firm converted from a private company into a worker cooperative.

The shares were bought from the family by the company at a cost of £5$\frac{1}{4}$m and placed in a trust—the **employee trust**. These shares are owned by the workers who work at the company and their interests are looked after by a number of **trustees** who themselves do not own shares. Up to 49% of the shares can be sold to individual workers at the factory who will then watch the value of these shares grow if the company makes a profit. The major decisions are made by the **'partnership council'** which comprises part trustees and part elected representatives of the workforce. The **trustees** appoint a managing director who in turn appoints his executive board to run the company. The trustees will always have

the majority vote of 51% of the shares but they cannot use this to out-vote the partnership council without a full meeting of all the workers where all sides of the arguments will be heard. This is a very complicated system since this is a large company with many workers but in principle it is like many others. The shares are owned by the workers, who have a say in the running of the firm. Profits are still shared as before, with cash bonuses.

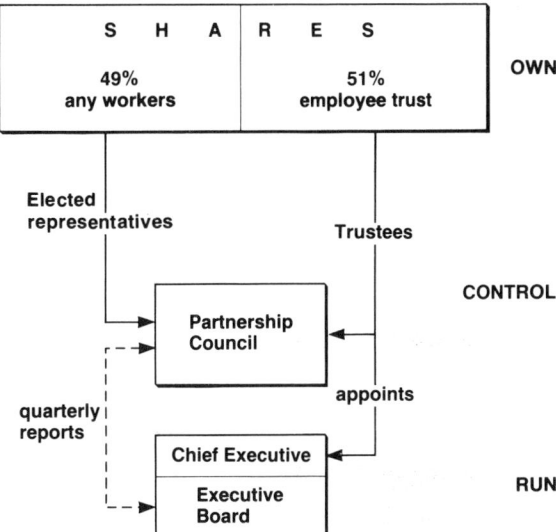

Baxi Heating was and is an efficient, profitable company. We can probably see that this form of enterprise has advantages for the workers but why did the family owners decide upon this form of enterprise? Why not 'go public'?

In their official publications about this conversion to a worker cooperative they give 2 main reasons for their actions:

- **Job security**

    If the firm became a large public company it might well be taken over by a giant company who could well decide to close down the plant or sack workers.

- **Efficiency**

    Since the workers own the firm they are likely to work harder, because they are working for themselves. It is interesting to note that there has never been a strike at this firm.

Exercise

The Baxi Heating example highlighted 2 major advantages of worker cooperatives. These were job security and efficiency. Assume you have just secured a job at Baxi Heating. A list of possible advantages of a worker cooperative follows. For each advantage award a mark from **1** to **5**, where **5** indicates that you think this advantage would definitely exist in your job, **4** it is likely to exist and so on until **1** it is very unlikely to exist in your new job.

Possible Advantages of a Worker Cooperative

Mark:	1	2	3	4	5
• Less boring work					
• Better labour relations					
• Job security					
• Workers work harder					
• More responsible workers					
• Workers produce better products					
• Workers earn more					

Your teacher will compare the results of the class and discuss your answers with you.

Types of Worker Cooperative

Baxi Heating is just one of the 500 or so worker cooperatives in the UK. Most are much smaller and employ on average approximately 18 people. In other countries like France and Spain there are many more cooperatives employing a more significant number of workers. All worker cooperatives are different, but the Cooperative Development Agency identifies 5 main types:

Conversions An old established firm is given or sold to its workers.

New Starts A group of workers set up in business as a cooperative.

Rescue An attempt to save a factory which has been closed by its owners, by the workers.

Phoenix An attempt to save part of a business which has been closed down.

Job Creation Schemes In areas of high unemployment local authorities often help unemployed people form cooperatives.

Sources of Finance for Worker Cooperatives

Exercise

By drawing up a list compare the various ways of raising money open to a public company such as Tesco with those open to a worker cooperative like Baxi Heating.

The methods of raising finance for a worker cooperative are limited not so much in the number of different methods available but in the amount of money that can be raised. Public companies can raise millions of pounds by selling shares, however a worker cooperative is unable to do this. The main sources are:

• Savings of workers
• Borrowing from friends, relatives, community groups, churches, trade unions and other sympathisers
• Borrow from a bank
• Trade credit, that is pay for supplies **after** using them and selling service or product
• Official sources—loans/grants from local authority
• Lease equipment, that is rent expensive items

Finance is a problem. The worker cooperative will find it difficult to raise the necessary cash for expansion unless it is already a profitable company, for then it can use some of the profits it is making. It will come as no surprise to note that the majority of worker cooperatives in this country are small and to be found in the service areas. Such production as house decorating, motor car repairs, computer software need very

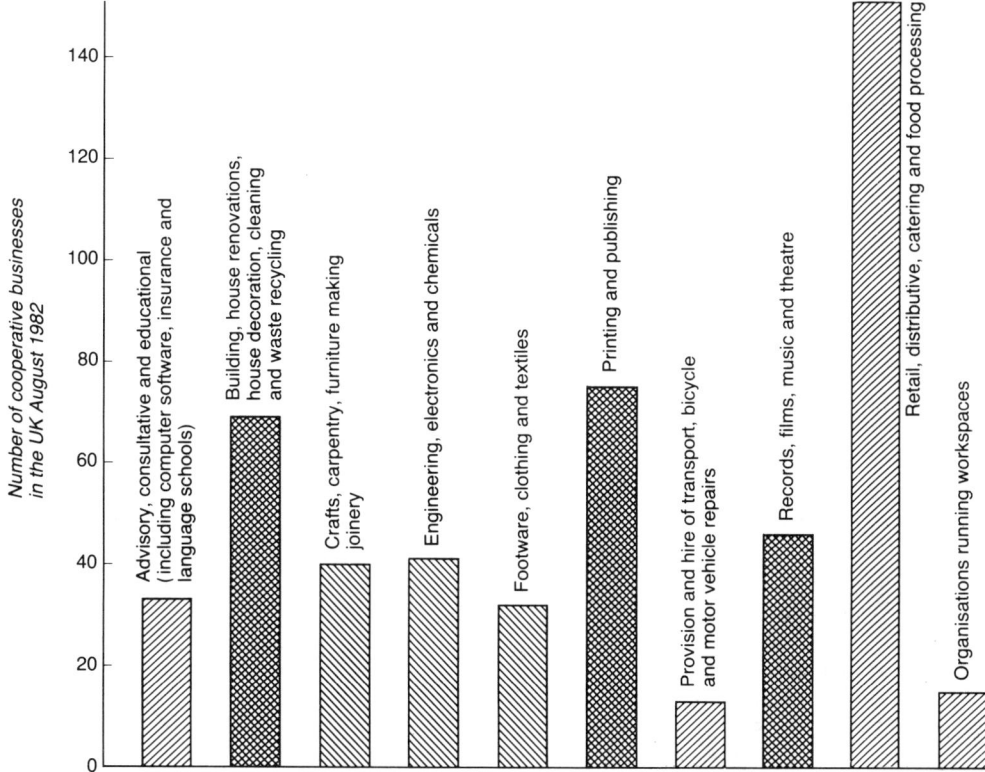

KEY:

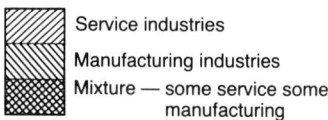 Service industries

Manufacturing industries

Mixture — some service some manufacturing

Fig 13 Types of worker cooperatives in the UK (1982)
Source: CDA 1982 Directory

little capital. They can be undertaken from home and need little specialised equipment. Figure 13 illustrates the types of worker cooperatives listed by the CDA in their 1982 Directory. Where they exist in industries which require large amounts of capital they are more often conversions or very old and have grown slowly over the years.

ASSIGNMENT

Read this article from *The Guardian* about *Instant Muscle* and then answer the following questions.

Instant Muscle, instant employment   Polly Toynbee

IT BEGAN with four school leavers from Farnham. They left school with a handful of failed A levels between them, and no prospect of a job. Looking around in that well-heeled part of Surrey they saw work to be done, though no actual jobs. They printed a leaflet and offered their services under the title Instant Muscle. The list of unskilled services they offered included: Mow the lawn, put up shelves, paint the house, sweep the leaves, paper the bedroom, unblock the drains, dig the garden, mind the baby — all the jobs you meant to do but haven't had time.

Within two days they had been asked to do 70 jobs in the area, charging a standard £2.50 an hour. So they called in some unemployed friends and went down to the Job Centre to bring in more young people to work with them. Last summer there were 40 of them working full time.

Peter Raynes, the father of one of the boys, became interested. He ran a management consultancy firm of his own and he saw how Instant Muscle could grow and spread all over the country. "There were mistakes at first," he says. "It started as a partnership, employing other people. But it gave the employees no sense of belonging, of doing their own thing. The whole point ought to be to get depressed unemployed young people to realise that there are things they can do for themselves. They just looked on the partners as bosses, and that was hopeless." Someone mentioned the word co-operative to him. "I didn't know anything about co-ops — just thought of them as rather tatty supermarkets."

He gave up his management consultancy and set to work on Instant Muscle full time, for no pay. For a year now he has worked non-stop, his small bungalow packed with filing cabinets. He sold his Lotus Elan, and has all but burnt up his savings, without grants or assistance. But there are now six flourishing Instant Muscle co-operatives around the country, and by the end of March there will be 18. Another 19 will follow shortly.

To get started each co-op needs about £500 as a cash float to acquire premises, telephone, and a few tools. This is usually forthcoming from local authority or local charity, but after that, the co-op sinks or swims on its own. Peter Raynes needs central government funding for his own operation. He has no secretary, and reckons five full-time workers are needed to travel around setting up new groups, offering two-day training courses on running co-operatives and co-ordinating their activities. "The whole point is that the young people should do it themselves, but we have learned the pitfalls from our mistakes and they do need help in the first stages."

In Wellington, Somerset, the Instant Muscle co-op now has nine members, three girls and six boys. Andrew Binding is 18 and joined at the beginning, three months ago. He had 3 CSEs.

He saw no prospect of a job, and drew supplementary benefit. He read about Instant Muscle at the Job Centre and applied to join. "I've been doing concreting and painting mostly. We got a lot of jobs right from the start when we began leafletting the area. Of course when the weather's bad there's not so much we can do. We've lists of jobs waiting to be done. In a good week I might get £50–£60, at £1.25 an hour, and £1 an hour into the co-op. I was on £23.50 supplementary benefit before." Their first money went into buying a Transit van, their most important capital investment. Now they are trying to get the money for a cement mixer.

---

1   What type of cooperative is *Instant Muscle*.

2   Peter Raynes, father of one of the original boys, is quoted as saying: 'There were mistakes at first—it started as a partnership employing other people.' Why was this a mistake?

3   What advantages does this type of cooperative offer to the young unemployed?

4   Peter Raynes would like some funds from central Government. What would he do with this money?

5   List the types of jobs *Instant Muscle* offer to do. Why are these most suitable?

6   We are told that each cooperative group needs about £500 to start working. Where is this money found?

7   Andrew Binding says he is paid £1.25 an hour and £1 an hour into the coop. What sort of things do you think the £1 that is paid into the coop buys?

8   Why do Andrew and the other members of the coop not 'go it alone'? What do they gain by being members of a coop?

CASE STUDY

The Retail Cooperative Society

Most high streets in the country have a Coop shop and at some time in your life you must have been into such a shop. They are not very different to any other supermarket or department store—the difference is in the ownership. Retail cooperatives are owned by their members. Anyone over 16 who shops in a Coop can become a member if they buy part of a share in the society which costs as little as 5p. The full shares cost £1 and one can own up to £2 000 worth.

The Cooperative principle for running shops dates back to the 1840s when a group of workers in Rochdale saved up enough money to start their own shop (below right). They hoped to grow into what we now call a commune owning their own land and houses and producing their own food. From these early beginnings the cooperative movement was formed and the societies of today are still based upon the same principles:

- Open membership—anyone over 16 can belong.
- Democratic control—the people who control the Coop, the Board, are elected by the members all of whom have **one vote** no matter how many shares they own.
- Fixed return on shares. Although interest is paid to those who own shares the amount is low and fixed.
- Profits are distributed in proportion to the amount **bought** from the society.
- Promotion of education.
- International cooperation with other cooperatives.

The shop in Rochdale was a great success and led the original members to buy a corn mill as a joint venture with others. As other retail societies were formed in different areas they began to act together in buying goods in bulk (wholesaling) and set up the Cooperative Wholesale Society and from there it was a logical step to become involved in producing their own goods. If you look at Fig 14 you can see just how many different goods are provided by their own factories now.

In 1872 the CWS started a loan and deposit department for member societies. This has since developed into a proper bank just like any other high street bank with branches and customers all over the country.

If you look at Fig 15 it shows just how the Cooperative movement works in the UK today.

In the early days and until quite recently any

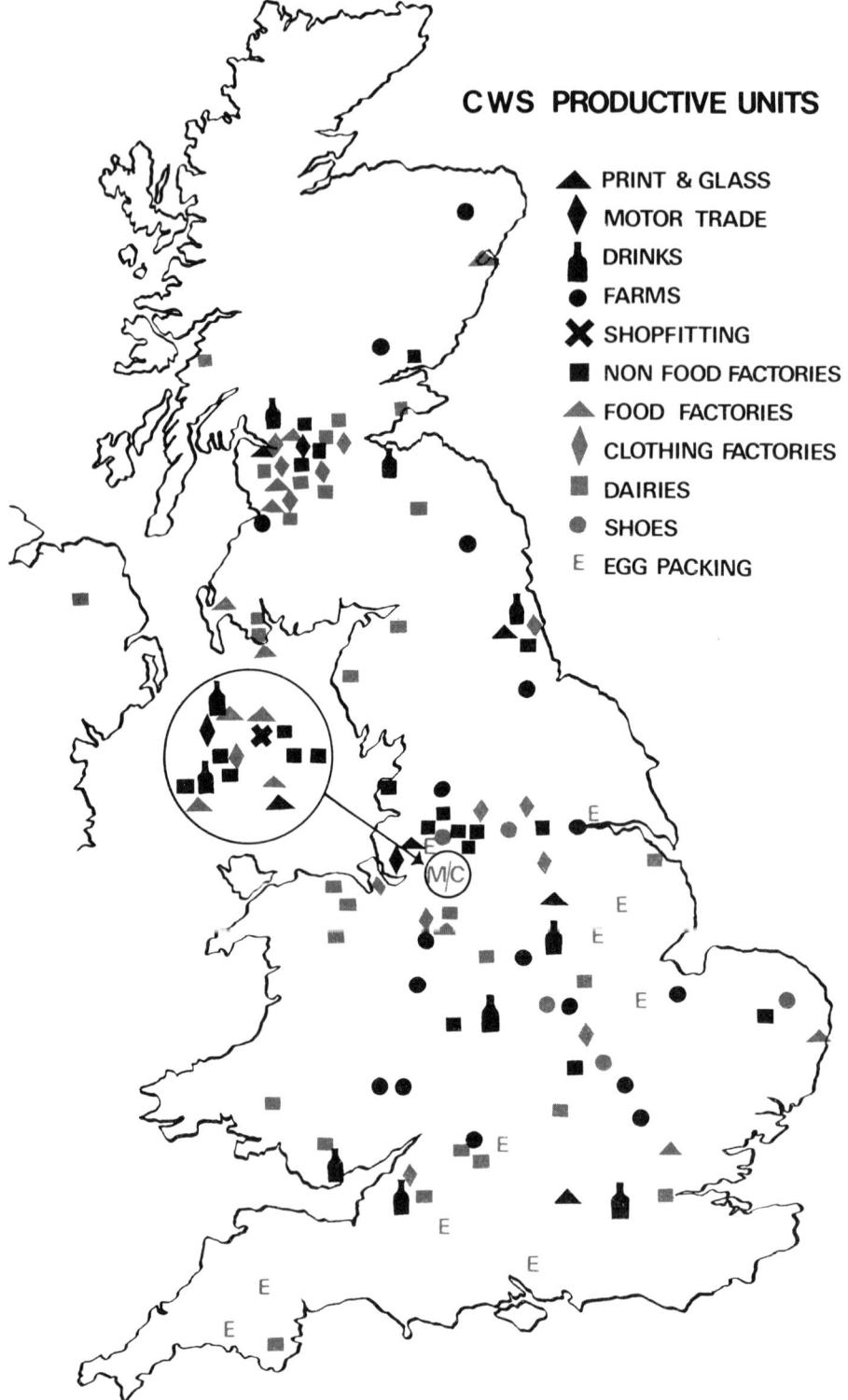

CWS PRODUCTIVE UNITS

▲ PRINT & GLASS
◆ MOTOR TRADE
🍾 DRINKS
● FARMS
✕ SHOPFITTING
■ NON FOOD FACTORIES
▲ FOOD FACTORIES
◆ CLOTHING FACTORIES
■ DAIRIES
● SHOES
E EGG PACKING

Fig 14

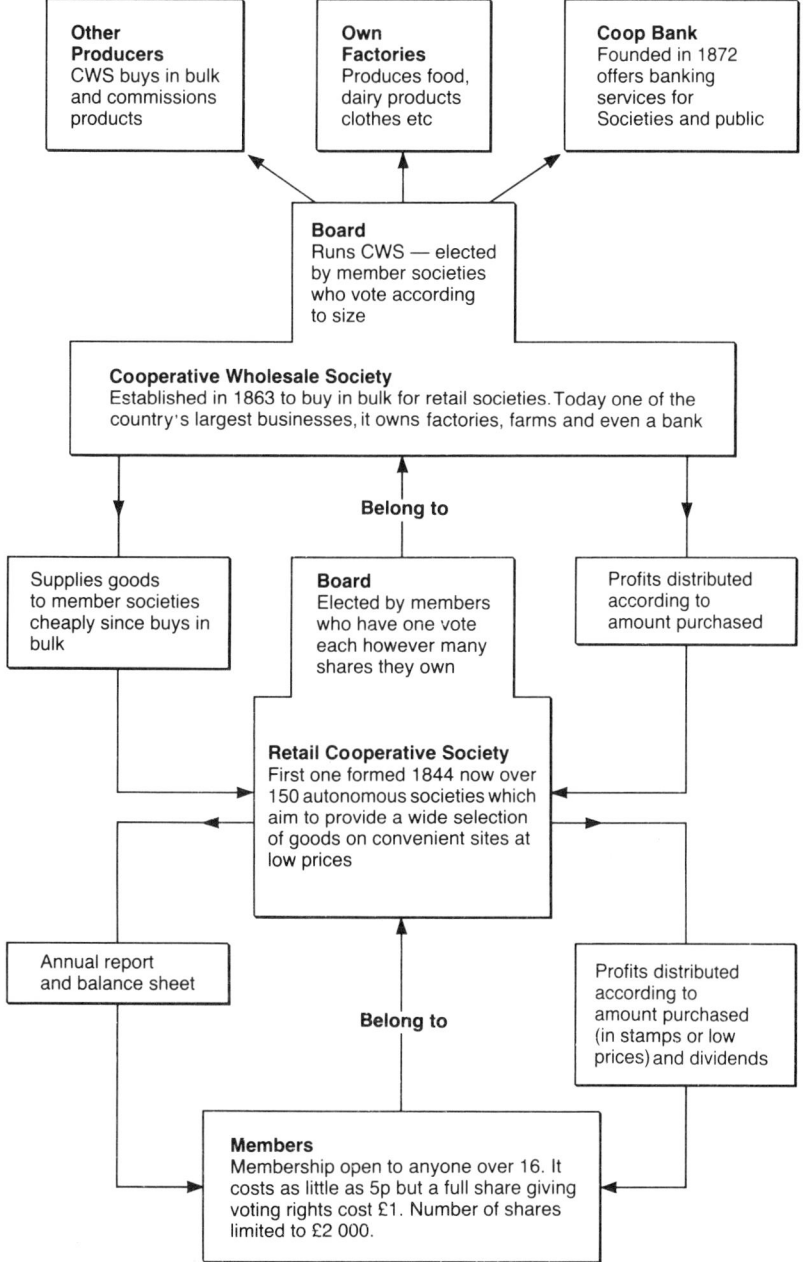

Other Producers
CWS buys in bulk and commissions products

Own Factories
Produces food, dairy products clothes etc

Coop Bank
Founded in 1872 offers banking services for Societies and public

Board
Runs CWS — elected by member societies who vote according to size

Cooperative Wholesale Society
Established in 1863 to buy in bulk for retail societies. Today one of the country's largest businesses, it owns factories, farms and even a bank

Belong to

Supplies goods to member societies cheaply since buys in bulk

Board
Elected by members who have one vote each however many shares they own

Profits distributed according to amount purchased

Retail Cooperative Society
First one formed 1844 now over 150 autonomous societies which aim to provide a wide selection of goods on convenient sites at low prices

Annual report and balance sheet

Belong to

Profits distributed according to amount purchased (in stamps or low prices) and dividends

Members
Membership open to anyone over 16. It costs as little as 5p but a full share giving voting rights cost £1. Number of shares limited to £2 000.

Fig 15

profit or surpluses would be distributed in the form of a dividend. Every time a member purchased something they would give the cashier their membership number which would be recorded along with the amount spent. Then, at the end of the year, their account would be credited with so much back in the pound. The member could either draw this out or leave it as part of their share capital. Later the system of stamps was introduced. Any shopper was given stamps which were stuck into a book and exchanged for goods or added to share capital or changed for cash. A member wrote their number into the book and received a bonus. In some areas this system has been replaced by lower prices.

In order to promote education of their members

and workers the Cooperative movement have their own college which runs courses along with local training.

The Coop is more than just a shop owned by its customers. It has been referred to already as a movement, which it is.

The CWS and the different retail societies belong to the Cooperative Union which looks after all the activities of the cooperative movement in Great Britain. These include not only those we have already discussed but also its own political party formed in 1917. This endeavours to return MPs to parliament so that the voice of the Cooperative movement is heard there. (In 1984 there were 7 such MPs.)

Lastly, the Cooperative Union is affiliated to the International Cooperative Alliance which has 161 members from 64 countries and represents a total of 336 667 519 individual members. The aim of this organisation, which was formed as long ago as 1895, is to gather information about cooperatives from all over the world and then pass this information on to people who wish to form a cooperative.

Exercise

The following is a chart which aims to compare public joint stock companies, about which you learnt in Chapter 2, and Cooperative enterprises about which you learnt in this chapter. As you will see it is incomplete. Using the information that you have been given in these 2 chapters try and complete it.

	Retail Cooperative	*Worker Cooperative*	*Public Joint–Stock Company*
Ownership			Large number of shareholders. Often pension funds and other institutions. There is no limit on the number of shares owned.
Control	Shareholders have only one vote however many shares. They elect a board which manages the society.		
Capital Source			Many different types of shares are sold. Also loans from the public—debentures and banks. Value of shares varies from day-to-day but can be sold.
Distribution of Profits		Profits distributed to workers in a bonus which is either a percentage of income or a fixed amount each.	

Exercise

Here is a sketch of an imaginary shopping centre:

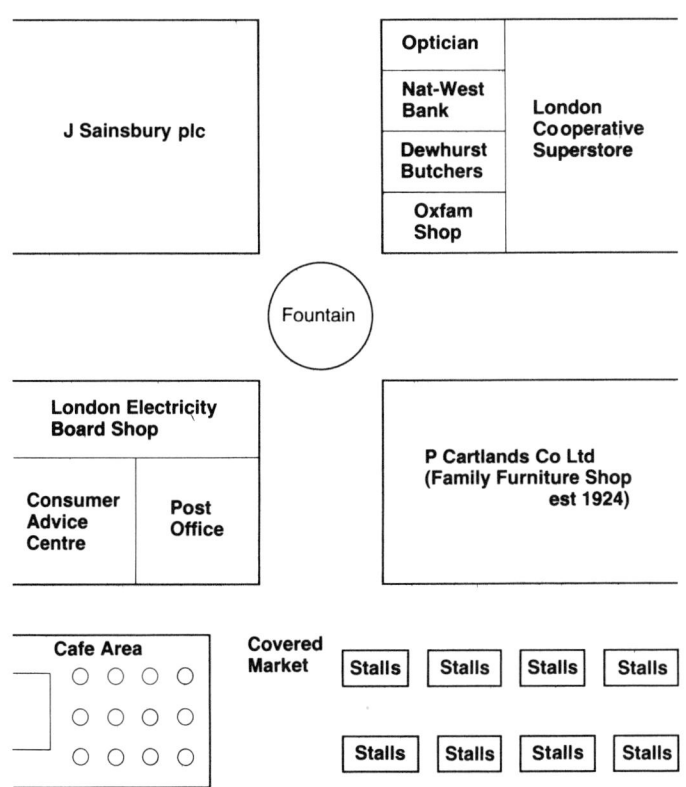

Either

From the imaginary shopping centre above find an example of:

a   a likely one-man business
b   a service which is likely to be provided by a partnership
c   a service provided by the local authority
d   a shop run by a public corporation
e   a shop which sells durable consumer goods
f   a shop run by volunteers
g   a shop which shares its profits with its customers

h   a shop which is part of a public company
i   a business which has obviously been involved in some form of horizontal integration
j   a shop which is likely to be a private company
k   a branch of a public corporation which was not formed as a result of nationalisation.

or

Draw a plan of your local shopping centre or high street and mark on it as many of the features listed in *a–k* above as you can.

SUMMARY EXERCISE

1 List the 4 main forms of cooperative enterprise in this country.

2 What are the differences between the following types of **worker cooperatives** in this country:

a Phoenix
b Conversion
c Rescue

3 Give 2 advantages to the worker of belonging to a worker cooperative.

4 Give 2 disadvantages to a worker of belonging to a worker cooperative.

5 What source of finance open to public companies is not open to a cooperative enterprise?

6 In what main industrial area are most British cooperatives to be found? Why is this so?

7 How are the profits of a retail cooperative distributed?

8 List as many differences as you can between a share in a retail cooperative and one in a public company.

9 How are the members of the Board of a retail cooperative selected?

10 List 2 other interests of the retail cooperative movement other than providing cheap goods for members.

ASSIGNMENT

Imagine that after working for a small engineering firm for a year it is announced the owners are making a loss and have decided to close the factory. Many of the workers are proposing to take over the firm and run it as a worker cooperative. Using the evidence given in this chapter decide whether you would be in favour of such a change. Write a brief summary of your reasons.

5 People at Work

Specialisation

People work in order to earn money to buy things they need and want. In the past families provided for themselves, each household being able to satisfy all of its members' needs. This is called **self-sufficiency**. It has great limitations and in general results in a poorer way of life. As people came together in groups and lived in settlements they gradually realised it was better for people only to work at one job—**to specialise**. There are many advantages:

- a person can fully utilise a natural ability
- a person can develop a skill and become very good at a job
- each person would only require one set of tools or piece of equipment
- no time is lost changing from task to task

All of these advantages combine to give the main gain from specialisation—greater output.

A doctor and an assembly line worker are both specialised workers. There is however, a difference. The doctor is a specialist, studying the subject of medicine in great depth for many years. An assembly line worker is quickly trained and performs one or two simple repetitive tasks day after day. The doctor probably finds the work interesting and rewarding, however, the assembly line worker may well become bored.

Exercise

1 Give one reason for working other than the financial reward.
2 List 3 jobs which are not paid. Suggest a reason why these jobs are not paid.

3 Give 3 examples of specialisation in depth, like a doctor.
4 Give 3 examples of specialisation by process, like an assembly line worker.
5 Give one disadvantage to the worker of specialisation.
6 Give one advantage to the community of specialisation.
7 Explain this statement: 'In the UK there is no shortage of work simply a shortage of paid employment.'

ASSIGNMENT

Conduct a class experiment.

1 Divide the class into 2 groups of equal size.
2 Give each group the same simple task which requires several stages. For example, the cutting out and manufacture of paper aeroplanes or the sorting and stapling of a booklet.
3 Let one team specialise—that is each member undertakes one stage only in the task. The other group is not allowed to specialise, each member must complete the entire task on their own.
4 Each group must be given the same equipment.
5 Count the final output of each group.
Write up the results of your experiment to include a conclusion. Comment upon the quality from each group and the feelings of group members.

The Working Population

In a developed economy such as ours not everyone works. Those people who offer themselves for work are collectively known as the **working population**. This includes those people unemployed since it is the potential work force (those who could work, not those who are working).

WHO WORKS IN THE UK (1981)

Total population 56 million people

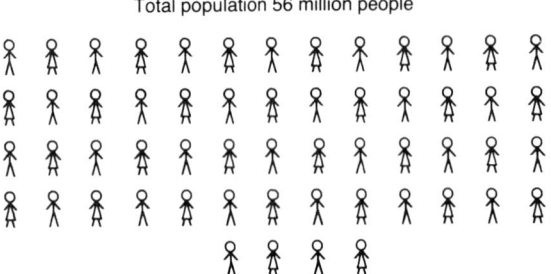

Not all of the population are the right age to work

less → Those under 16 and over 60/65

Total in working age group

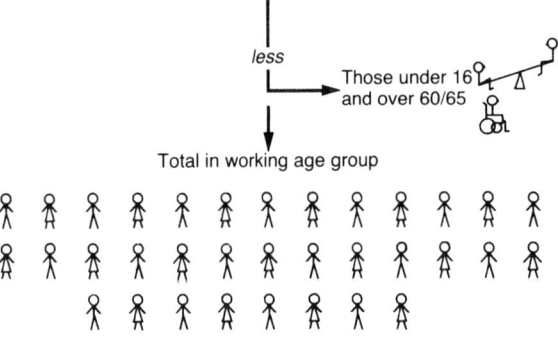

Not all those people of the right age do work

less → Housewives Students

Those of retirement age who still work

plus

Total working population (26 069 000 people)

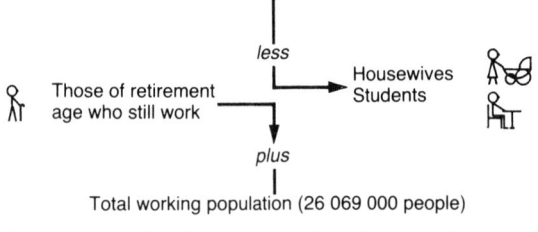

Not all those who want to work can find work. Of this 26 million, potential work force 13% are currently unemployed.

Fig 16 Source: Britain: An Official Handbook, 1983, HMSO

The size of the working population is very important. A country with a large working population has the ability to produce a great number of goods and services. Those people who are unable to work—the very young, the old and parents bringing up children—are known as the **dependent population**. The working population must support the dependent population. In 1981 the working population of the UK was just 26.1 million which is 60% of the population over 16 years old or 47% of the total population.

FACTORS WHICH AFFECT THE SIZE OF THE WORKING POPULATION

1 The size of the total population

A larger population will in general contain more workers. The size of a country's population will depend upon the number of people entering (being born or immigrating) and the number of people who leave (die or emigrate. See Fig 17).

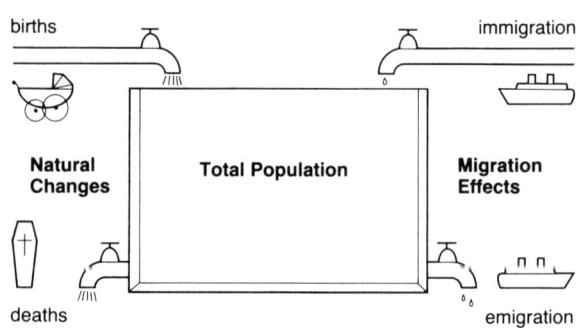

Fig 17 Factors affecting total population

The effects of births and deaths are called **natural changes** and are the major influence upon total population. The chart that follows shows that since 1962 the number of births in the UK have been falling sharply. Many people think this is part of a long-term trend. As people become better educated they realise that a smaller family can lead to a higher standard of living. More reliable forms of contraception have become generally available and many more women wish to pursue a career. Other people believe that the difficult economic conditions over the last few years have caused couples to postpone having children.

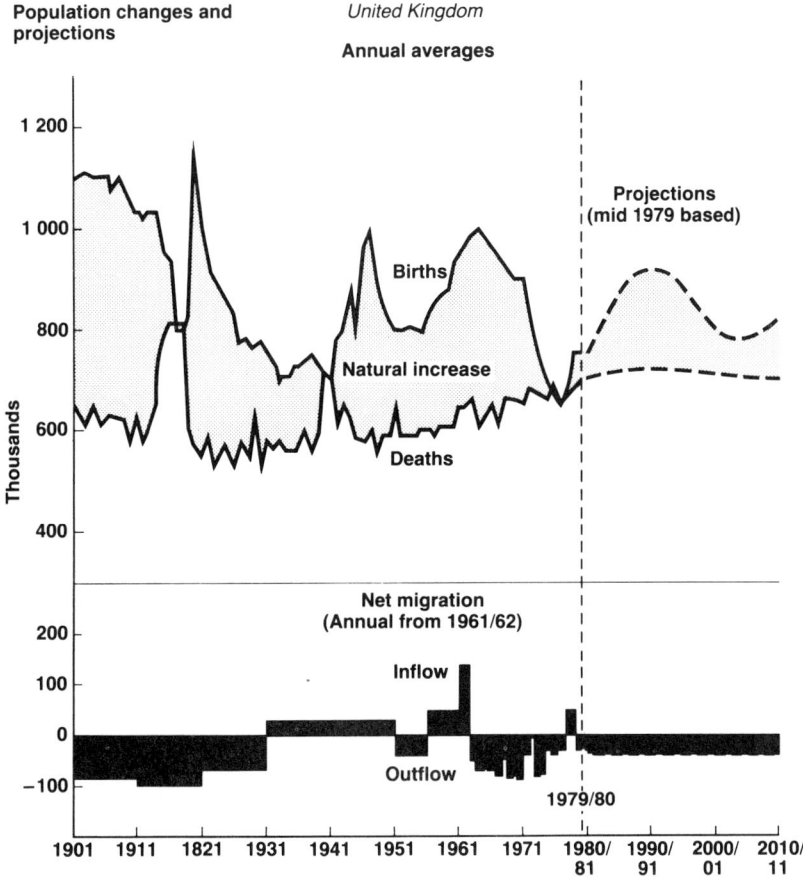

Population changes and projections

United Kingdom

Annual averages

Projections
(mid 1979 based)

Births

Natural increase

Deaths

Net migration
(Annual from 1961/62)

Inflow

Outflow

1979/80

Thousands

Migration effects, immigration and emigration, are relatively small and have little effect upon the total population. It is a great expense and upheaval to move to another country and most, including our own, have strict laws which restrict immigration. Since 1962 more people have emigrated from this country than have immigrated *to* this country. Only on a few occasions has there been a net migration into the UK. For example, during the Second World War when Europeans fled from Hitler (see above and page 48).

2 The age distribution of the population

Only people of a certain age work. In the UK full-time employment starts when children reach the age of 16 and usually ends at 60 for women and 65 for men, the age at which a state pension can be drawn. A population could be growing not because more children are being born but

because people are living longer. Over the last 100 years life expectancy for both men and women has increased dramatically in the developed economies. In the UK the percentage of people who are above the retirement age has increased from 5% in 1901 to 15% now. This has, however, been matched by a fall in the birth rate leaving a dependent population roughly the same size. If this trend continues the dependent population will increase in size in proportion to the working population. With fewer children being born fewer will be available to work but more and more old people will need to be supported.

3 Social changes

Women now form a high percentage of the total working population and this is increasing. It is not considered unusual for a woman to return to work after having children nor for the man in a

Population Changes and Projections

	Population at start of period (millions)	*United Kingdom* Average annual change (thousands)				*Millions and thousands*
		Live births	Deaths	Net natural change	Net civilian migration and other adjustments	Overall annual change
Census enumerated:						
1901–11	38.2	1091	624	467	−82	385
1911–21	42.1	975	689	286	−92	194
1921–31	44.0	824	555	268	−67	201
1931–51	46.0	785	598	188	+22	213
Mid-year estimates:						
1951–61	50.3	839	593	246	+6	252
1961–66	52.8	988	633	355	−15	339
1966–71	54.5	937	644	293	−71	222
1971–72	55.6	862	661	202	−30	171
1972–73	55.8	808	672	136	−4	132
1973–74	55.9	752	664	88	−78	10
1974–75	55.9	721	671	50	−71	−22
1975–76	55.9	689	681	7	−22	−15
1976–77	55.9	655	660	−5	−28	−33
1977–78	55.9	664	665	—	−17	−17
1978–79	55.8	720	673	47	—	47
1979–80	55.9	744	658	86	—	—
Projections:						
1979–81	55.9	743	692	52	−15	37
1981–91	56.0	857	710	147	−29	117
1991–2001	57.2	861	713	148	−30	118

Fig 18 Source: Social Trends 1981, HMSO

partnership to look after those children. Laws passed during the last 15 years have ensured that women are paid the same as men, cannot be discriminated against and are allowed maternity leave to have a baby and return to their old job. Changes in the law and attitudes have, therefore, increased the number of economically active women (either working or looking for employment) and therefore the size of the working population.

4   Government influences

The Government will influence the size of the working population in several ways. It is the Government which decides the official retirement age, school leaving age, number of further education places and level of grants. The Government has rarely changed the school leaving age; 1947 to 15 and 1972 to 16, but between 1960–61 and 1975–76 the percentage of young people leaving school and *not* seeking employment rose from 14.1% to 22%. This was probably not due to increases in grants but the increased availability of places in higher education.

Exercise

1   Give 2 reasons why very few people **migrate**.
2   From the graph (Fig 18) in which year did the UK experience a **natural decline** in population?
3   The UK has a growing number of old dependent people. List **two** problems this might cause.

4 Between 1961 and 1979 the percentage of economically active women (either working or looking for work) between the ages of 25 and 44 rose from 40.3% to 61.9%. Give **one** reason for this change and **one** consequence.

5 In the year 1975–76 19% of boys leaving school entered some form of full-time education but 25.6% of girls leaving school entered some form of full-time education. Explain the difference.

CASE STUDY

Mothercare and the falling birthrate

We have seen that the age distribution of a country's population will help to determine the size of its working population. It will also effect what that population wants. A change in the age distribution will cause changes in the pattern of consumption. If there is a fall in the birth rate it will affect certain businesses more than others. Mothercare, for example, specialise in providing clothes and other products for expectant mothers and their babies. The Chairman of Habitat/Mothercare, Sir Terrance Conran, was quoted in June 1983 as saying:

'It's only unsuccessful retailers who get worked up about it. These statistics about the ageing population are true but the changes in the market are not going to take place suddenly . . .'

Even so, many people feel that the fall in the birthrate will restrict Mothercare's natural growth. They are also facing increased competition from other stores like Boots, Marks & Spencer and C & A. Mothercare, however, aim to go on expanding and opening new shops.

Exercise

You are a member of the management team of Mothercare who has been asked by Sir Terrance Conran to suggest ways of overcoming the problems of increased competition and a falling birth rate. Remember you wish to keep expanding and to make greater profits for your shareholders.

How many ways did you think of? Here is what Mothercare actually did during 1983–84:

- Revamped shops with attractive new interiors.
- Produced higher priced, more fashionable maternity dresses (£29.95 as well as £19.95). In the words of Sir Terrance, 'the signs are that Mothercare is retrieving the middle classes.'
- Produced clothes for older children 10–13.

THE GEOGRAPHICAL DISTRIBUTION OF THE POPULATION

The population of the UK is unevenly spread throughout the land. There is an uneven distribution between the 4 countries of the UK. England not only contains the majority of the

population (83%) but is more densely packed. The majority of people live in towns or urban areas as opposed to the open country; about three quarters of the total population now live in towns. Some cities have expanded to include the

(1979)	England	Wales	Scotland	Northern Ireland	United Kingdom
Population (millions)	46.4	2.8	5.2	1.5	55.9
Population Density (number per sq km)	356	134	66	109	229

Source: Social Trends, 1981 HMSO

surrounding towns leaving one vast **conurbation**. There are 7 such areas in the UK: Greater London, West Midlands, West Yorkshire, South-East Lancashire, Merseyside, Clydeside, and Tyneside. Between them they hold over one third of the country's population.

During the industrial revolution there was a movement of people towards the major coal fields since coal was the major source of energy and difficult to transport. Since the beginning of this century there has been a gradual southward shift of the population with Outer London and the South East growing rapidly since the Second World War. The fastest growing regions are now East Anglia and the South West.

The large conurbations do cause problems though. Transport is difficult due to bad congestion. At their centres the conurbations often have poor housing. To help the situation the **New Towns Act (1946)** gave the Secretary of State for the Environment the power to designate areas of the country for development into new towns. By attracting industry to new areas and building new homes for rent or purchase close at hand people would be encouraged to move away from the conurbations. New towns can be planned

Exercise

Study the following table:

Population and population density: regions and metropolitan counties

| | Mid-year estimates (millions) | | | | |
	1961	*1971*	*1976*	*1978*	*1979*
England:					
North	3.1	3.1	3.1	3.1	3.1
Tyne and Wear MC	1.2	1.2	1.2	1.2	1.2
Yorkshire and Humberside	4.7	4.9	4.9	4.9	4.9
South Yorkshire MC	1.3	1.3	1.3	1.3	1.3
West Yorkshire MC	2.0	2.1	2.1	2.1	2.1
East Midlands	3.3	3.6	3.7	3.7	3.8
East Anglia	1.5	1.7	1.8	1.8	1.9
South East	16.1	17.0	16.9	16.8	16.9
Greater London	8.0	7.4	7.0	6.9	6.9
Outer Metropolitan Area	4.4	5.2	5.3	5.3	5.3
Outer South East	3.7	4.2	4.6	4.6	4.6
South West	3.7	4.1	4.3	4.3	4.3
West Midlands	4.8	5.1	5.2	5.2	5.2
West Midlands MC	2.7	2.8	2.7	2.7	2.7
North West	6.4	6.6	6.5	6.5	6.5
Greater Manchester MC	2.7	2.7	2.7	2.7	2.6
Merseyside MC	1.7	1.7	1.6	1.5	1.5
Scotland:					
Central Clydeside	1.8	1.7	1.8	1.8	1.8

Source: Social Trends, 1981 HMSO

1 List 3 areas where there has been a stable population.

2 List 3 areas where there has been a fall in population.

3 List 3 areas where there has been a growth in population.

4 For **one** area in your answer to question **2** suggest one reason for the fall in population.

5 For **one** area in your answer to question **3** suggest one reason for the growth in population.

with modern needs and problems in mind. Cars can be kept away from shopping centres and adequate parking can be provided. The urban sprawl was further halted by the establishment of **green belts**—areas of countryside upon which building has been prohibited—around London, Birmingham and Liverpool.

Types of Employment

There are well over 35 000 different occupations in this country, and these occupations can be split into 3 different classifications. One convenient and quick way is to distinguish between 3 levels of production.

To produce anything one must start with raw materials, manufacture them into some good or service (often through many different stages) and then distribute and sell the product. The manufacture of a desk, for example, illustrates this process. The desk started life as a tree which had to be cut down. This is the first stage of production or **primary production**. Then it was turned into planks of wood and finally the desk. This we call **secondary production**. The last stage was to sell and deliver it to the school. This is the third or **tertiary stage**. The following diagram illustrates this process more clearly.

Primary Production
Industries concerned with obtaining raw materials or food eg agriculture, mining, fishing, forestry etc.

|

Secondary Production
Industries concerned with manufacturing building and construction, or in other words the stage at which things are made.

|

Tertiary Production
Industries concerned with distribution and services, including civil servants.

Consider the percentage of the working population engaged at each level. An interesting and perhaps surprising picture emerges:

Distribution of Employment by Sector

Category	% of working population 1971	1981
Primary	4.8	4.1
Secondary	42.2	36.6
Tertiary	53.1	59.2

(These figures exclude unemployed and armed forces and take public utilities as secondary.)

Source: Department of Employment, HMSO

The percentage of the working population employed in the primary sector is small and falling. This is not perhaps surprising since the UK has very few raw materials and a small land area. What is perhaps surprising is that well over half the working population are employed in the tertiary sector. Increased mechanisation has replaced workers in the primary and secondary sectors but the move towards tertiary employment is part of a long-run trend.

In the days before industrialisation most people worked on the land. However, industrialisation brought the growth of the manufacturing sector. Increased wealth and the fall in price of manufactured goods brought about by mass production meant that everybody wanted goods. As incomes continued to grow so the desire for services grew. The UK has specialised in fact in financial and professional services such as insurance and banking which results in more employment in the tertiary sector (see chart overleaf).

Exercise

Look at the chart overleaf carefully and then answer these questions:

1 Which 3 industries **lost** the most manpower over the decade shown?
2 Which 3 industries **gained** the most manpower over the decade shown?
3 What, if anything, do the industries in your answer to question 1 have in common which explains this loss of labour?
4 What, if anything, do the industries in your answer to question 2 have in common which explains this gain in labour?

Analysis of Civil Employment in Britain 1971 and 1981

Industry or Service	1971 Thousands	1971 Per cent	1981 Thousands	1981 Per cent
Primary sector				
Agriculture, forestry and fishing	734	3.1	657	2.7
Mining and quarrying	397	1.7	345	1.4
Manufacturing industries				
Chemicals and allied industries	483	2.0	471	1.9
Metal manufacture	558	2.3	402	1.6
Textiles, leather and clothing	1 147	4.8	831	3.4
Engineering and allied industries	3 650	15.2	3 150	12.9
Food, drink and tobacco	777	3.2	690	2.8
Other manufactures	1 565	6.5	1 385	5.7
Other production industries				
Construction	1 594	6.6	1 672	6.9
Gas, electricity and water	377	1.6	347	1.4
Services				
Transport and communications	1 639	6.8	1 582	6.5
Distributive trades	3 088	12.9	3 159	13.0
Professional, financial, scientific and miscellaneous services	6 512	27.1	8 081	33.2
National and local government service	1 509	6.3	1 596	6.5
Total in civil employment	24 031		24 367	
of whom employees	22 122		22 511	
Self-employed	1 909		1 856	

Source: Britain: An Official Handbook, 1983 HMSO

5 Many people believe that those industries which have had a growing workforce over the last decade will have a falling workforce over the next. Give one reason why this should be? What would be the result for the country if this is so?

A second way of looking at employment is to break jobs down into **job families**. This is how we approach the classification in careers lessons. You will find that somewhere in your school you have what is called a 'signposts' box file issued by Careers Research and Advisory Centre (CRAC), in which some 800 or so jobs are classified under 10 headings. Some jobs will fit into more than one section. It is often fun to try and think of a job which could fit all 10—perhaps a first division football manager? This is a very useful way of looking at employment for those who are choosing a career. If, for example, you wanted to work outdoors you would look at section J, or with numbers, section G. Here is the complete list with a few examples. Try to think of further examples as you go through. You can always check with the signposts box.

A **Scientific**—Air traffic controller, chiropodist, physicist

B **Social Service**—Nurse, dietition, social worker, youth leader

C **General Service**—Accountant, telephonist, sales assistant

D **Persuading/Influencing**—Estate agent, insurance salesman, journalist

E **Literary**—Archivist, barrister, interpreter

F **Artistic**—Fashion designer, dancer, photographer

G **Computational**—Accountant, actuary, surveyor

H **Practical**—Boatbuilder, cook, dental technician

I **Nature**—Farm worker, market gardener, botanist

J **Outdoor Active**—Merchant navy, army, building worker

LEVELS OF ENTRY

For every job family there are different levels of entry depending upon the academic ability or qualifications of the person concerned. These different levels of entry may differ in name from occupation to occupation, but they conform roughly to the pattern below:

Level of entry	Qualifications	Training
Operative	Nil	'on the job' for a few weeks
Craft	4 CSE grades 1–3	3–4 years including part-time college of Further Education, TEC/BTEC, City & Guilds
Technician	4 GCE grades A–C or CSE grades 1	As craft but higher level courses
Student	4 GCE grades A–C with 2 at A level	4–5 year professional training
Graduate	University degree	Further professional training

> ### ASSIGNMENT
>
> With the aid of the chart opposite and the following table from the Engineering Careers Information Service give examples of jobs from each level for the following:
>
> a Your own school
> b Your local general hospital
> c A large car manufacturer (like Fords)

Engineering Industry—Career Opportunities

Category	Typical Entry Requirements	Training and Further Education Recommended	Job Opportunities
Operator	No specific academic requirements. Entry age: 16 years and over. Indication of aptitude for working with metal. Headmaster's report.	Under 4 weeks—training programme. Over 4 weeks—training derived from job analysis. Under 18 years of age: 15–18 days of further education. Juvenile Operator Scheme (Broad Based).	No specific career pattern: machinist, assembler, welder, mate to a craftsman, etc. Long term prospects: foreman/supervisor.
Craft	Normally CSE preferred in maths. Other useful subjects: science, tech. drawing, physics, metal/woodwork, English. Entry age: 16–17 years.	First-year off/job training followed by module training covering at least two modules. Further education: normally City & Guilds craft courses. Duration of training: 3–4 years.	Dependent on module training, ie, fitter, turner, miller, welder, sheet-metal worker, electrician, maintenance engineer, etc. Additional training to develop further skills may be undertaken at any age, by using the appropriate modules. Long term prospects: supervision/management.

Engineering Industry—Career Opportunities

Category	Typical Entry Requirements	Training and Further Education Recommended	Job Opportunities
Technician	GCE/CSE O level (CSE Grade 1), passes in maths and a science subject. Other useful subjects: tech. drawing, metal/woodwork, engineering, English. Entry age: 16–17 years.	First-year off/job training followed by a specialised programme of technician training, to include manufacturing practice, design appreciation, communications, specific training. Further education: technician certificate course.	Mechanical laboratory technician, technical assistant, tool draughtsman, instrument technician, quality assurance technician, test engineer, junior contracts engineer, scheduler assistant work measurement engineer, development technician, etc. Long term prospects: supervision/management.
Technician Engineer	a 4 GCE/CSE O level passes (to include maths, a science subject and English). *or* b 6 GCE passes—maths and physics must have been studied to A level, and at least one passed. (For Scotland, 5 SCE passes are required, including maths and a science subject at H grade.)	First-year off/job training, followed by a specialised programme of technician engineer training, to include: manufacturing practice, design appreciation, communications, control techniques, commercial subjects, specific training. Further education: a Tech. Cert. & Tech. Dip. courses, bridging if required to— b higher technical certificate or higher technical diploma courses.	Development technician engineer, design draughtsman, estimator, work study, process planning, production control, test engineer, technical sales, service engineer, technical author, buyer, commissioning engineer, project engineer, etc. Long term prospects: supervision/management.
Professional Engineer or Technologist	University entrance and faculty requirements. Entry age: 18 years or over.	Thick or thin sandwich course, giving a combination of practical experience and University study leading to a university or CNAA degree. Duration of training: 4–5 years.	Production engineer, works manager, research engineer, designer, project engineer, overseas representative, consultant engineer, etc. Long term prospects: management.

Fig 19 Source: Engineering Careers Information Service (sponsored by EITB, EEF and CSEU)

Mobility of Labour

In a modern economy the demand for goods and services is constantly changing as new products are invented. This means that the jobs people are required to do also change. Ten years ago most schools did not have a computer, most now do. New products are now being invented more quickly than ever before which means that society does not expect workers to remain in the same occupation all of their working lives.

Labour needs to be **mobile**; that is the ability to change quickly from occupation to occupation and area to area, so that industry can adapt to the new technology and take advantage of the benefits it will bring.

Changing jobs can mean one of two things:

a A completely new occupation—**occupational mobility**
b A similar occupation in a different industry—**industrial mobility**

Either can be associated with a change in the area in which a worker lives—**geographical mobility** (see Fig 20).

There are many obstacles or barriers to mobility which prevent a smooth movement of workers from unnecessary jobs to new jobs. Lack of knowledge of the opportunities in different areas or industries for example. One of the major barriers is the **cost** of changing a job. Most people train for an occupation when they first leave school. They are young and have few responsibilities. They are able to survive on the low wage or grant they receive whilst they train. However, an older person, perhaps with financial responsibilities such as a family or home to support might not be able to survive on these low incomes. Moving house is a further problem. Not only does it cost thousands of pounds to move but it might be impossible because of the

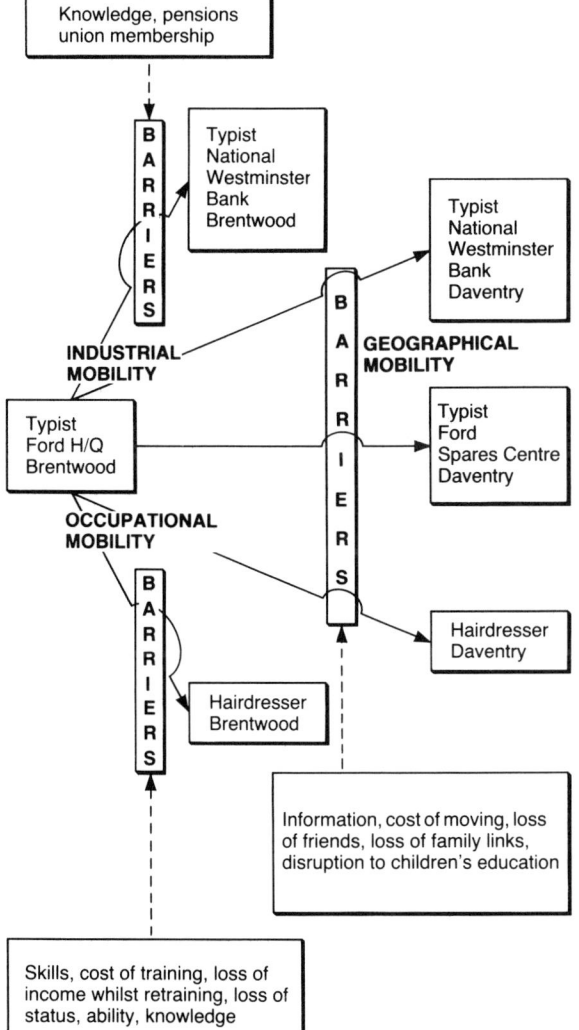

Fig 20 Types of labour mobility

Average House Prices 1983

Region	£
Greater London	34 640
South West	28 000
East Anglia	25 830
South East	33 764
Northern	20 032
Yorks & Humber	20 863
North West	22 832
East Midlands	22 026
West Midlands	23 131
Wales	22 556
Scotland	23 713
Northern Ireland	20 859
United Kingdom	26 471

Fig 21 Source: BSA Bulletin 38

different prices of houses in different parts of the country. Figure 21 shows that in 1983 the average price of a house in Greater London was 42% higher than in the North of England. It would be almost impossible for an unemployed shipbuilder in Newcastle to move to London even if he could find employment since he would not be able to afford a house.

Exercise

1 List **3** occupations/jobs which were common 50 years ago but are no longer required today.
2 List **3** occupations/jobs which are common today but were not required 50 years ago.
3 Give an example of something that you could do to ensure that you remain mobile as a worker.
4 Give one effect on the country if workers remain immobile.
5 Look at the figures below. Give **3** reasons why young people are more mobile than older people.

In 1979 11% of male workers and 13% of female workers changed their jobs at least once. The Government tries to increase mobility through the Department of Employment with such schemes as TOPS and the jobcentres (discussed later in the book).

ASSIGNMENT

Draw Fig 20 *Types of labour mobility*, but use examples from your own area.

Job mobility: full-time employees* who had changed employers in the previous 12 months, 1973, 1976, and 1979

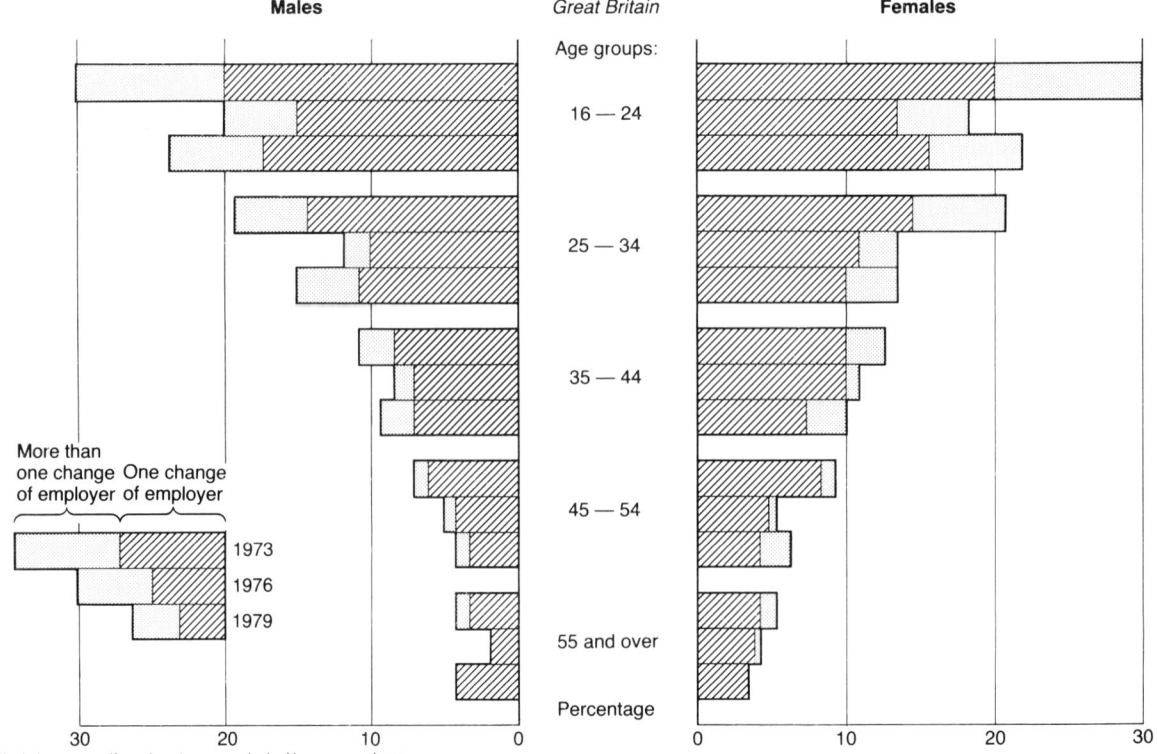

* Includes some self-employed persons who had been an employee during the previous 12 months. Excludes fulltime students who were working in the reference week.

Source: Social Trends, 1981 HMSO

Finding Work

Can you think of the ways people find work? One can:

- write to or approach the employer directly and ask
- go to the employment office (job centre) or careers office
- go to a private agency
- visit the school's careers teacher
- hear of the job through relatives or friends

One other important way to find work is through advertisements. These can be found in most newspapers—local and national. These often appear in categories, eg Hotel and Catering, etc. Some professions and trades have their own journals in which you would find advertisements for jobs in that specific field. An example of this is *The Times Educational Supplement* where teaching jobs are advertised. Also trade unions often have their own newspapers where specialist jobs are advertised. The National Union of Teachers has a weekly paper called *The Teacher* in which some teaching jobs are advertised. The following variety of jobs appeared in a local paper. Read through them carefully and then answer the questions.

Exercise

1 *Read the job advertisements.*

a Why do they ask for attractive bar staff and not a bar maid?
b Can you see any problems with the *Everest* job?
c Would you like the first cook's job? If not why not?
d Why do the Estate Agents want a car driver?
e Can you see 2 advantages in the Technician job?

GOVERNMENT HELP IN FINDING EMPLOYMENT

The Government provides various facilities for helping people find a job. The following paragraphs explain these services.

1 For the school leaver

At school Schools do not have to employ a careers teacher, but most do. It is not the job of a careers teacher to find employment for school leavers, this is the responsibility of the Careers Advisory Service. The role of a careers teacher in the school is to help students select the correct courses, decide upon a future career and apply for jobs. They arrange interviews with the Careers Advisory Service and organise careers displays and conventions. Often special careers lessons are given in the senior school where students learn how to write a letter of application, present their best image at interviews, etc. Most schools have a careers library where information about different occupations is kept.

The DE Group and its Functions

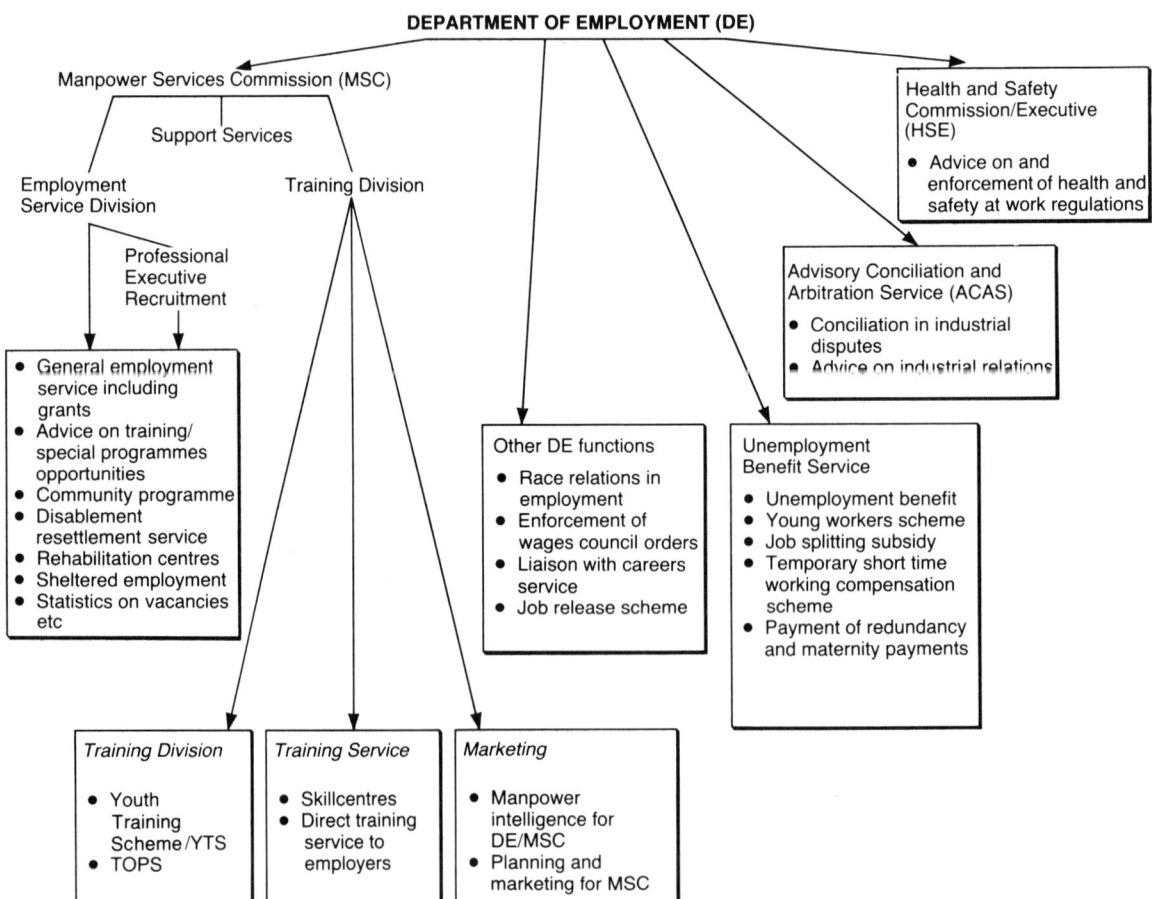

The Careers Advisory Service (CAS) This was established in 1909 and was called the 'Youth Employment Service'. It is run and financed by the education department of your council. Each area has a careers office from which careers and employment officers work. It is their responsibility to help young people find their first employment. A list of suitable jobs and training schemes is kept and visits are made to firms and colleges so that each officer has up-to-date information. Careers officers visit schools, take group discussions, interview school leavers and give advice. Often computers are used to help sort out appropriate jobs for students. Special careers officers help find employment for disabled students and older pupils.

2 For adults changing employment

Help is given to adults changing jobs by the Manpower Services Commission which is part of the Department of Employment. The diagram opposite shows that the MSC is split into 2 main bodies—the employment division and training division. The training division will be discussed later. The employment division runs well over a thousand **jobcentres** which provide information for the unemployed and those seeking a change in job or employment opportunities in the local area.

Most jobcentres have display boards like an estate agency but instead of houses they advertise jobs. Often these are arranged in types like the ones shown on this page. There are sections for local employment, part-time employment, jobs covering a wider area and jobs for the self-employed. People can just walk in and look around in their lunch hour or when they are out shopping. In this way all sorts of people are encouraged to use them, not just people who are redundant. Part-time work may suit someone with young children for example.

This is a completely free service. Employers do not pay to advertise nor do clients who find a job. If one of the cards seems suitable the person simply asks at the counter for further details and an interview is arranged. For the more serious job hunter an interview will be arranged with one of the experts who work at the jobcentre during which they will fill in a form (an *SR1/LNE*)

containing the relevant details, eg experience and qualifications. It is then the centre's task to try and match the unemployed person to a suitable vacant job. Computer terminals in the centre enable centres to keep in touch so that all the jobs in a whole area are known to each centre. The client is given help and advice on such things as training and even how to go for an interview if it is needed. There are also a small

---

SELF EMPLOYMENT

```
       JOB:  LIFE UNDERWRITERS (SELF EMP)        MAN OR

  DISTRICT:  15 MILE AREA OF LOCAL DISTRICT       WOMAN

      WAGE:  £80-£100 (3 NIGHT
             THEN COMMISSION O

     HOURS:  TO SUIT APPLICANT

   DETAILS:  AGE 25-40 EXPERIENCE NOT NECESSARY TO COLD
             CANVAS BUSINESSESS/HOUSEHOLDERS TO OBTAIN
             LIFE ASSURANCE & PENSION CONTRACTS, CAR OWNER
             & OWN PHONE PREFERRED, SMART APPEARANCE

             *** SELF EMPLOYED ***

ASK THE RECEPTIONIST FOR JOB NO
```

LOCAL JOBS

```
       JOB:  MOTOR PARTSMAN.                      MAN OR

  DISTRICT   LOCAL DISTRICT                        WOMAN

      WAGE:  £1.25. P.H. DEPEND-
             ING ON EXPERIENCE

     HOURS:  8.30.AM TO 6.30.PM.MONDAY
             TO SATURDAY.

   DETAILS:  MOTOR PARTSMAN AGE 20 - 40 REQUIRED.
             ESSENTIAL TO HAVE KNOWLEDGE OF THE MOTOR
             TRADE  AND PARTS TO WORK IN STORES. MUST ALSO
             HAVE EXPERIENCE OF HANDLING CASH. REFERENCES
             WILL BE TAKEN.

ASK THE RECEPTIONIST FOR JOB NO
```

---

number of professional executive recruitment offices where unemployed or even employed people of professional or executive status are given advice on availability of jobs which are kept on a special register.

When a firm moves into an area or if it needs to recruit labour for some reason, such as winning a new contract, it can set up a recruitment stall inside the jobcentre and undertake some initial interviewing and selection. This is clearly an efficient and cheap way of recruiting.

By offering this service the Government is clearly increasing the mobility of labour by giving people better **knowledge** of the jobs available and by helping them apply for them.

Exercise

Find out the following:

1 Where is the careers library in your school?
2 What jobs need a knowledge of economics or commerce?
3 What is the COIC library classification for banking?
4 Where is your local careers office?
5 Where is your nearest jobcentre?

ASSIGNMENT

Study the following article published in the *Sunday Times* in 1980 and construct a bar chart or pie chart to show the education or training of school leavers in the UK in 1980. The chart should have 4 sections:

- No training
- Full-time higher education
- Time served apprenticeships
- Full-time vocational education

Now answer these questions:

1 What is a **time-served apprenticeship scheme**?
2 Give an example of **full-time vocational education**.
3 What evidence is there to suggest that training of school leavers was poor in the UK?
4 Suggest one economic result of poor training for the UK.
5 What evidence is there to suggest that training has improved since 1980?

UK training is 'West's worst' Report by Robert Taylor

BRITAIN'S system of industrial training for workers is the worst of any major country. Sir Richard O'Brien, chairman of the Manpower Services Commission, warned last week that unless Britain transforms the way it trains its workers, it will cease to be an industrial trading power of any importance by the end of the Eighties.

Apart from Ireland, Britain has the highest proportion among Western countries of school-leavers receiving neither an apprenticeship nor any full-time vocational education as a preparation for a job, and it has the lowest proportion of apprentices in the working population.

As many as 44 per cent of young people go into the labour market in this country straight from school with no training at all, while 14 per cent win a time-served apprenticeship, 10 per cent go into full-time vocational education and 32 per cent into full-time higher education.

In Britain training is mainly left for individual employers to decide with government acting on the margin and in support of what employers see as their own needs. By contrast, in West Germany training is based on the collective employer needs viewed in national terms through powerful industry-based organisations.

With three times as many apprentices as in Britain (1 500 000) the West German economy benefits from having two out of every three men and one out of every two women in the labour market with vocational qualifications through practical and theoretical testing.

The most impressive feature of the West German system is the commitment to a basic vocational training year provided free for 15- or 16-year-old pupils in 13 broad occupational fields. By 1982 as many as 100 000 youngsters will be covered by this scheme. The State plays a vital part in the provision of suitable training through grants and subsidies.

In the United States there is a substantially better system than in Britain.

Americans enjoy a uniquely high rate of enrolment in tertiary education, with about 66 per cent of school-leavers proceeding to some form of post-secondary education and about 50 per cent going to college.

As the needs of industry are for more technical expertise from workers, greater flexibility and mobility between jobs, the archaic *laissez-faire* system which Britain developed in the first industrial revolution looks increasingly moribund and irrelevant.

Training

The article from the newspaper shows that most young people leaving school have no formal training. This does not mean that they will have no training at all before they start work—they will, after all, be 'shown the ropes' at least! There are, however, different types of training available. The following paragraphs show the main types.

'ON-THE-JOB' TRAINING

Here youngsters are shown what to do, while they are actually doing it. A firm might run a short course to teach new employees about the firm and what it produces, and to show them where things are and where to go for help. This is called an **induction course** and might last a few days. If this is all a young person receives it is very cheap for the firm but the worker might find it difficult to get another job since they have gained no recognised qualifications, only experience.

APPRENTICESHIPS

The apprenticeship is one of the oldest forms of training. Here a craftsman will take on a young helper who will perform many of the easy tasks like making the tea, fetching and carrying tools etc whilst learning the trade at the side of the craftsman.

Although this is a fine way to learn, it very much depends on the professionalism of the craftsman. Now, although the principle is much the same, some industries have an **Industrial Training Board** supervised by the Department of Employment, which monitors training in the industry and sets standards (eg the Engineering ITB).

The apprentice has to undertake training at a college where they learn the fundamental theory behind the craft. Sometimes this is full-time for a number of weeks (**block release**) or all day for one day per week (**day release**). When at work the apprentice has to complete a number of progressively more difficult tasks which are written up in a log book. The college courses often lead to City and Guilds certificates or the Business and Technical Education Council's (BTEC) general, national and higher national awards. After 4 or 5 years (depending upon the industry) if apprentices reach a satisfactory standard, they will be recognised as a qualified craftsman and would be able to find employment all over the world. It is tempting to think of apprenticeships operating only in the manual, male dominated areas such as engineering and construction industries; and it is true these are important areas of apprenticeships but do not forget hairdressing and floristry for example.

FULL-TIME VOCATIONAL EDUCATION

Vocation in this sense simply means employment, trade or profession. It is possible to leave school and go to a college or institute and learn one specific job. This is called **full-time vocational education** and accounts for about 10% of all school leavers. There are numerous examples such as physiotherapy, medical schools, secretarial colleges etc. The advantage is that a student becomes very highly skilled but the disadvantage is they only possess one skill which might limit mobility. However, competition is often high to enter such colleges and places are limited which means that, in most cases, a job is almost guaranteed.

There are also some private training colleges, many of which are excellent. Students have to pay for these but most people believe it to be a worthwhile investment for the future.

HIGHER EDUCATION

After school some 32% of students continue to study in an academic sense. This may mean attending University or a Polytechnic to study for a degree or a College of Higher Education to study for BTEC national or higher national awards, or perhaps even a College of Further Education to re-take O and A levels or study for general and national awards.

GOVERNMENT TRAINING SCHEMES

The Manpower Services Commission (MSC) has a training division which offers 2 very important types of training. There is the comparatively new Youth Training Scheme (YTS) and the much older Training Opportunities Scheme (TOPS). We shall look at both.

1 The Youth Training Scheme (YTS)

The very high levels of youth unemployment over the last few years have led the Government to introduce special schemes for school leavers who cannot find work. Such schemes started in 1978 after pilot schemes in some cities. They were known then as the Youth Opportunity Programme (YOPs) and lasted for 6 months although youngsters were allowed to go on more than one if they remained unemployed. These schemes fell into a variety of different forms. Some were just work experience: WEEPs (Work Experience on Employers' Premises) or included some sort of training at a local college of further education. Some areas had training workshops where vocational skills were taught as well as a combination of college courses and training workshops with community projects and work experience as well. These were called 'Work Orientation Resource Centres' (WORCs). Community projects were very popular since the young people on them were able to gain experience in skills and feel useful at the same time. In such projects young people were engaged in special projects which helped the community, eg converting an old bus into a 'playbus'.

These schemes were aimed at preventing those young people who left school and could not find employment from becoming disillusioned or even unemployable. If school leavers take too long looking for a job, employers begin to wonder why they have not been employed or gained any experience. The YOPs scheme gave young people experience and introduced them to employers through WEEPs. A large proportion of young people completing these courses, at least 50%, did find employment or go on to further education.

Since September 1983 YOPs has been replaced by the Youth Training Scheme (YTS). The main reason was to combine the best elements of YOPs and offer them to *all* unemployed and some employed school leavers as part of their training. The separate elements of YOPs have been replaced by a longer, one-year training and experience programme which could be counted by many employed school leavers as the first year of an apprenticeship or any other training scheme, with City and Guilds certificates possible upon completion of the year. Unemployed school leavers would follow exactly the same course. It must be remembered that the YOP scheme was only a temporary measure and led to the new YTS. The Government planned for 460 000 places in the first year with priority given to 16-year-olds but some 17-year-olds being accepted onto places where they had lost a job. Each scheme includes:

- Induction Course — Explains the content.
- Assessment — At several points the individual is assessed to determine his/her peculiar needs and aspirations.
- Work Experience — A maximum of 39 weeks which can be with one or more firms.
- Guidance/ Support
- Off-the-job Training — A minimum of 13 weeks relevant training to include basic skills and appropriate college based training in one or more broad vocational areas such as office work or engineering etc.
- Records of Achievement — All trainees keep a full record of all work/lessons completed in a diary/file and on completion are given a certificate.

Trainees are given £25 per week and all expenses for travelling over £4 per week are refunded.

Most places are with established firms who are given grants towards the cost of training and to cover the £25 a week allowance. The grant is

£1 850 per trainee. If, however, the firm would have taken on 2 school leavers anyway but will now take on 3 extra trainees they receive the grant for all five. Some schemes are based on the old YOPs community projects and training workshops.

The Ford Motor Company runs a scheme in clerical duties for 20 trainees over two 9 month periods at their Dunston research establishment in Basildon whilst Marconi of Chelmsford run a scheme also for 20 trainees in basic engineering. In 1986 the YTS scheme was expanded to last a full two years.

ASSIGNMENT

Your careers teacher and local careers office should have a list of all the firms participating in YTS in your own area. Find out how the scheme is run in your area.

---

2 The Training Opportunities Scheme (TOPS)

One of the problems faced by a modern society is the fact that demand for products changes over time. Whereas a few years ago televisions and radios were full of glass valves today they are full of transistors. The demand has changed and society no longer needs some skills, however there is a shortage of others. We have also seen how expensive it might be for someone to retrain. If they had financial responsibilities they might not be able to afford a long apprenticeship for example.

This is where the Skillcentres can help. Run by the Manpower Services Commission they offer courses for unemployed workers to retrain in a new and hopefully more needed skill. There are more than 500 different courses available nationwide in over 90 MSC Skillcentres and 700 colleges and specialist training centres with some based on employers' actual premises. Obviously, not all 500 courses are available in every area; the skills required in different areas vary. The courses last for up to 12 months and trainees receive allowances whilst on the course.

To go on a course a person must be:

- Over 19
- Away from full-time education for more than 2 years
- Not have been on a TOPS course in the last 3 years
- Have been unemployed for more than 2 years

Here are some of the courses offered at a typical Skillcentre:

Construction	Bricklaying, carpentry and joinery, heating and ventilation, house painting, plastering, plumbing
Engineering Production	Automatic lathe setting, capstan setting/operator, centre lathe turning, milling setting/operator, grinding, sheet metal working, tool fitting and machining, welding
Engineering Servicing	Draughtsmanship, engineering inspection, fitting, tool maintenance
Electrical/ Electronics	Radio TV and electronic servicing, electrical installation and maintenance
Plant and Automotive Trades	Agricultural machinery maintenance, contractors plant maintenance, heavy vehicle repair and maintenance, body repair/ paint spraying, motor vehicle repair and maintenance, mechanical skills
General Servicing	Air conditioning and refrigeration, typewriter repair and maintenance, watch and clock repair, domestic appliance servicing, office machinery repair
Miscellaneous	Boat fitting, commercial cookery, hairdressing, storekeeping, screen process printing

In addition to these skills, TOPS offer courses in clerical and commercial skills at colleges and such office skills as audio typing, general clerical work, secretarial work, shorthand/typing and bookkeeping.

Courses also exist in such things as basic reading/writing and arithmetic for people who perhaps missed out at school. These are called **preparatory courses**.

Other courses include:

Short Industrial Courses	13 week preparation in a skill before employment
TOPS Small Business Course	For those thinking of starting their own business
Non-Craft Courses	These include accounts, catering, computer training, electronics, exporting
Special Courses	Run for the disabled and some for the young unemployed
Management and Postgraduate Training	Courses are run for graduates and management leading to such qualifications as the Diploma in Management Studies

Also a number of **skillplus for craftsmen** courses are run either for the unemployed craftsman or for firms who wish to improve the quality of their work force. These are like refresher courses which help bring craftsmen up-to-date. They last for about 6 months.

Whilst on a TOPS course the basic allowance is £38.00 per week with free meals (£41.55 without meals) and travelling expenses over £4 per week. An extra £24.70 is paid for those who are married and have to support a spouse plus an extra £40 per week for those living away from home. National Insurance is paid and trainees may also be entitled to rent and rate rebate and supplementary allowance. A special 'premium' of £17 per week is paid for some higher level courses. A trainee is probably better off than being unemployed!

Unemployment

There are very many people who cannot find paid employment in this country and all over the world. The reasons for this are many and are often different for different people. This section deals with the problem of unemployment. It is important to point out that to an individual it does not matter what 'type' of unemployment the economist labels his or her problem—they are unemployed and that means probably a lower standard of living than those in employment. It means boredom, a sense of frustration and even inadequacy which will in turn affect relationships. Looked at like this, one person out of work in human terms is a very considerable problem to that individual. When this problem is magnified to over 3 million people out of work it is a very considerable human problem and an economic problem. Unemployment benefit is paid in a country which does not allow people to starve or go homeless when they become unemployed. This has to come from those who are working through taxation and when the numbers rise to this level it becomes very expensive. Not only does the country have to pay people to do nothing it also has the added cost—an opportunity cost—of the lost output. Every man-hour lost through unemployment is lost for ever—time is not a commodity which can be saved. With 3 million unemployed 3 million working days are lost every day. It is not surprising that governments put a high priority on solving this problem. Statistics are gathered every month on the numbers unemployed region by region and economists discuss the various causes so that a cure can be found.

MEASURING THE UNEMPLOYED

Until October 1982 the unemployed were counted as those people who registered at jobcentres. Since then registration has been voluntary and unemployment has been measured as the number of people claiming benefit. This has meant that unemployed people looking for a job through the jobcentres but who are not entitled to a benefit—like married women returning to work after having a family—are no longer counted but it also means that people who find a job are removed from the statistics quicker than before. It also means that some severely disabled people are now counted. It was estimated that the new count is about 190 000 lower than before.

Our figures have never been very reliable since large numbers of unemployed people cannot claim any benefit and therefore are not included.

The new scheme is at least cheaper (£10 million) and quicker since it is computerised.

Look at the table below, and graph opposite:

UK adult unemployment

Underlying increase

	Millions				Thousands	
	New basis	%	Old basis	%	New basis	Old basis
1981 Q4	2.61	(11)	2.75	(12)	+25	+26
1982 Q1	2.68	(12)	2.82	(12)	+20	+18
1982 Q2	2.74	(12)	2.88	(12)	+28	+30
1982 Q3	2.84	(12)	2.98	(13)	+31	+42
Oct	2.9	(12.4)	3.1	(12.8)	+24	+44
Nov	2.9	(12.5)	—	—	+23	—

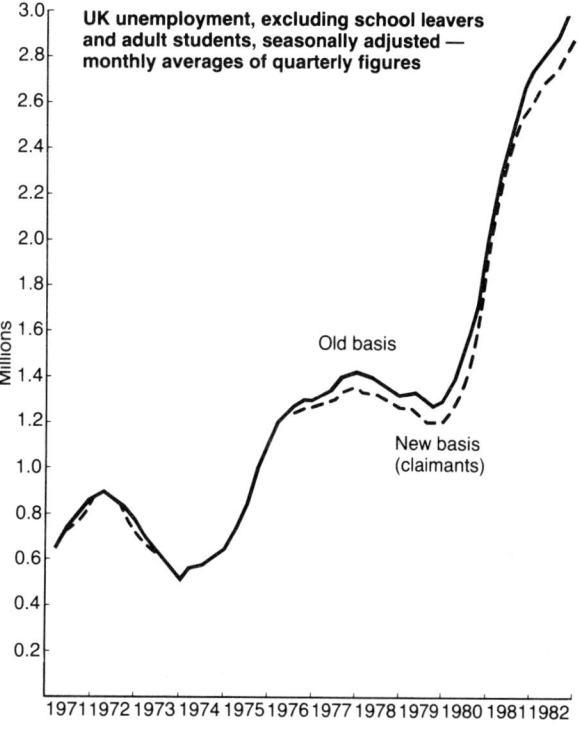

Source: Economic Progress Report No 152, December

It is also important to note that the young people on the YTS scheme (looked at earlier) are not included on the unemployment register although it is likely that less than half will be in a full-time job at the end of the year. School leavers in July are not entitled to benefit until September, so these do not count either. For these reasons some people feel that our unemployment figures are a considerable understatement of the true figures. On the other hand the figures do include the disabled and some people who have retired early and 'sign-on' to avoid paying National Insurance. Added to this some people would not work if they were offered a job because low pay means that they receive more on unemployment benefit. Still more are just changing jobs—we call this **frictional unemployment**. Estimates show that every month some 400 000 join the register only to leave again. These represent no problem. Indeed, these facts seem to suggest that the level of hard-core unemployment is less than the figures would suggest.

TYPES OF UNEMPLOYMENT

Seasonal A hotel owner in Blackpool would not expect to employ waitresses in November. An apple grower in Kent would not need fruit pickers in January. A builder would not pay bricklayers to huddle inside a hut during December when it is too wet to lay bricks. For these reasons there is seasonal unemployment in agriculture, tourism and the building trade. The climate is to blame and there is very little that can be done about it.

Structural Just as the sort of goods and services people want are constantly changing, so it is a fact that people can decide to buy those goods and services from different places whether it be another country or shop. If the good a person helps to make is no longer wanted either because it is out-dated or another country can produce the good more cheaply, then they will be out of a job. It is called **structural unemployment**

because it is caused by the changing structure of demand. It is most unfortunate for the UK that some of our most important industries at the beginning of the century have gradually suffered from this fate.

Foreign competition and falling demand has caused much unemployment in the shipbuilding, textile and iron and steel industries. This problem is still further aggravated by the fact that these industries are all concentrated in a few areas of the country. This leads to **regional unemployment** discussed later in Chapter 8. The Government tries to help this problem through the MSC TOPS schemes.

Technological You will learn about robots in Chapter 7 which are clever enough to build cars. These are called UIMs (Ultra Intelligent Machines). Already in America there are typewriters into which you just speak and the words are automatically typed. This also causes unemployment, as people are replaced by machines. One solution may well be earlier retirement or a shorter working week.

General Unemployment If the population of a country does not buy all of the goods which it can produce and the surplus cannot be sold to other countries then the only solution is to lay-off workers in all industries until people start spending again. When this happens a country is said to have **general unemployment** and be suffering a **slump** or **depression**. Some people believe that when a country is in such a situation it should try to export a way out of it. To do this the country must have lower prices than its competitors. It becomes very important therefore to control inflation and to become more efficient. Other people believe that the Government should try to encourage people to spend by reducing the level of tax or spending more itself perhaps by building hospitals and schools.

Youth Unemployment We have in this country very high levels of youth unemployment with over half of all school leavers unable to find employment. One solution is to put them on YTS places. For many this will provide them with the skills necessary to find employment, but for others the result will be just another queue for benefits. Why have we got such high youth unemployment? Here are some suggestions:

1 Look back at our graph of population changes (see page 47). If you count back 16 years from the present time you will notice that there was a high birth-rate period. This means very high numbers of young people coming onto the job market in the 1980s just when the country is going through a recession.

2 During a depression when less workers are needed it is cheaper to take on fewer new employees rather than sacking older workers because redundancy money has to be paid to older workers. Also older experienced labour has skills the firm helped them to acquire so why lose these? So it is the school leaver who is sacked before he even has a job!

3 More and more married women are seeking employment after having children. Again this forces out school leavers because the married woman has skills and experience and is seen by employers to be more reliable.

4 Technological progress means that fewer workers are needed, and again, rather than sacking older workers firms simply employ less trainees.

5 The wages of young people have risen over the last 50 years which means they are not a cheap alternative, for example, to married women returning to work.

It is not surprising then that so many young people are without a job at least now in the early 1980s. Perhaps the end of the slump will have come by the time you read this and things will become better. Also the fall in the birth rate in the 1970s will mean fewer young people seeking jobs. The problems of technological progress, wages and married women will not go away and perhaps could become worse.

Exercise

1 If you were Prime Minister what measures would you suggest to help more young people to find work? Think about using grants, subsidies, changes to retirement age, job sharing etc. How would each of these help and how would you implement them?

2 On 1 August 1983 the Government introduced the **Enterprise Allowance Scheme**. If unemployed people try to start up their own business they lose their benefits straight away, even before their business makes any profit. This scheme gives £40 per week for 52 weeks to anyone who has been unemployed for at least 13 weeks, is between 18 and retirement age, is receiving some benefit already and has £1 000 to invest. Will it reduce unemployment of any sort? Give reasons for your answer.

CASE STUDY

The GLC 'Jobs for a Change'

It is not only central Government which can try to help with the problem of the unemployed. The former Greater London Council (GLC) initiated its own programme to try to bring jobs to the country's capital city. Concerned that between 1971 and 1981, London lost one third of its jobs in manufacturing industry with 33 million square feet of factory and warehouse space lying empty the GLC launched its own campaign to try and reverse this trend.

One method adopted by the GLC was to create the Greater London Enterprise Board. This was quite separate from the GLC although it was committed to GLC policy. It had about £30 million a year to spend which came from the rates. The idea was to help new firms starting up or firms which were closing down. It gave help by buying shares or giving loans. More money was given to firms taking on apprentices or training young workers in other ways.

Many firms were helped by the Board, for example Third Sector. Third Sector used to be called Associated Automation, a factory owned by General Electric Company (GEC) which made telephone equipment. When GEC decided to close this factory because of falling orders (it made the old telephone coin boxes now being replaced by card boxes made elsewhere), the GLC helped the formation of a workers' cooperative. Of course, there is still the problem of demand for the product so the workers are themselves trying to develop new products which they can produce and sell. One example at Third Sector is alarm systems for use in old people's homes.

The GLC calculated that for every week a Londoner is out of work it costs £250, the cost of benefits plus the cost of the lost production he or she could have produced. Given this cost they felt that to spend £30 million a year on creating or saving jobs was a good idea.

ASSIGNMENT

1 Explain how the size of a country's working population might change even though the total population of the country stays the same. For what reasons might a Government engineer such a situation?

2 You are a fully qualified, unemployed chef. Explain in detail all the ways in which you would attempt to find employment.

3 Having just left school you are looking for your first job. List all of the ways you and other school leavers might seek employment. Mention the people who could be of help and say who would be most helpful and why.

4 Outline the different sorts of training you could receive after leaving school either as a young employee or as part of the Government's YTS programme.

5 It is important that the workers of a country can change their jobs easily. We call this the **mobility of labour.**

a State why it is important for workers to be mobile in a modern society.

b State clearly the 3 types of mobility, giving an example of each.

c Describe 4 barriers to mobility which might affect your mother or father.

6 Study the following figures:

Manpower and Income		1973	1978	1983
Total working population	('000's)	25 614	25 798	26 704
As % of total population	(%)	45.8	47.2	47.4
Total employees in employment	('000's)	22 664	22 777	21 163
of which:				
men	('000's)	13 773	13 389	11 909
women	('000's)	8 891	9 388	9 254
Wholly unemployed	('000's)	557	1 343	2 984
As % of working population	(%)	2.2	5.1	11.2

Source: The British Economy in Figures 1983, Lloyds Bank

a Define the term **working population**.

b The working population grew over the 10 year period as a % of the total population. Suggests 3 reasons for such a growth.

c Although the total employment fell during the 10 year period the number of women working increased. Give 2 reasons why this should be true.

d Unemployment in 1983 is approximately 5 times as much as that in 1973. Give 3 commonly held reasons why this happened and indeed has continued to happen.

7 Look at the table.

Economic Indicators (months or monthly averages)

	1981				1982		
	1st qtr	2nd qtr	3rd qtr	4th qtr	1st qtr	Mar	Apr
2 Unemployed (million)	2.3	2.5	2.6	2.7	2.8	2.8	2.85
3 Unemployed (%)	9.6	10.4	11.1	11.5	11.8	11.8	11.9

Source: Economic Progress Report No 146, June 1982 COI

a The above figures show the number of **registered unemployed** (excluding school leavers). There are, however, a large number of unemployed who do not register. Give an example of such a person and state why they do not register.

b Why might these figures be higher at certain times of the year than others?

c Name and describe a scheme run by the Government to train unemployed people to take new jobs. Are there any problems with this scheme? If so, what are they?

SUMMARY EXERCISE

1 We live in a society in which we have specialisation amongst our workers. Give 3 advantages to society of this specialisation and 3 disadvantages to the individual worker.

2 Name 2 categories of people of working age who do not work and one category who are not of working age but do work.

3 Since 1901 there have been 'peaks' or 'booms' in the number of babies born. Give 3 problems this may cause on both the supply of goods and services and the demand for labour?

4 Give examples of primary, secondary and tertiary production found close to your school.

5 Explain how the Government's TOPS programme attempts to increase the occupational mobility of labour. State which 2 types of unemployment it attempts to cure.

6 On a radio phone-in programme a caller asks why it is that the unemployed ship-building workers in Newcastle do not come down to Dagenham as there are always jobs in the local paper. Write down some of the points you would make if able to answer his question.

7 What is **frictional unemployment**. Is it a problem?

8 Give an example of a **private employment agency**. Which group of workers often find employment this way?

9 Give an example of a full-time vocational training course other than teaching.

10 Give an example of people who register as unemployed but cannot ever be expected to work and a group who do not register but do very much want to work. Why does this situation occur?

6 Trade Unions and Employer Organisations

Trade Unions

About 13 million working people belong to trade unions in the UK. A trade union is an organisation of working people who join together because they have something in common such as a skill or craft and by so doing are able to increase their power and influence in discussions with an employer.

Exercise

You and a few friends decide that one of the school rules is silly and ought to be changed. After considerable discussion you arrive at 3 plans of campaign:

1 You go and see the head teacher as soon as possible and ask that the rule be changed.
2 Ask that it be discussed in form/tutor group and if

there is general agreement send a group of students (picking the best speakers!) to see the head teacher.
3 Write the request for a rule change on sheets of paper and ask as many people in the school who agree with it to sign and take all of these signatures to the head teacher.

Which of these alternative plans would you choose and why?

In the example above it is likely that you would choose option **2** or **3** because joining together with other students who feel the same would strengthen your argument. This illustrates the principle of trade unions. By joining together workers have increased power and influence when discussing such matters as wage rates, holidays and working conditions with employers.

CASE STUDY

The Transport and General Workers Union

The Transport and General Workers Union (TGWU) was formed in 1922 through the amalgamation of 14 different unions. A further 80 merged with the TGWU over time to produce by far the largest and arguably most influential union in the UK today. The TGWU has nearly 2 million members and represents many different types of worker from all over the country and several industries. It is known as a **multi-industrial union**.

It cost 62p per week to belong to the TGWU in 1984. What are the members buying?

Collective bargaining All unions will negotiate

with employers about wages (this is what we hear about most in the news). The TGWU also negotiates such things as overtime, hours of work and holidays, redundancy, health and safety, working conditions and pensions.

Individual help Members of the TGWU are given help in such matters as securing compensation from employers if they are injured at work. If they are ill or on strike the union will pay out cash benefits (the Union has its own recuperation centre in Eastbourne). It also runs education courses for members and gives free legal aid and advice to members.

ORGANISATION OF TRADE UNIONS

No two trade unions are exactly the same but most are organised in a similar way to the TGWU outlined above. This organisation or structure is outlined below:

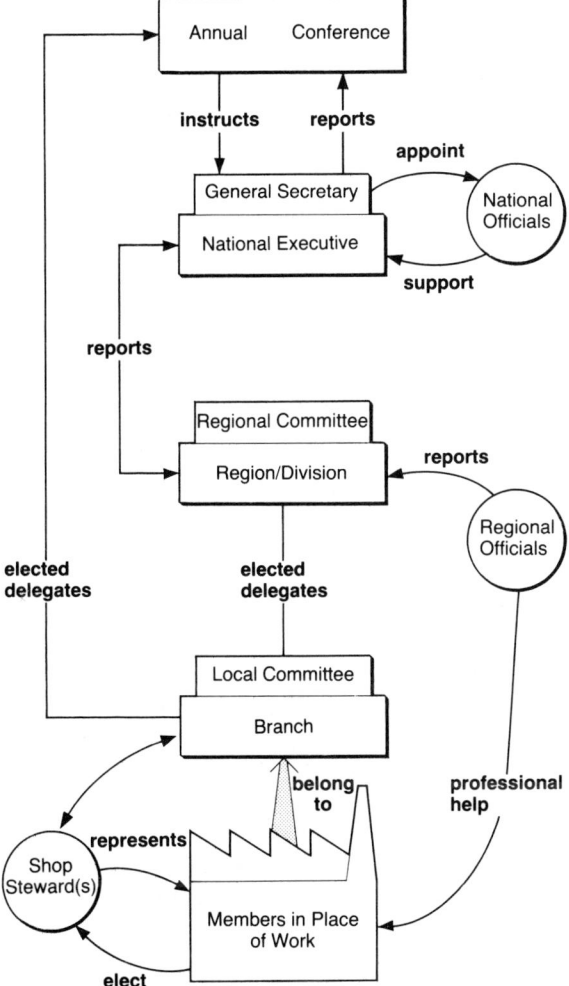

Fig 22 The organisation or structure of a typical trade union

The members of a trade union will elect a shop steward in their place of work. This worker will continue with his/her normal work but will be given some time and facilities by the employer to carry out union work. They will keep their members in touch with union policy and tell them when branch meetings are to be held. It is their responsibility to negotiate with the employer on issues which affect members like new working conditions, holidays, discipline of members etc. They also recruit new members and collect subscriptions.

Each member belongs to a branch which meets regularly to make decisions about both local and national issues which affect members. This is done by members putting forward motions or statements which are then formally debated and voted upon. The branch will elect a committee and officers (President, Secretary etc) to run the branch each year.

Large unions will group branches geographically into regions or divisions to look after all members in an area. Most employ the services of full-time officials who are paid to look after the interests of members, in particular any legal and technical matters where their expertise can be invaluable. Branches send delegates to regional meetings where a committee is elected to look after regional matters.

The most important body in any union is the Annual Conference. Each branch will send delegates to this large meeting which normally lasts a week. The delegates will discuss motions sent by branches and if passed they will form the policy for that union. Since the Conference only meets for one week the union elects a group of members to put into effect the policies it decides upon. This group is known as the National Executive Committee. It may be elected by secret ballot, at Conference by ballot or even by divisions/regions. Legislation now before Parliament seeks to make secret ballots of all members compulsory for the election of all voting members of such executive committees.

The National Executive is aided by full-time national officials who are paid to carry out union policy. The Conference or membership will elect or appoint a General Secretary, a full-time figurehead who will represent the union in negotiations with employers and Government nationally. They often become household names as they are seen on television so often.

It can be seen therefore that unions are organised on democratic lines. Any member has the right to attend branch meetings and vote for or against motions and stand for election to office in that union.

Exercise

1   Name the General Secretary of 2 unions stating which union they represent.
2   Give 2 benefits an individual member might expect from joining a trade union.
3   How is national policy decided in a trade union?
4   Give one task a regional official of a trade union might undertake.
5   Describe how a worker might become a regional or divisional president of the union and name one task they might perform in this office.

SUMMARY OF THE FUNCTIONS AND OBJECTIVES OF TRADE UNIONS

The TUC describe the general objectives of trade unions, those goals they are working to achieve, as follows:

- Improved conditions of employment—better wages, shorter hours and longer holidays
- Improved physical environment at work—heating, lighting, ventilation, health and safety
- Job security
- Job satisfaction and prospects—personal fulfilment, elimination of boring repetitive work, training and retraining
- Income security—protection of income when work is interrupted by illness, accident, old age, redundancy or unemployment
- Full employment
- Redistribution of national income and wealth between those who provide labour and those who provide capital
- A share in the planning and control of industry
- Improvements in the standard of living such as standards of education, health service and the provision of housing
- The defence of trade unions' right to operate freely

Such overall aims should not be confused with their day-to-day functions which can be summarised as:

- Collective negotiation on wages, pensions, health and safety and conditions of service
- Individual representation and help if a member faces redundancy, discipline, etc or has been injured at work
- Free legal aid and advice
- Financial payments if on strike, ill or retired and in need of help
- Collective purchasing schemes—often cheap insurance, travel etc
- Education and training of officers and members
- Research into problems of industry and representation on national and international bodies

Classification of Trade Unions

A trade union was defined as a group of workers who have something in common. The type of trade union will depend upon what its members have in common (see below).

Type of union	*Common link of members*	*Examples*
Craft	Skill or trade	Card Setting Machine Tenders' Society National Union of Scalemakers
Industrial	Same industry	National Union of Railwaymen (NUR) National Union of Mineworkers (NUM)
General	None—other than all work	Transport and General Workers Union (TGWU) General and Municipal Workers Union (GMWU)
Non-manual	Nature of work	Association of Scientific, Technical and Managerial Staffs (ASTMS) Association of Professional, Executive, Clerical and Computer Staff (APECCS)

Craft unions represent workers who have a skill, usually acquired after a long apprenticeship.

They are known as **closed unions** and aim to protect their skill and maintain standards. They are very small and can result in one firm having several different unions. In some cases it can lead to disputes between unions about who should do what. In our modern technological world machines have replaced many skills and so the number of craft unions has fallen. An industrial union will recruit from a whole industry. This can mean a company negotiates with only one union—which is obviously of benefit to both sides. General unions, like the TGWU are **open**. Anyone in any industry can join. They are very large and can offer a wide range of services to members and have a great deal of power. Over the last 20 years non-manual or white collar unions have grown rapidly. In 1965 they represented only 18% of total union membership. Now it is closer to 40%. This reflects perhaps the change in the nature of employment. The success of manual unions in increasing pay levels also encourages non-manual workers like teachers and local government workers to form unions.

ASSIGNMENT

1 Take 2 trade unions. One that someone you know belongs to and one a person working in your **school** belongs to (a teacher, cleaner, secretary, cook, laboratory assistant). For each list:

a The name of the union and type
b The cost to join
c How it is organised
d Services offered to members
e Last time union called a strike

2 Add the results in answer **1** to the results of 4 of your friends.

a Is there a pattern in the organisation of unions?
b Are certain types of unions more expensive than others?
c Do expensive unions offer a greater range of services than smaller?

Collective Bargaining

Keith once owned an old Triumph 2000 motorcar. He wanted to sell it and thought that it was worth about £650. He advertised it in a local paper for £700 ono (that stands for 'or near offer' and means that he was prepared to negotiate—haggle the price). The man who bought it told Keith that he would not give more than £750 for the car! He obviously did not understand the game. If he had offered *less* than £700, say £650, Keith would have said that he would take £675 and they could have settled. Instead the buyer offered more than Keith wanted so he took it with both hands.

The above example is not what happens exactly in collective bargaining but similar. If Keith and the buyer had followed the rules Keith would have known that he had sold his Triumph for as much as he could and the buyer would have known that he had spent as little as he could and still bought the motorcar.

When a trade union negotiates a wage claim for its membership it is called **collective bargaining**. Often a union will claim a pay rise which is a maximum, or in other words, the most they would like. The employer will often offer the least amount that they would like to pay. Both sides will then negotiate. Perhaps the employer will offer more but with certain conditions, such as harder work from the employees. This is known as a **productivity deal**. Clearly the employer can pay more if the same number of workers are producing more goods.

Exercise

Which of the following occupations could not negotiate a productivity deal? State your reasons in each case.

- car workers
- coal miners
- nurses
- school teachers
- bricklayers
- bus drivers

A union might accept a lower offer than the claim plus longer holidays or tea breaks. In most cases a compromise is reached which is called a settlement and work will continue as normal. In a few cases agreement cannot be reached. This is called

deadlock. To indicate their strength of feeling and to try to force the employer to make a better offer the members of a union can take **industrial action**. All members of a union are asked to vote for or against such action and it has to be agreed by the union's Executive. (If individual members of a union take action without permission of their executive it is unofficial action and the workers taking action are not protected by the union nor do they receive any strike pay.) Figure 23 shows the course taken by the wage bargaining process.

FORMS OF INDUSTRIAL ACTION

Strike   Union members stop work. Strikes can be *'all out'*—all members involved until employer makes a better offer. *'Selective'*—some workers are called to strike and others stay at work (often those who stay at work pay into a fund to help support those on strike). *'Token'*—workers leave

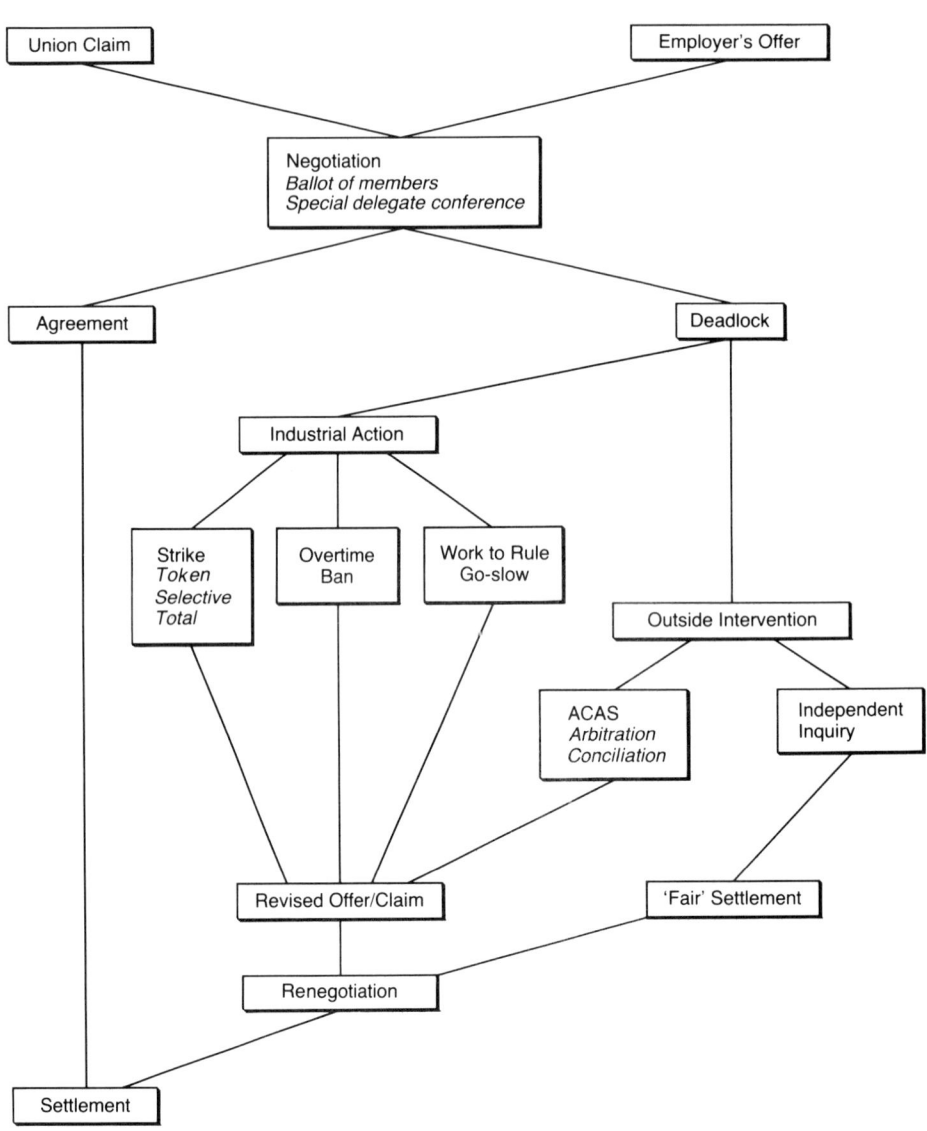

Fig 23 The wage bargaining process

work for a day or even an hour (often used by caring professions, such as nursing to prevent suffering).

Note Although unions often have strike funds to help striking members who obviously receive no pay whilst on strike very few unions have enough to support an all out strike for more than a few days.

Overtime ban Union members only work normal hours accepting no overtime. (Clearly only effective in industries where overtime is common place.)

Work to rule/contract Union members adhere very closely to the letter of the rules or contract which govern their work. They withdraw 'good will' in effect undertaking no work they do not *have* to do.

Go slow Union members deliberately take their time in performing tasks.

Exercise

Take each of the above forms of industrial action and in each case think of an occupation where it would be both appropriate and effective. State why it would be effective and if possible give an example.

The recently passed Trade Union Act (1985) makes all forms of strike action unlawful unless a majority of members of the union have voted in favour of such action by means of a secret ballot no longer than 4 weeks before the action commences.

The **1982 Employment Act** makes industrial action lawful only when it is in connection with a trade dispute (as listed by the Act) and between the workers and their employer. Trade disputes include such matters as pay, conditions of work, discipline, allocation of work etc. Certain disputes cannot lawfully be pursued through industrial action, such as disputes between workers and workers and **secondary industrial action**, that is workers from one employer taking action to help workers of another employer (unless the second firm is either a customer or supplier of the firm in dispute).

PICKETING

Union members taking industrial action are allowed to try to persuade fellow workers to support their action. If a group of workers are on strike they may well **picket** other workers who are employed by the same employer by positioning a small group of striking workers at the factory gate to try to dissuade others from working during the dispute.

The **1980 Employment Act** restricts picketing to those workers directly affected by the action and to their own place of work. Picketing is only for the purpose of obtaining or communicating information or peacefully persuading a fellow worker to work or not to work. Trade union officials and workers who have been dismissed are also allowed to picket.

When a dispute reaches deadlock the Trade Union Congress (TUC), a body which represents most unions, might step in and offer help in bringing both sides together. If both parties agree the services of ACAS the Advisory, Conciliation and Arbitration Service, may be sought.

ACAS is an independent body established by the **1975 Employment Protection Act** to help improve industrial relations. In a situation of stalemate 2 services can be offered. Conciliation—where an independent person or persons will talk to both sides and try to bring them together to negotiate again. Arbitration—where independent people listen to the case put by both sides in the dispute and then suggest what can be considered a fair settlement.

CASE STUDY

The 1982 Health Service Workers' Pay Negotiations

The National Health Service employs about one million workers of whom approximately two-thirds are members of a trade union or professional organisation. Fourteen unions which have members in the health service and are members of the TUC have formed the TUC Health Service Committee. The major unions in this committee are:

National Union of Public Employees—represents 300 000 nurses, ancillary workers and ambulance men (NUPE)

Confederation of Health Service Employees—represents nurses and other workers (COSHE)

Association of Scientific Technical and Managerial Staffs—representing professional technicians etc (ASTMS)

National and Local Government Officers Association—representing clerical and administrative staff (NALGO)

The Royal College of Nurses—professional body representing nurses (RCN)

Plus 9 other unions representing specialised groups.

(*Note* NUPE, COSHE, NALGO and RCN collectively represent 75% of NHS staff)

Wages for health service workers are negotiated in bodies called **Whitley Councils**. Each council deals with a separate group of health service workers and has representatives from the unions, National Health Service and Government. Wages are negotiated from April each year.

The 1982 Negotiations

During 1981 the TUC Health Service Committee agreed that a joint claim for a 12% pay rise for all workers in the Health Service should be lodged with all Whitney Councils for the 1982 pay negotiations. By March 1982 the employers had offered a pay rise of 4% for most workers and 6.4% for some grades of workers and nurses. In real terms an increase in take home pay for a typical cleaner of 79p per week. The unions rejected the offer and mounted a campaign to try to win public sympathy.

The TUC called for a one day token strike from non-health service workers in support of their health service colleagues and many unionists stopped work on 19 May 1982. The campaign showed that some health service employees were better off financially unemployed! A health service gardener working in the Wigan area calculated that he would receive £17 per week more if he were unemployed. In July 1982 the employers made an improved offer of a 6% pay increase for most workers and $7\frac{1}{2}$% for some grades and nurses. Once again the unions rejected this offer. The unions made it clear that other public sector workers had been awarded far higher settlements during that year:

Miners	8.6% increase—accepted
Water workers	9.1% increase—accepted
Firemen	10.1% increase—accepted
Police	13.2% increase—accepted
Senior civil servants	14.3% increase—accepted
Judges	18.6% increase—accepted

NUPE calculated that whilst a 6% rise in pay for a health service domestic meant an extra £3.54 per week a 4% rise in pay for the Secretary of State for Health would mean an extra £27.98 per week.

In response to this sort of pressure and further industrial action a third and final offer was made in September 1982. Although no improvement was made upon the 6% and $7\frac{1}{2}$% originally offered in July certain promises were made. These were a guaranteed 4% increase in the following year (since this, it was argued, would be higher than any other public sector worker would be offered it was an improvement) plus the agreement to establish an independent pay review body for the nurses similar to that which exists for doctors. (The review bodies pay suggestions would *not* be binding.)

During December 1982, one year after the original claim of 12%, the various Whitney Councils agreed upon this final settlement which was back dated to (the increase paid from) August and not April. In effect the health service workers lost the 4% and 6.4% increase which would have been paid from April 1982 until August 1982 in order to gain an extra 2%.

Summary of the 1982 Health Service Pay Claim

Autumn 1981	TUC Health Service Committee agree on joint 12% claim
January 1982	Union side 12% claim submitted to Whitney Councils
March 1982	Employers' side offer: 4% most 6.4% some grades + nurses
	Union side reject offer
May 1982	TUC Day of Action Campaign
July 1982	Employers' side revised offer: 6% most $7\frac{1}{2}$% some grades + nurses
	Unions side reject offer
	Campaign continues
September 1982	Final offer as above but with 4% guaranteed offer for following year + nurses pay review body
December 1982	Whitney Councils reach agreement on final offer— Union side reluctantly accept
	Increased pay back dated to August only

Exercise

1   In 1982 miners were offered, and accepted, an 8.6% increase in wages whilst health service workers were offered 4%. Why do you think miners were offered such a large rise?

2   Why did the health service workers use a campaign of one day token strikes and trying to gain public support to win higher wages rather than opting for an all out strike?

3   After the guaranteed rise in April 1984 of 4% 1st year nurses now earn £50 per week. In view of this do you feel that the unions have been successful?

4   Why did the TUC call for non-health service unionists to take action?

5   Given that the unions in the health service have so little power, why might it still be worthwhile for a health service worker to join a trade union?

ASSIGNMENT

1 Take a current wage negotiation and keep a diary of the events. By reading the newspapers and watching the television news you should be able to establish:

a The union claim
b The employer's offer
c The nature and extent of any industrial action

d Any revised offer/claim
e Whether ACAS or any other body was involved
f The final settlement

Write a conclusion to your diary of events in which you decide whether the union was successful or not and why.

2 Study the following 2 tables below and opposite and then answer the questions:

Days lost through Industrial Action 1970–1980 (United Kingdom)

Year	No of disputes beginning	People involved	No of days lost
1970	3 906	3 793 000	10 980 000
1971	2 228	1 171 000	13 551 000
1972*	2 497	1 722 000	23 909 000
1973	2 873	1 513 000	7 197 000
1974	2 922	1 622 000	14 750 000
1975	2 282	789 000	6 012 000
1976	2 016	666 000	3 284 000
1977	2 703	1 155 000	10 142 000
1978	2 471	1 001 000	9 405 000
1979**	2 080	4 583 000	29 474 000
1980	1 262	785 000	11 910 000

* 10 800 000 days are accounted for by the 1972 miners' strike

** 17 863 000 days are accounted for by the 1979 industrial action of the engineering unions

The Trades Union Congress (TUC)

TUC is one of the best known abbreviations in Britain, but many people have little or no idea of what the Trades Union Congress actually is or indeed what it does. Some think it is a union which it is not; others a Government body, which it is not. Some even think that it is a political party, which it is not.

In 1868 individual trade unions joined together to form a club or organisation which could be a spokesman for all trade unions. This we call the TUC. Today 107 of the country's 438 unions belong to (or are affiliated to) this central organisation. The TUC has its own head office and staff and is divided into 7 main departments. These gather information which is used in discussions with Government and to help member unions. Although less than a quarter of all unions belong to the TUC most of the larger ones do which means when the elected leaders of the TUC speak with Government they are representing the views of over 11 million workers.

In order that the leaders of the TUC know what member unions feel about current issues and problems (and indeed so that those leaders

Average working days lost through industrial disputes per 1 000 employees in selected industries (mining, manufacturing, construction and transport) in 18 countries 1974–1978

	Average for years 74–78
United Kingdom	758
Australia	1 452
Belgium	462
Canada	2 134
Denmark	198
Finland	922
France	304
Germany (FR)	96
India	1 470
Irish Republic	1 114
Italy	1 658
Japan	224
Netherlands	30
New Zealand	660
Norway	140
Spain	1 678
Sweden	18
United States	1 183

Source: Department of Employment Gazette, January 1981

a Given that the working population of the UK is about 26 million what percentage of the working population was involved in industrial action in 1980?

  i 3%   *iv* 30%
  ii 10%   *v* 50%
  iii 20%

b In 1978, 419.4 million working days were lost through illness. How many were lost through industrial action?

c In the second table how many of the 18 countries had **less** days lost through industrial disputes per 1 000 employees in those selected industries than the UK.

d Name one way in which the **employer** loses during a strike and one way in which they gain.

e Name one way in which a **worker** loses during a strike and one way in which they gain.

might be elected) the member unions each send delegates once a year to an annual conference. Unions send one delegate for every 5 000 members in their union and have one vote for every 10 000 members. Individual unions put forward motions which are discussed in formal debate and are then voted upon. If a motion is carried it becomes TUC policy. Between conferences the day-to-day running of the Congress is left in the hands of a General Council which has 44 elected members representing all industries and types of employment. Four seats are also reserved for women. The Congress has an elected General Secretary who is the figurehead and voicepiece of the TUC.

It is also affiliated to a large number of international organisations and nominates representatives to various government and public bodies including the National Economic Development Council (NEDC) and ACAS.

Employers' Organisations

Employers often join together to form organisations based upon industries. For example, the

British Hotels', Restaurants' and Caterers' Association. These organisations represent the member companies in that industry in negotiations with trade unions on wages and conditions of work and the Government when discussing standards etc. They will also give advice to members on legal matters. Some, such as the British Carpet Manufacturers' Association perform a dual role since they not only undertake the work mentioned previously but also act as Trade Associations which means promoting their product and helping to sell it.

The Confederation of British Industry

The CBI was formed in 1965 by the amalgamation of 3 smaller organisations and is now the largest central employers' organisation in Britain. It represents about 300 000 companies and defines its role as:

'. . . an independent, non party-political body financed entirely by industry and commerce. It exists primarily to ensure that Governments of whatever political complexion, and society as a whole, understand the needs, problems and intentions of British business, and the contribution it makes to the prosperity of the country.'

Members of the CBI come from 5 main areas:

1 Individual industrial companies
2 Individual commercial companies
3 Public sector—nationalised industries/ public corporations
4 Employers' organisations and trade associations
5 Commercial associations—like local Chambers of Commerce.

CBI policy is determined by its members. The governing body of the CBI is the Council which has 400 members drawn from regions and member organisations. All policies must be approved by the Council. For the last few years the CBI has held a delegate conference which acts as a forum for debate.

Like the TUC the CBI nominates representatives to government and public bodies and belongs to international employers' organisations. The CBI also provides many services for its members. By employing specialists it is able to give advice on such things as taxation, overseas trade and legal problems.

ASSIGNMENT

1 You have been made President of the local branch of a trade union. Part of your responsibilities include speaking to local workers in your field and trying to recruit new members. Write a 5 minute speech you might make to try to convince people to join your union.
2 With reference to a current dispute, or one about which you have learnt, describe and explain the process of **collective bargaining**.
3 The trade union official most workers come into contact with is the **shop steward**. If you were to become a shop steward what would you consider to be your main duties and responsibilities as an official of a trade union?
4 When you start work you may well join a trade union.

a How could you as an individual member influence the running of your union?
b Explain fully 3 benefits you as a member would expect to gain which non-members would not gain.

5 The Government has changed the law regarding picketing.

a What is **picketing**. Why and when is it employed?
b Why and how has the Government recently changed the law regarding picketing?
c Why do the unions, in general, oppose such changes?

SUMMARY EXERCISE

1 Trade unions are concerned with anything which affects the material well-being of their members. With reference to the TGWU case study on page 70 list 4 such areas of concern for the modern British trade union.

2 Small craft unions such as the National Union of Basket, Cane, Wicker and Fibre Furniture Makers of Great Britain and Ireland are often said to be bad for industry and the trade union movement. Give 2 reasons why such small craft unions are criticised.

3 Give 3 examples of **industrial unions**. What advantages are there for the employer if he negotiates with one industrial union rather than several smaller craft unions?

4 The Transport and General Workers Union is the largest union in the UK with nearly 2 million members. It is an example of an open, general union. Give 2 reasons people join such large unions.

5 The Association of Scientific, Technical and Managerial Staff (ASTMS) is an example of a **non-manual union**. (Sometimes called **white collar** unions because the jobs undertaken by members are so clean.) In recent years such unions have grown. In 1965 non-manual unions had 1.8 million members (18% of total union membership). By 1977 this had grown to 4.3 million members (36% of total union membership). Give 3 reasons for this growth.

6 The **shop steward** is an ordinary worker who is elected by fellow union members to represent them on the shop floor. Name 2 other duties the shop steward performs for the union.

7 List 3 factors a union might bear in mind when considering a pay claim.

8 A strike, groups of workers collectively withdrawing their labour, is one form of industrial action. List 3 further forms of industrial action and give examples of where such action has recently been used.

9 The Advisory Conciliation and Arbitration Service is an independent body which can be requested to help in a dispute between employers and trade unions. Assistance can be given in the form of: *a* arbitration and *b* conciliation. Distinguish between these 2 terms and indicate situations where either would prove useful.

10 Why are some unions in some occupations considered more powerful than others? What effect does this have upon their members' wage rates?

7 Mass Production and Automation

Many of the goods we buy have been produced using **mass production** techniques. What does this mean?

Henry Ford wrote that mass production is:

The focusing upon a manufacturing project of the principles of power, accuracy, economy, system, continuity, speed and repetition.

If a very large quantity of a good is to be made then the production can be organised in a very efficient way so that the maximum amount can be produced at the lowest cost. When such principles are used the workers are each given a very simple task to perform. It is easy to learn and they soon become proficient. The factory is organised so that raw materials and components arrive at one end and the finished product emerges at the other. As the good is made it passes from one stage to another often on a conveyor belt. Sometimes it will not even stop moving whilst the next job is performed. (This is often called **assembly line production**.)

CASE STUDY

Mass production at Fords

Henry Ford did not invent mass production but he was one of the pioneers in its use, in particular for a product as large and complicated as a car. Henry Ford manufactured his first car by hand in his garden shed but by the time he moved into his first factory in 1903 he had already started experimenting with more efficient methods of production. At first he looked at small complicated parts and how to improve production. The magneto flywheel, for example, which had previously been assembled by one man in 22 minutes, was now assembled in 29 separate operations which altogether took only 13 minutes. The principle was to divide assembly into as many simplified operations as possible, to keep parts on the move and bring work to the men. For the chassis itself, Ford used a rope and windlass to drag it along the floor. Six assembly workers kept pace with it as it moved, picking up whatever parts were required from the piles of components brought to the assembly line by trucks. The system was continually being improved. Power driven conveyor belts were installed which now carried both the chassis and men. As each operation was completed the men would move back to the next car on the line. Further splitting of the work into less and less complicated procedures enabled the total assembly time of a Ford car to fall from 12 hours and 28 minutes to just 1 hour 33 minutes!

In Fig 24 the principles of mass production experimented with at the turn of the century in the Ford plant in Detroit are very much in use in a modern Ford assembly plant like Dagenham. On this Fiesta trim assembly line the cars are mounted on a conveyor belt which takes them past the assembly workers who in turn fix their particular piece of trim to the body. Notice that on both sides of the line there are wire baskets full of component parts waiting to be fixed. The lines move fairly slowly so that each worker can per-

Fig 24

form his task and get ready for the next car. At the Dagenham plant there are many such assembly lines. Some assemble the steel panels, which have been pressed into shape, onto the body shells. On others the engines are assembled and test run. The engine plant can produce an engine every $12\frac{1}{2}$ seconds. Each worker has a simple task and spends no more than 30 seconds upon each engine (the actual engine assembly line is $4\frac{1}{2}$ miles long). In other parts of the factory seat and internal trim is manufactured and of course in the paint shop the body shells are given their beautiful colour, again on an assembly line principle. Such innovation by Henry Ford and others resulted in the price of the motor car falling so that the average man could afford one. It brought about a revolution in personal transport. Today there are 255 cars for every 1 000 people in this country. Mass production of motor cars and other consumer goods changed our way of life at home. Everybody could now enjoy the luxuries of life, however, the old-fashioned craftsman at his work was gone forever.

Mass production is really a form of specialisation. The benefits of such a process were noted as long ago as 1776 by Adam Smith in his book *The Wealth of Nations* where he analysed how the production of pins could be improved.

By visiting pin making factories he found that the process could be split into about 18 distinct operations. Any unskilled worker could perform one or 2 of these jobs but if you asked them to make a whole pin each they would only be able to make about 20 a day. If 10 workers were asked to perform just one or 2 jobs and then pass the unfinished pin on to the next worker Smith found they could make up to 48 000 pins a day or 4 800 for each worker.

(*Note* We divided the total output by the number of workers, in this case 10, to find the output per man. You will need to be able to do this in the next exercise.)

Exercise

Number of workers	Output of umbrellas (*per day*)	Output per worker
5	10	2
10	50	
50	1 000	

1   Copy out the previous table and calculate the missing output per worker.
2   Is output per worker increasing or decreasing?
3   Explain in your own words why output per worker is changing as more workers are employed.
4   100 workers can produce 2 000 umbrellas per day and 200 workers 3 500 umbrellas per day. Add this information to your table and calculate output per worker. Explain what is happening to output and suggest why?
5   You find that most umbrella factories are very small even though the price of umbrellas might fall if they were mass produced. Explain why this might be so?

Advantages of Mass Production

Mass production makes it possible to increase the amount of goods or services that it is possible to produce from a given number of factors of production. This in turn makes them cheaper, for the following reasons:

● practice makes perfect
● no loss of time changing tools or reorganising work for different tasks
● less training for each worker is needed since they only need to learn one task rather than several
● special machines can be used to help perform one simple task making the worker quicker and more accurate
● labour becomes potentially more mobile as a person can be retrained easily enabling him to work in many different industries

Problems Associated with Mass Production

Mass production is not without problems however. Work in a factory which uses such methods could be very boring and if a country had little unemployment it might be difficult to persuade workers to perform such monotonous tasks. This is not the only problem. Others include:

● boredom—mindless repetition of the same simple task may lead to workers becoming bored and less efficient
● less skilled craftsmen are needed, however, industry does need skilled machine designers and maintenance staff
● risk of unemployment—if machines replace workers who only have one skill it could result in unemployment
● greater interdependence—each production stage is dependent upon the last. A walk-out and strike in the paint shop at Fords will probably cause the rest of the 17 000 workers to be laid off
● slow workers in a team will have difficulty keeping up with the others

Perhaps you can think of other advantages and problems to add to this list.

Such problems are taken very seriously by large firms for it can lead to an unhappy workforce, poor quality, absenteeism and high job turnover. For this reason some firms have introduced job rotation schemes where workers change their task every few weeks. Also **job enrichment** schemes have been tried where workers are given more say in the running of their section in the factory and more interesting work. In some factories the boredom is reduced by having piped music and excellent recreational facilities.

Limits to Mass Production

There are some products which are not mass produced even though it would be possible to do so. In the exercise above you were asked why the umbrella factory might only produce very few a day although clearly it would be cheaper to produce a large number. The answer was because they might only be able to *sell* a small number each week they would only produce a small number each week.

The size of the market is a very important factor when deciding whether mass production is possible. It would not be worthwhile, for example, mass producing riding hats. Although this might make them cheaper it would be unlikely to increase the number sold since only a few people ride horses today and their hats last a very long time.

For other goods and services which are not mass produced the reason is simply that they cannot be mass produced. For example, it would be impossible to mass produce hair styling or doctors consultations.

Automation

The use of specialist machinery goes hand in hand with mass production since more and more of this machinery works automatically. Automation is the replacement of tasks performed by workers with automatic machinery. Look at the following picture:

This is part of the new Ford automatic welding machinery in use at Dagenham for the production of the Sierra. Look carefully at the picture. These are very sophisticated machines which each perform several tasks, in this case welding the body shell. They form part of a multi-million pound modernisation programme undertaken by Fords at Dagenham before the launch of the new Sierra. This includes automatic presses which stamp out the body panels and special carts which transport the body panels around the factory without drivers. They stop if anyone gets in the way and play a little tune to warn workers that they are coming. The main thing that you notice when looking at the picture above is the lack of workers, the machines have replaced men at Fords and all over the country. In many cases workers are not sacked but given early retirement and new workers are not taken on. This has meant very high levels of youth unemployment all over the country.

As time passes it is certain that much more production will become automated which has very important implications for our lives.

ADVANTAGES OF AUTOMATED PRODUCTION

There are many advantages such as:

- Increased output—automated production is quicker than manual production techniques
- Reduced cost—prices should be lower
- Boring jobs can be done by machines
- Less workers needed should lead to more leisure

PROBLEMS CREATED BY AUTOMATED PRODUCTION

Automation also brings problems. These include:

- Technological unemployment—although we will need people with the skills to build and maintain the machines, we will not need the unskilled worker in the future as their job will be done by machines. This is part of a trend which has been going on for many years but in recent years the process has been speeding up.
- Too much leisure—would we all become bored if we only had to work 3 days a week?
- Them and us; workers and unemployed—perhaps we will move to a period where work is not shared through greater leisure but will be done by a few, who will have money, leaving many to permanent poverty and unemployment

THE WORKING WEEK

Year	Hours worked per week by	
	Men	Women
1969	45.7	37.9
1974	44.0	37.2
1979	43.2	37.2

When you think that our grandfathers probably worked a 55–60 hour week we can see what a dramatic change there has already been. Will this trend continue? Will you be working a 30 or 25 hour week?

THE WORKING LIFE

At the moment most people spend 10 or 11 years at least in full-time education and then move on to a job where they receive training of some kind and then expect to spend the rest of their lives in the same job, as many as 40–50 years, before they retire and enjoy 20 or so years leisure. We can show this diagrammatically:

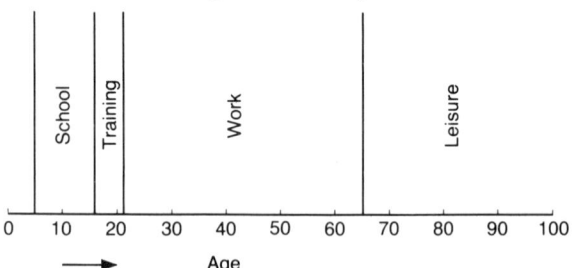

This is the typical work pattern we enjoy at the moment. Many people feel that we will experience the pattern below with periods of work interspersed with periods of leisure and re-training as there will not be enough work for us all to work all the time due to automation.

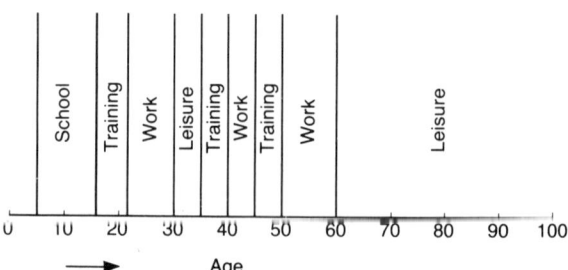

Others feel that we will all work a 3 day week and enjoy 4 days leisure every week. This sounds fine but how is it to be paid for and are there enough leisure activities to keep us all from being bored.

It has also been suggested that with less work and more free time we will all be able to spend more time helping others less fortunate like the handicapped.

EDUCATION FOR LEISURE

Some people believe that as we will have more leisure time in the future we should be educated to enjoy it and use it properly. Perhaps a school timetable should have more sports and games and less academic study. What do you think?

Other people feel that as the world is running out of raw materials automation will not last and we will all be forced to work harder in the future.

SUMMARY EXERCISE

1 The main advantages of mass production are that they reduce costs and increase output. Explain why this is true.
2 If you were to work in a factory using mass production techniques state 2 characteristics you would expect your work to have.
3 Does mass production *always* cause unemployment? Explain your answer.
4 What is meant by the term **interdependence**? Give your own example to explain this.
5 Give an example of a good, other than riding hats, for which the demand is so low that it is not produced using mass production.
6 Services like hair-stylists are not mass produced. Can you think of 3 more examples?
7 Some skills like typing are needed in many different industries. Can you think of 2 other examples.
8 We are told mass production can lead to boredom. Can you think of 2 ways in which a firm can try to prevent its workers from becoming bored? Explain why the firm would want to prevent boredom.
9 Define **automation** and give an example of industries where it can, and cannot be introduced.
10 Can you give one example of each of the following:

a A car produced with little or no mass production techniques
b A car produced using mass production but little automation
c A car produced using fully automated production.

ASSIGNMENTS

1 The assembly line at Fords Dagenham is **automated**.

a What do we mean by **automation**?
b Give an example of how recently Fords have increased the level of automation.
c Describe 2 jobs at Fords which are not as yet automated and show why this is so.
d Write about 2 advantages and 2 disadvantages to the worker of increased automation.

2 With reference to a firm you have studied explain:

a What is meant by the **division of labour**.
b Show, using your example, 4 benefits such division of labour brings to the owners of the business.
c Again using your example, give examples of 2 problems which may affect the workers in a factory where there is a great division of labour.

8 The Question of Location

One important decision to be made by any entrepreneur is where they should locate a new plant or factory. This is true whether it is a small one-man business or large public company. Entrepreneurs want to make the largest profit they can. The choice of site will be very important, for some types of business, in determining just how large this profit will be. It would be very foolish to open a travel agency in a small back street out of town. People would not be prepared to search out such a service and one couldn't rely on passing trade. Far better would be a unit in a busy shopping centre in the middle of town. This would be convenient for people and give you a chance to catch the eye of the passer-by. Let us consider 2 firms whose names are known all over the world: British Petroleum and Ford Motor Company. If we take a major factory for each and ask why the site was chosen we can perhaps learn important lessons.

CASE STUDY

Ford Motor Company, Dagenham, Essex

Ford cars were first produced, or at least assembled, in Britain as long ago as 1911, not at the Dagenham site, but in a small factory in Trafford Park, Manchester. After the First World War the demand for cars began to grow and the Manchester factory, although capable of producing well over 6 000 cars a year, was still too small so that by 1925 the Dagenham site was chosen. As you will see later, work did not start on the site until 1929, however, and the first vehicle, the Model AA truck, rolled off the production line in October 1931. Dagenham was to become world famous, the major production site for Ford and a most successful factory.

It must at first have seemed a rather strange choice since much of the 500 acre site was low-lying marsh into which engineers had to sink 22 000 concrete piles 40 feet deep. The factory was therefore neither cheap or quick to construct and a special share issue was required to pay for it. (Much of the technical details can be seen in

the newspaper article which follows on page 91.)

The map (Fig 25) which follows and this aerial photograph of the site clearly show why Dagenham was chosen.

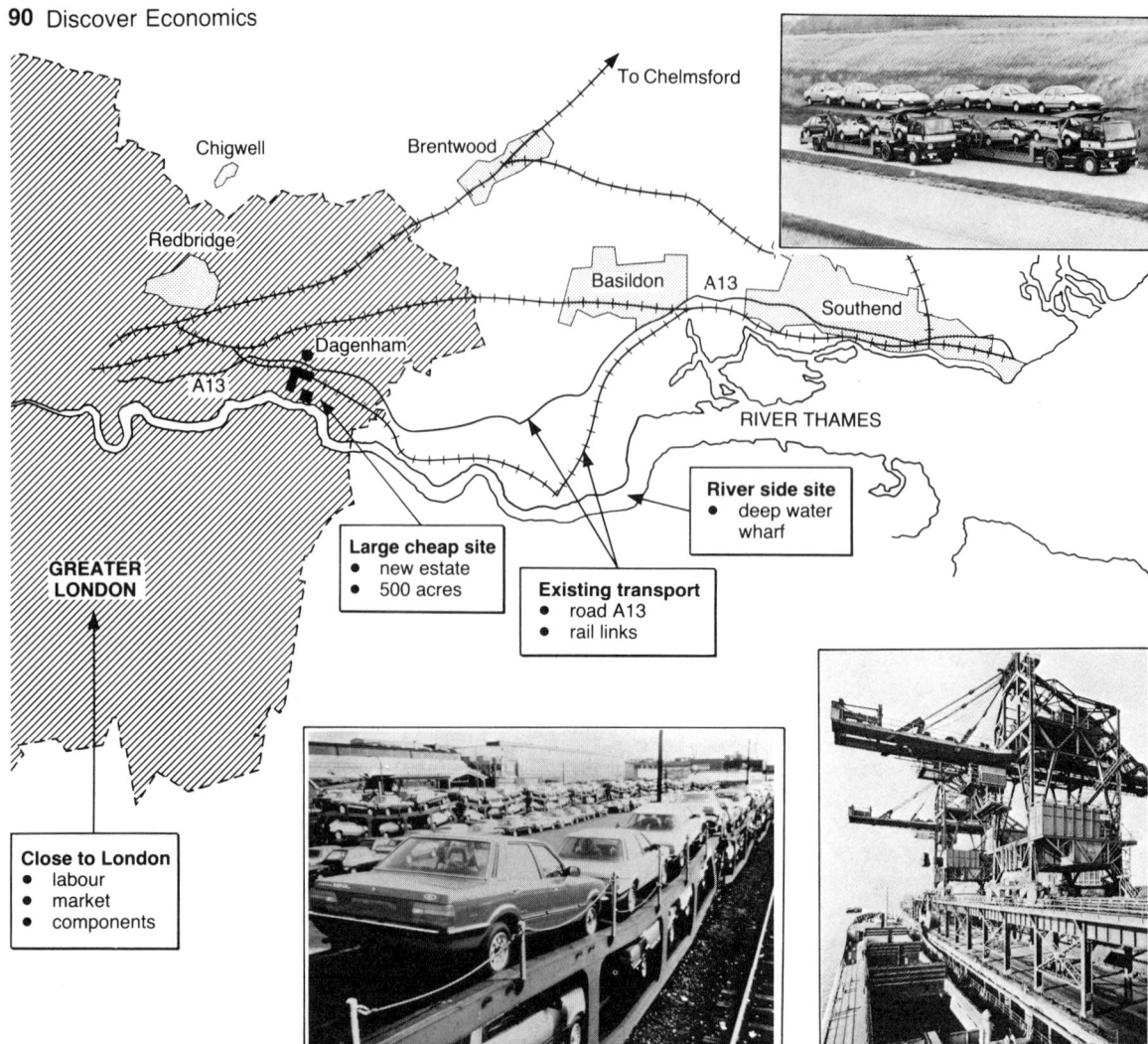

Fig 25 The location of the Ford Dagenham site

Here is a summary of the chief reasons:

Transport facilities

- Deep-water wharf—The photograph clearly shows the factory right on the River Thames. The factory was constructed with its own wharf capable of berthing ocean going ships of up to 10 500 tonnes cargo carrying capacity. The site can therefore export finished cars (often in kit form for reassembly in foreign countries) and import raw materials by sea which is a cheap method of transport. Henry Ford thought this to be most important and even turned down a site in Rotterdam because it did not have these facilities.

- Railway—Ford were able to construct their own sidings from existing railway lines and, by using the specially designed rolling stock shown on the map, were able to deliver finished cars throughout the UK.

- Road—The site is adjacent to the A13 and full use is made of road transport. Car transporters, like those shown, and lorries delivering rolls of sheet steel for body pressings are familiar sights in and around Dagenham.

Labour supply

- The LCC (now GLC) was at the time constructing a huge estate next to the village of Dagenham. This and its proximity to London guaranteed a large labour supply.

Size and cost of site
- It was a large site, suitable for expansion and being of poor quality relatively cheap.

Close to Greater London
- As we have seen being close to London meant a ready labour supply but it also meant being close to a large number of small engineering firms. Such firms still flourish on the outskirts of London and could therefore supply components. The capital with its vast population also represents a large market.

Study the aerial photograph on page 89 carefully. In the foreground is of course the River Thames.

Notice the company's own wharf complete with cranes but alas, in this shot, no ships! The building immediately behind the wharf is the original plant where today engines of all sizes are built. To the right is the foundry. As you look, follow the company road on the left, over the man-made lake— all that remains of the marsh—to the railway sidings where there are whole lines of full transporter trucks. The building on the left behind the rail lines is the body shop and on the right the assembly shops; the 2 being linked by a bridge through which the completed body shells glide to meet up with their chassis and engine after several coats of paint. In the background you can see the old Dagenham council estate with a few modern tower blocks.

ASSIGNMENTS

1 Draw in your notebooks a sketch-map of Dagenham to show the main reasons for the choice of site.

2 Read this article from the *Ilford Recorder* 3 May, 1929.

THE RECORDER, FRIDAY, MAY 3, 1929.

THE FORD FACTORY.

Start To Be Made This Month.

A GIGANTIC SCHEME.

Employment For Local Men.

DAGENHAM WORKS TO COST THREE MILLION.

An industrial development of immense magnitude, and one that will provide employment for thousands of workpeople in the south, is foreshadowed by the announcement that a start will be made on the new Ford factory, at Dagenham, on May 16th.

It is computed that for the first two years from 3,000 to 4,000 men will be employed in laying down the necessary plant. The number will be increased to 15,000 when the factory is fully in action.

The whole scheme, it is estimated, will cost between two and three millions sterling, and its completion will mark the most important landmark in the industrial history of the district.

The official announcement that a definite start is to be made on the erection of the new Ford factory— the advent of which has for so long been rumoured—on May 16th, was made at a meeting of the Dagenham Council on Friday.

What such a factory means to Ilford and Dagenham it is, at this

early stage, difficult to visualise. One thing that is certain, however, is that it will bring to the towns, and their environs, a measure of prosperity that will be the envy of other communities.

This week, in a special interview, Major Caink, of Ford Motors (England), Ltd., who is responsible for the arrangements in connection with the Dagenham developments, gave the "Recorder" an outline of the magnitude of the scheme. He quoted figures, which, by their immensity, are almost incomprehensible but which convey an idea of the vastness of the undertaking. The works, when completed, will be enormous.

THE PROPOSALS

"How many men will be employed?" Major Caink was asked by our representative.

"For the next couple of years," he replied, "three to four thousand men will be employed in laying down manufacturing plant. When that work is completed, we shall employ about 15,000 men.

"The rate of production is estimated at 500 cars a day, but about two and a half years will elapse before we can start producing the cars."

Asked what work will be first put in hand, Major Caink replied that already he had given out contracts for the levelling of the ground and the laying of the railway tracks. "Then," he added, "there would be bridges to build, followed by the erection of assembling sheds."

A COOL £60,000

"Will the men employed on this work be local men?"—"Yes, as far as possible Dagenham men will be employed."

Major Caink said that a river wall would have to be built, as well as two jetties, before operations could begin in earnest.

"What will be the cost?" was our representative's next question.

"Oh," replied our informant, "the levelling, the laying of the track, the building of the river wall and so on will only cost about £60,000. Of course, the whole scheme will cost much more; probably between two or three millions."

Seeking further information about the new Ford enterprise, our reporter interviewed Mr. Francis, the surveyor to Dagenham Council.

AN AGREEABLE SUBJECT.

"You've come to see me about Ford's," he said, proffering a cigarette.

"Yes," replied the reporter.

Mr. Francis appeared to enjoy talking of Ford's and he soon warmed to his subject in a smoke-filled room. After describing an imaginary picture of a future Dagenham, he discussed the preliminary arrangements that have already been made for the starting of the project.

"Well, Major Caink and Mr. Brooks saw me last week on behalf of Sir Percival Perry, the chairman of Ford Motors (England), Ltd. They told me that there would be a ceremony on May 16th. Mr. Edswold Ford is to cut the first sod on that day.

CUTTING THE FIRST SOD.

"They propose to erect a big marquee inside which a portion of the ground will be roped in, and here the first sod will be cut. The remainder of the marquee will be set aside for refreshments for the guests.

"A fleet of 15 Ford cars will be sent to Valence House at 11.45 a.m. to take the councillors to the site. They are also making special arrangements for the transportation of the representatives of the L.C.C., P.L.A., and Essex County Council."

"Mr. Edswold Ford," he continued, "will make a speech outlining the proposals of the firm, and his speech will be followed by one from Sir Percival Perry.

"Councillor C. Dellow (chairman Dagenham Council) will respond on behalf of the district."

IMMEDIATE PREPARATIONS

"What plans have you had in for approval?" asked the reporter.

"The information which we have in regard to the immediate proposals is that they will put down three assembly sheds, 300ft. wide by 1,000ft. long. There will be a railway loop-line serving all sheds. A reinforced concrete riverside wall and a private road are to be constructed, the latter from Ripple-road, opposite Marsh Green Farm, down to the riverside crossing Dagenham Breech.

"That's all I can tell you," concluded Mr. Francis.

Do you think that everybody in the community would greet the news of a giant factory on their doorstep with the same enthusiasm shown in this article? If you read the newspapers or watch television news programmes you would probably have seen reports about such groups as Greenpeace and the Ecology party. Many people today are worried about the environment and the way we are polluting it.

You are a reporter on your local paper and a new car plant is to be built very close to your school. Write a short article about this decision bringing out both good and bad points.

CASE STUDY

BP Oil, Llandarcy Refinery Ltd, Neath, West Glamorgan

Until BP (then the Anglo–Persian Oil Company) started refining crude oil in 1921 at their South Wales site such refining was carried out close to the oil fields. For several reasons, however, BP decided that it would be better to refine the crude oil actually in the British Isles, some 6000 miles away from the oil fields in Persia, but in the marketplace for the finished product.

This not only meant more profit but greater security of supply for the consumer. It is not only petrol for the motorist that comes from such refining but also high grade lubricants, fuel oils and chemicals for industry. Having decided to refine in the UK the company had to look for a site. After looking at several the 650 acre site at Skewen, near Swansea in South Wales was chosen. Again look at the map (Fig 26) and then read the summary of reasons for the choice that follows it.

Transport facilities

- Crude oil is, as we all know, shipped in large special ships which need a special terminal to unload safely. BP were able to sign a 99 year lease for the south side of Swansea's Queen's Docks, for this purpose.

Labour supply

- Adequate labour supply was available in the area both to build and staff the refinery. When one considers that it now employs 1600 workers it shows how important labour is.

  At the time the South Wales area was suffering from very high levels of unemployment due to contractions in traditional local industry like coal mining.

Land

- Adequate cheap land was available, at the time only waste land.

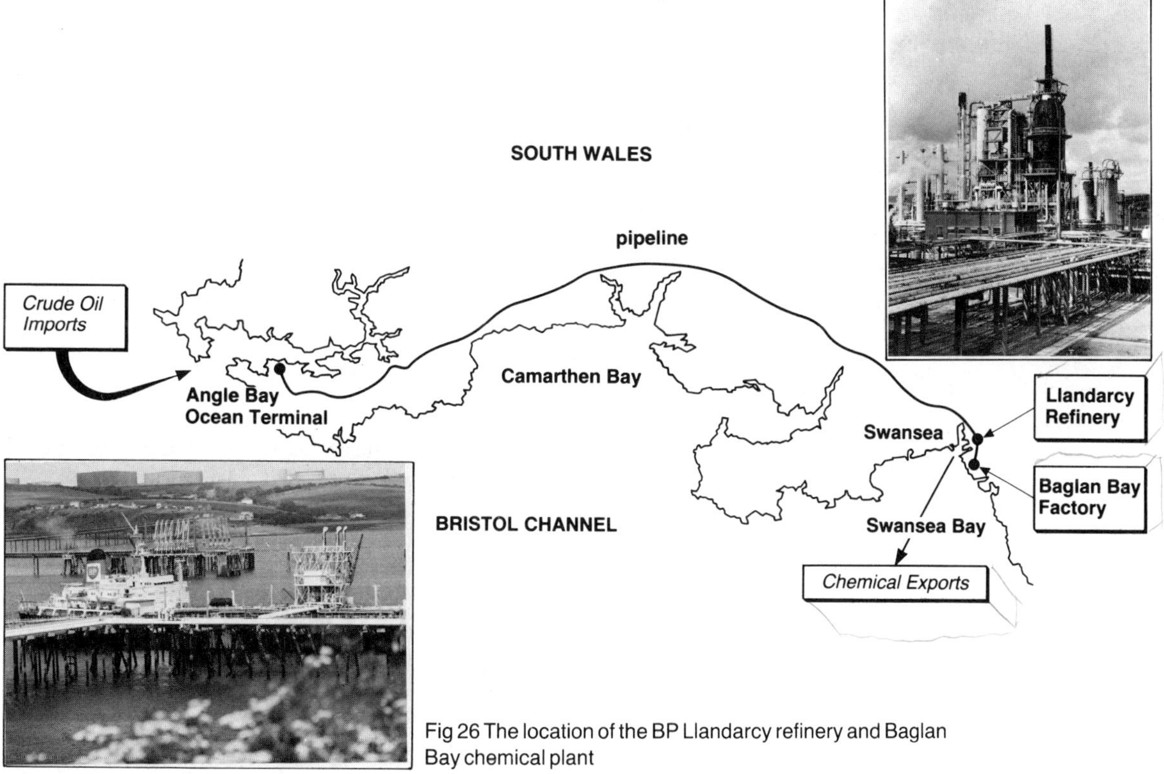

Fig 26 The location of the BP Llandarcy refinery and Baglan Bay chemical plant

During the late 1940s and early 1950s it became possible to build very large tankers to ship crude oil from the Middle-East. Unfortunately the Swansea docks were not capable of taking such large ships but it was so much cheaper for the company to transport oil in this way that a new larger terminal was needed. In August 1960 the Ocean Terminal at Angle Bay on Milford Haven was opened. This site was capable of dealing with ships of up to 250 000 dwt.

The crude oil is pumped from the ships into storage tanks, cleverly landscaped into the beautiful countryside of the Pembrokeshire National Park, and from there underground by pipeline 62 miles down the coast to the old Llandarcy refinery. It would have been impracticable to move a giant refinery but in this way BP have been able to use the largest oil tankers.

Similar pipelines carry one of the refined products, naphtha, a little further down the coast to the BP Chemicals Ltd plant at Baglan Bay. Here, with other raw materials, the company manufactures chemicals for the world's plastics industry. Baglan Bay, opened in 1963, was chosen because it is so close to its main supply of feedstock (raw material) and because of its supply of land. This was a 500 acre site with a prime coastal position making waste disposal possible through a $2\frac{3}{4}$ mile pipe out into the Bristol Channel. The export of chemicals via an extended Queen's Docks was also possible. Added to this adequate labour supply in the area made it a logical choice of site. Another related factor was that South Wales was (and still is) a **development area**. This means that Central Government provides grants to companies moving to these areas to help with such things as building costs etc.

It must be stressed that BP take pollution of the environment very seriously and do not just dump waste out at sea. The waste is treated and the company has a full-time environmental control team which samples water in the Bristol channel as well as checking the atmosphere and noise levels in the area.

From this development of BP we can learn 2 important lessons. Firstly, when a large established plant finds that one or more of the original reasons for choosing the site no longer apply it will often continue to produce there. We call this **industrial inertia**. It is obvious that once built, once the original location decision has been made, particularly with heavy, capital intensive industries like the petro-chemical industry, it would be very difficult and expensive to close down and move. This is, of course, not so with our original example—the travel agency. If we rented a shop in the wrong district it would be easy to move. We could even take all our fixtures and fittings.

Secondly, and perhaps more importantly, once the refinery was established other chemical factories followed. This is not only true for Baglan Bay. Other chemical companies now operate in the South Wales area. In this way an area develops a reputation and becomes associated with a product.

Exercise

Answer the following questions in complete sentences.

1 In 1925 Henry Ford found it necessary to look for new British premises. Why was this?

2 Many people would have found the choice of Dagenham strange for the construction of the Ford manufacturing plant. Why was this and how were the problems of the site overcome?

3 Can you think of at least 2 raw materials imported into the Dagenham area by Ford?

4 What 3 types of modern transport method does the Dagenham site enjoy?

5 Can you think of one type of modern transport for which the Dagenham site is not ideally situated? Does this matter?

6 Why, before the BP Llandarcy refinery was built, was crude oil usually refined close to the oil fields?

7 Can you see 2 reasons which attracted BP to Llandarcy which are similar to those which attracted Ford to Dagenham?

8 Why, when super-tankers were introduced did BP not move or close down the Llandarcy refinery?

9 BP still use the Queen's Docks in Swansea. What for?

10 Why was the Baglan Bay site chosen for chemical production by BP?

ASSIGNMENT

Consider any local business. (It could be a sweet shop or huge company.) Think of all the reasons which may have influenced the entrepreneur to choose that locality or particular site. Was it a good choice? Is it part of an industry in that area or just one isolated plant? How does it affect the area? You could perhaps write a case study.

Location Factors

In the case studies 3 common factors emerged which had influenced the choice of site—**land, labour** and **transport facilities**. There are many other factors which might affect this choice, but this will depend upon the type of firm. Some firms may need to be close to their markets or to sub-contractors, others may need special waste disposal facilities.

Here we shall look at these factors in a little more detail.

LAND

The term land refers to all naturally occurring factors of production eg, the actual land, the climatic conditions, the minerals and raw materials under the ground. For some industries such as oil, the position of raw materials will decide the location. Agriculture is obviously dependent upon the type of soil and the climate but in a country as small as Britain this will not have too great an influence. Some industries are dependent upon agriculture themselves and will thus be in certain areas, like jam making and sugar beet refining. Manufacturing industry will just want good, cheap building land often with room for expansion.

LABOUR

All industry needs labour and it is expensive to move people around. Labour intensive industry, like clothing manufacture, will tend to locate close to large centres of population. Sometimes a firm has to move the labour, such as with North Sea oil wells.

TRANSPORT COSTS

Some firms might cause raw materials to lose weight during the productive process. That is they start with heavy or bulky inputs and end up with a much lighter finished product. These **weight or bulk reducing** firms will clearly be able to minimise transport costs if they are sited close to the raw materials since it would be silly to pay for the transport of waste. An example would be the production of pig iron from iron ore where much of the weight of raw material goes up the chimney in smoke. Such firms are often called **material orientated**. In this country this can mean being sited close to a port since we have so few raw materials. The opposite to this would be a firm which adds weight during the productive process, for example brewing as the majority of beer is water. Why pay to ship water around. For this reason breweries are found around most centres of population. Such firms are often called **weight gaining** and tend to be **market orientated**.

It is difficult to think of too many examples of firms where transport cost are very important to us here in the UK since this is such a small country and has such good communicaton networks. In general transport costs will be more important to firms which produce cheap, heavy goods as opposed to light, expensive goods since, for the latter, transport costs represent such a small proportion of the final cost. Consider the difference between brick manufacture and diamond cutting.

MARKET

Some firms, weight or bulk gaining firms, will reduce transport costs by situating themselves close to their markets. There are a further two types of business which will tend to be close to the market for the product. Firstly, it would be foolish to mass produce a product like bread in just one area and transport it to other areas to sell—it would arrive stale. Even in a relatively small country such as the UK some goods, **perishable goods**, will need to be produced as close to their place of consumption as possible. In fact, there has been a return to small retail bakers producing their own bread on site. (Hot oven bread can now be smelt in most high streets and even inside some famous supermarket chains.) The second type of market orientated good is, in fact, not a good at all but a service. **Service industries**, like hairdressers, are spread out all over the country in every town and city. You would not travel miles just to get your hair cut, would you?

Exercise

It costs £20 to move one tonne of iron ore 10 miles, £10 to move one tonne of coal 10 miles and £15 to move one tonne of limestone 10 miles. If for each tonne of pig iron you need 3 tonnes of iron ore, 2 tonnes of coal and one tonne of limestone and these raw materials were located at the different sites as shown in Fig 27 where do you think would be the best place to site a blast furnace so as to minimise transport costs? Site **A, B, C** or **D**?

Copy out the following table and complete it:

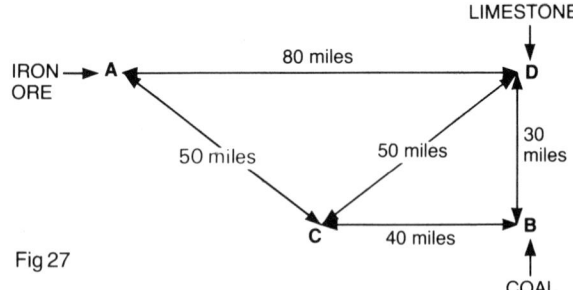

Fig 27

	Cost to move 3 tonnes of Iron ore to:		Cost to move 2 tonnes of coal to:		Cost to move 1 tonne of limestone to		Total transport cost
Location **A**	£—	+	£180	+	£120		=£300
Location **B**	£	+	£—	+	£45		=£
Location **C**	£	+	£80	+	£		=£
Location **D**	£480	+	£	+	£—		=£

At which site are transport costs least?

If the local planning authority would not give permission for a blast furnace to be built at the cheapest site where then would you suggest it be situated?

WASTE DISPOSAL AND SAFETY

Considerations about these 2 factors can be very important for such firms as chemical manufacturers. One important waste of an atomic power station is heat so that these buildings are usually located on the coast. They are also kept well away from large centres of population because of potential danger.

SUB-CONTRACTORS AND OTHER ACQUIRED ADVANTAGES OF AN AREA

If an area attracts a large number of firms from the same industry it will change or acquire additional advantages which will often attract still further firms. Sub-contractors offering specialised services will set up in the area together with component manufacturers. Educational facilities, such as specialised training in local colleges, will make the area of greater importance to the industry. Special transport facilities and even markets may be constructed. In the end the area will become famous for that product and the name will help to sell the product, eg Sheffield steel, Northamptonshire shoes etc. This will often mean that the acquired advantages of the area become more important than the original advantages of the area so that if these original advantages disappear firms will stay where they are. As we have seen this is called **industrial inertia**.

PERSONAL INFLUENCES

Often none of the factors looked at will decide the location for an entrepreneur. The choice of site will depend simply upon the personal likes or dislikes of the entrepreneur. It could well be the area in which they were born and live which is chosen and no other reason at all.

CASE STUDY

Daventry—a town which set out to attract new firms

This case study shows how a *town* can demonstrate to entrepreneurs its locational advantages, improve them and successfully attract new enterprise to the area and thus provide employment for a growing population. Look at the maps of England contained in some of the early advertising literature given out by Daventry District Council (see below). You will see that the town of Daventry is situated in the middle of the country. It grew up as an important staging post and crossroads during the era of the stage coach but, by the 1950s the town was in decline with only a

small population. Birmingham, a mere 40 miles away, had begun a slum clearance programme during the 1930s but needed new areas to build modern housing for various reasons away from the city itself. Daventry was chosen in 1963 to be a Birmingham overspill town with a planned rise in population of 30 000 by 1981. If the town were to grow at this rate it was necessary to create many new jobs in the area since people could not commute 80 miles a day to and from work. The town set out to attract what are called **footloose businesses**, that is types of businesses which

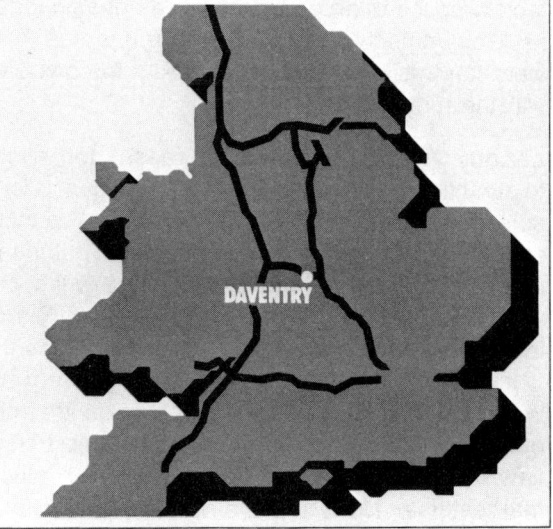

in the heart of things

Daventry is situated in Northamptonshire and provides easy access to the two major industrial areas of Greater London and the West Midlands. Daventry, located on the A45, with easy access to the M1, is an ideal national distribution centre. This is evidenced by Ford Motor Co., and Green Shield Ltd., who have national distribution centres in the town. Daventry's proximity to the M1 at the centre of the UK's motorway system links it to the M6 and M5.

Within half an hour's motoring you are in the industrial centres of Coventry, Leicester, Northampton; the tourist activity of Stratford-upon-Avon; the farming environment of the National Agricultural Centre and the international trading world of the National Exhibition Centre, Birmingham.

Inter-City trains are available at nearby Rugby and local services at Long Buckby, 4 miles from Daventry. British Rail can speed you to London (Euston) in less than an hour. Forty miles to the north you have the choice of two airports, Birmingham international airport (Elmdon) and Castle Donnington. By road, rail and air Daventry can be reached easily and conveniently. Bring your firm to the heart of things.

DAVENTRY

can operate in any area and are not tied to one specific area. Daventry was not in a development area and therefore could not offer grants or tax concessions like say Liverpool or Newcastle. The Council had to rely upon 3 main advantages which they stressed in their advertising literature.

Such advertisements were placed in trade magazines and quality newspapers like the *Financial Times*. The staff of the town's development office took stands to exhibitions in Birmingham and London and would attend any event where potential business converts would attend. Glossy brochures were produced to send in response to enquiries which stressed the following 3 advantages:

Transport costs Being in the middle of the country means that Daventry is not far from most regions of Britain. The town is only 3 miles from the M1 giving easy access to London and the West Midlands. It is only 10 miles from the British Rail (BR) freight terminal at Rugby and 12 miles from the one at Northampton. BR passenger services to London run from Long Buckby only a few miles down the road. Birmingham airport is just 40 miles away.

Land The Council with the help of Birmingham City Council initially built 2 industrial estates with all services. Unit factories, warehouses and offices of different sizes were built. The development department also helped to build factory space to order. Prices were not as cheap as Government aided development areas but were kept as low as possible so as to compete with the surrounding areas.

Labour This was the original reason for trying to attract new businesses. As a Birmingham over-spill town Daventry had built a number of council and private estates. In the early days the potential employer was helped with staffing his new firm by the Council which kept records of people in Birmingham wishing to move and their qualifications.

In addition, the town itself was being improved by the construction of a new shopping centre and other amenities whilst a new by-pass and traffic flow scheme much improved access to the industrial estates. New schools were built for the children with parks and open spaces for recreation. Looking to the future, additional housing and industrial areas were planned which are in the process of being developed (see opposite).

SUCCESS?

The town has expanded as planned and managed to attract new firms. Both of the original industrial estates are full and a third is under construction. Although many different types of firms have been attracted 2 of the largest employers were companies which needed good transport and communications. Fords opened their national parts centre, from where spare parts are sent to garages all over the country. Green Shield Stamps, now Argos, also set up a national distribution centre. Both companies enjoy the convenient location close to the motorways and central position. Also, small engineering and manufacturing companies were attracted both from the local area, the South East and London. The full picture is shown by these 2 tables:

Origins of Firms on Industrial Estates in Daventry

Originating area	% of total companies	% of total employment
Local area	43.0	12.0
Remainder of county	4.6	4.5
Birmingham	4.6	2.3
Remainder of West Midlands	11.6	4.0
East Midlands	2.3	1.4
London & South East	20.3	58.9
Elsewhere in Great Britain	2.9	6.8
Abroad	3.5	9.4
Unknown	7.2	0.7

Employment in the Main Sectors in Daventry's Industrial Estates

Jobs in manufacturing industry	2 418	47.7%
Jobs in national and regional services	2 465	48.7%

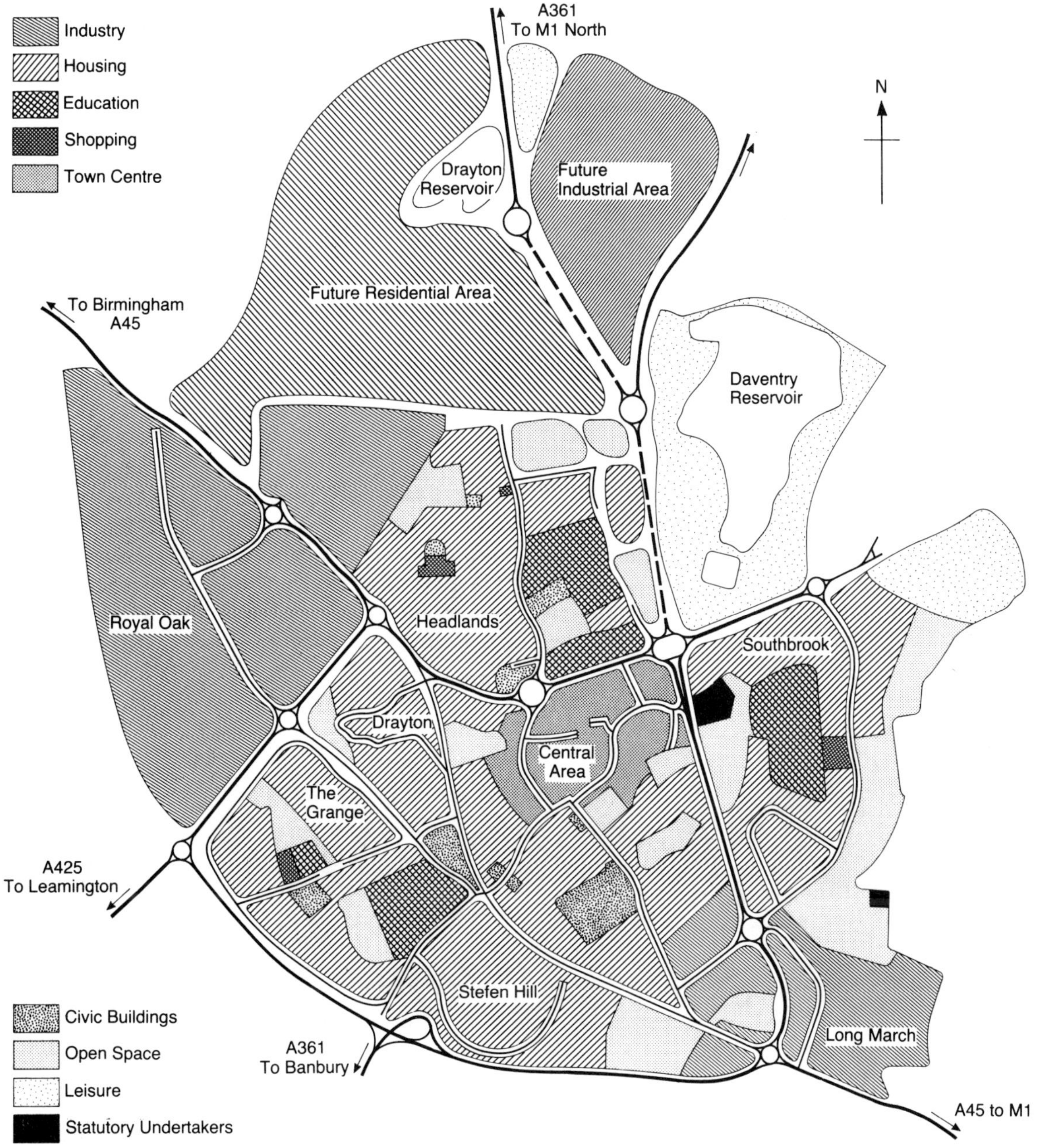

Industry

Housing

Education

Shopping

Town Centre

A361
To M1 North

Drayton
Reservoir

Future
Industrial Area

N

To Birmingham
A45

Future Residential Area

Daventry
Reservoir

Royal Oak

Headlands

Southbrook

Drayton

Central
Area

The
Grange

A425
To Leamington

Stefen Hill

Long March

A361
To Banbury

A45 to M1

Civic Buildings

Open Space

Leisure

Statutory Undertakers

Jobs in local services	182	3.6%
Total employment	5 065	100.0%

Source: Daventry Planning Department Survey, January 1977

Since 1977 the country has been going through a recession with very high levels of unemployment throughout the entire country. Daventry has enjoyed unemployment rates consistently below the national average because of its development programme and in spite of the current recession the district council is going ahead with the third industrial area hoping to attract still more firms. In many respects this is vital for the future of the town. The early years of the programme in the

1960s attracted very many young married couples to the area. They have had their own families who will need jobs well into the 1990s. It has been estimated that by 1991 *two thirds* of the population of Daventry will be between 20 and 29! These young people will need their own homes and employment. This strange age distribution is reflected in the **activity rates**. The activity rate is the percentage of the population over the minimum working age who are either in work or actively looking for work. As the following table shows, the activity rate of Daventry is considerably higher than that of the UK.

Activity Rates 1971

	Daventry	Great Britain
Male	88.98%	81.37%
Female	45.03%	42.73%

Source: 1971 Census, HMSO

The Council is well aware of the task ahead and in a recent report by the chief planning officer suggestions were made not only to extend industrial building but also to introduce new initiatives including tourism, the setting up of training workshops and wider promotion.

Industrial Location

We have looked at the factors which influenced the choice of sites for the Ford, Dagenham plant and BP refinery and chemical plants at Llandarcy and Baglan Bay. The map below however shows the location of car assembly plants and oil refineries throughout the UK. It can be seen that they are spread out over the country. This is because no one area is uniquely suited to this type of production. It is possible to produce cars and refine oil in a variety of different locations. Costs are not minimised in just one area. This is

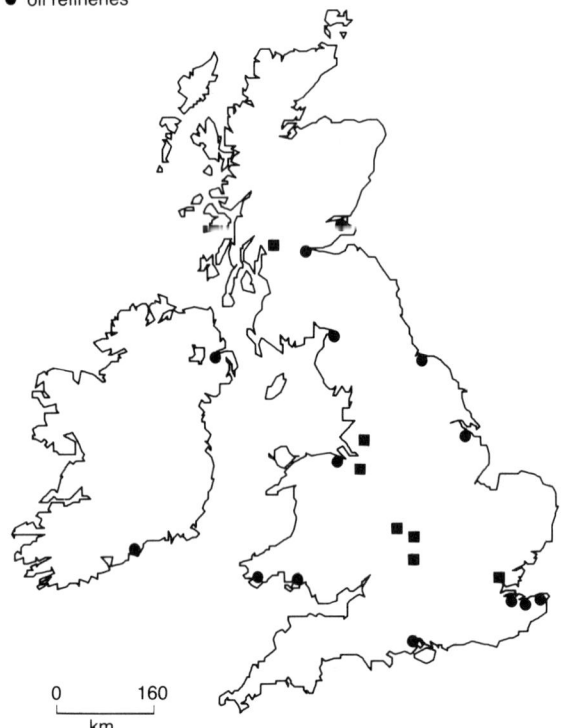

The location of major car assembly plants and oil refineries

The location of major ship building and iron and steel works

true for the majority of industries. These are called **scattered** or **dispersed industries**.

For a few industries however, for various reasons, not all sites are equally attractive and many firms from the same industry tend to congregate in a few areas. These industries are called **concentrated** or **highly localised**. Examples include the textile industry, coal mining, ship building and to a lesser degree iron and steel. With some smaller industries it may be due to historical reasons, for others it will be because of the natural uneven spread of raw materials throughout the country. Ship building will need deep, safe estuaries and centres of population close to steel production. Iron will need to be close to one or more of the heavy raw materials or a port for imports. The second map opposite shows the location of ship building and iron and steel.

CASE STUDY

The knitted textiles industry

The knitted textiles industry is not evenly spread throughout Britain as the map shows. There are firms scattered around Scotland, the North and South of England and in Wales, but the main centres of production are the East Midlands, where 60% of knitted textiles are made, and the Scottish Borders.

When presented with this information for the first time it is not easy to see why there is such an uneven distribution in this small but important industry. The reasons are in the main historic and a matter of chance.

The migration of lace makers from Flanders into the East Midlands area led to the development of the lace making industry and therefore a pool of skilled workers. Coupled with this it was in a small village just outside Nottingham that the first knitting frame was invented and of course there was a supply of local wool.

Source: Knitting, Lace and Net Industry Training Board

Government Influences on Location

Some areas become dependent upon a very few industries. Newcastle on ship building, Corby on steel, Nottingham on textiles for example. Although this might restrict the choice of careers in such areas, and perhaps lead to pollution, so long as the industry survives the area will prosper and attract firms in similar and allied fields. If the industry were for any reason to collapse then the area would fall into decline as well. It would not only be the people who were employed in the declining industry who would be affected. Component manufacturers, service industries and even the public sector would be faced with falling demand, unemployment and decline. This we call **regional unemployment**. Three of Britain's most highly localised industries: textiles, ship building and iron and steel have been in decline due to foreign competition for many years now. When one considers that at the end of the Second World War textiles represented over 30% of our exports by value and now forms just 3% you can see how

this industry has declined in importance. Look at the map below and you can see how uneven unemployment is.

Notice the figure for Northern Ireland—more than twice the unemployment of the South East. The problem is not as simple as this. Within some areas there are unemployment black spots like Corby in the Midlands due to the closure of the British Steel plant. Even within cities there are run down areas perhaps due to high rents/rates which have forced firms out to the cheaper sites. What can be done to remedy regional/localised unemployment such as this?

It is clear that firms left to make their own

Regional Unemployment November 1984 (% of working population)

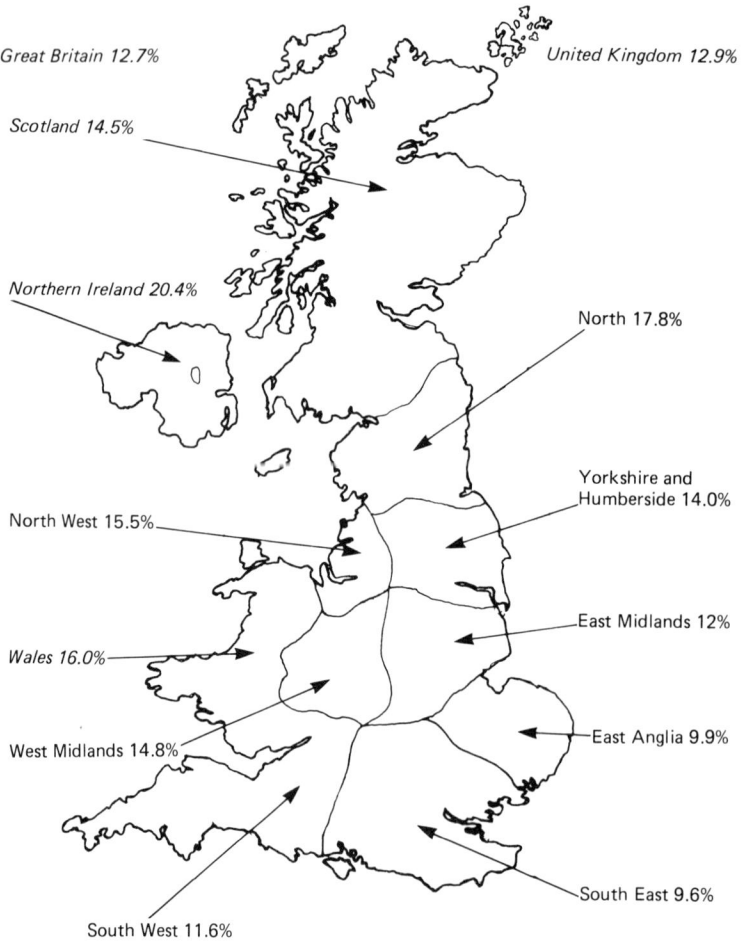

Regional unemployment, November 1984, Source:
Department of Employment, 1984 HMSO

rational decisions will choose the cheapest site. For the new expanding industries this will not necessarily be the areas which suit the older declining industries. If nothing were to be done this would leave wasted factors of production. Land would be wasted; and there would be empty industrial estates. Capital would be wasted; roads unused, factories closed down. People in these areas might be unemployed for months, even years, which not only means wasted labour but also hard times and a low standard of living for the families concerned.

The only body which can do anything to help is the Government. There are 2 alternatives for the Government: move the people who are unemployed to where there are jobs *or* move new industry to the unemployed people.

The first alternative can be rejected since not only would it be very impractical and perhaps cause emotional upset for families who would be split up, but it would also leave whole areas of the country wasted. Schools and hospitals would lie empty in, say, Newcastle but there would be over-crowding in, say, London.

The Government has therefore for many years now tried to encourage industry to move to areas

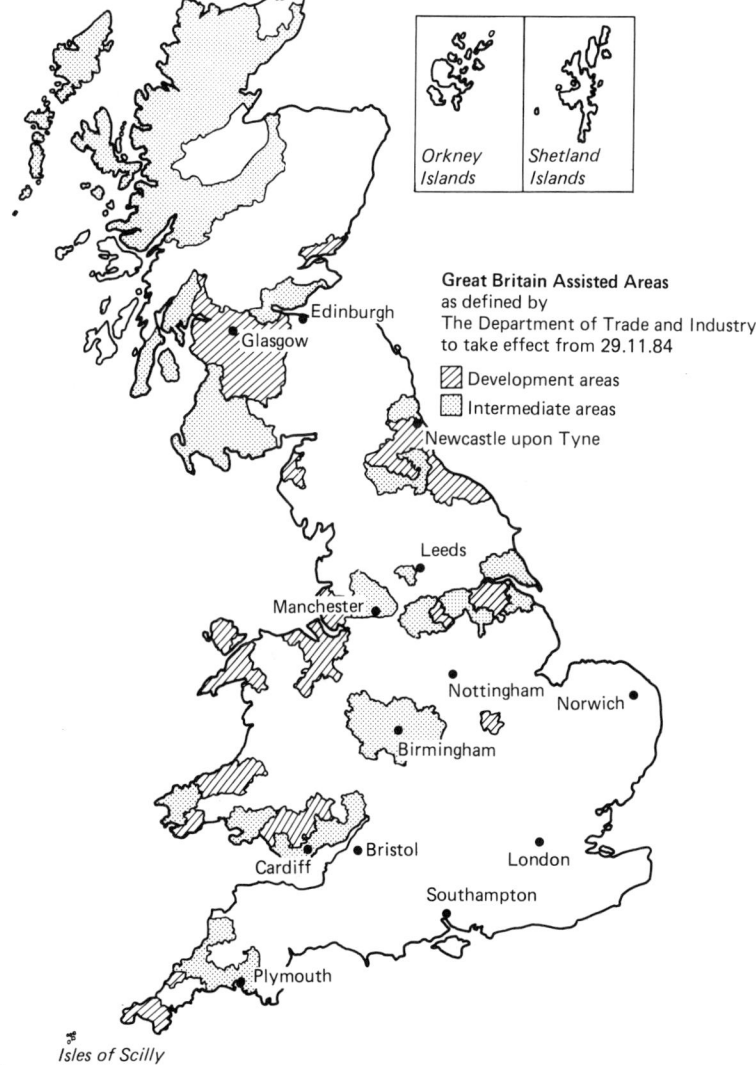

Great Britain Assisted Areas
as defined by
The Department of Trade and Industry
to take effect from 29.11.84

Development areas
Intermediate areas

Great Britain assisted areas

of high unemployment. With the public sector this is easy since such industries are controlled by the Government. (I find that my income tax inspector works in Newcastle although I live in Essex. I pay my car tax to Swansea along with my television licence and the National Giro Bank is in Bootle. These sites were chosen by the Government to provide employment.) The private sector industry, however, needs to be persuaded and the most effective method is to make areas of high unemployment financially attractive. Paying something towards the cost of moving and setting up a factory in areas of high unemployment will in the end save the Government money since they will not have to pay unemployment benefit to the people who now find work (see previous map).

Certain areas of high unemployment are called **assisted areas** by the Government. These are of two types:

a Development areas—areas of very high unemployment eg Liverpool, Newcastle, Glasgow etc
b Intermediate areas—areas of high unemployment eg Birmingham, Plymouth, Cardiff

The Government offers financial help to firms which decide to move to these areas in an attempt to create more jobs in such places.

FINANCIAL ASSISTANCE IN ASSISTED AREAS

Development areas In these areas a firm is able to claim *either* a 15% grant towards the cost of new buildings and machinery—a regional development grant *or* a job grant of £3 000 per job created. The Goverment will pay which ever is the greater. It must be noted however that the 15% grant is subject to a 'cost per job limit' of £10 000 although this does not apply to very small firms. New firms are also allowed to apply for selective assistance.

Intermediate areas In these areas firms are eligible for selective assistance only.

Selective assistance Any firms in assisted areas can apply for grants if an investment project creates jobs or protects existing employment.

Note To qualify for a grant a firm must be designated a **qualifying activity**. Until November 1984 this meant that service industries were not eligible. Since then some service industries have also been eligible along with manufacturing industries.

Government built factories In many assisted areas the Government has built factories and smaller workshops. It is sometimes possible to arrange rent free periods.

Contracts preference scheme Companies in development areas receive preferential treatment if they tender for contracts placed by government departments or the nationalised industries. Remember the Government is a very big spender and has to buy millions of pounds worth of manufactured products. The firms who supply these products are guaranteed large regular orders.

Finance from the EEC It is possible for firms in the assisted areas to borrow up to 50% of the total costs of a project from the European Investment Bank at fixed rates of interest for 7 years.

In addition to these measures and others not mentioned here, Northern Ireland is treated as a very special case. Grants are negotiated with the Government and special projects which offer a high number of jobs created can receive up to 50% grants.

Enterprise zones A number of enterprise zones have been established as part of a 10 year experiment. The main idea behind them is that the Government wishes to see whether business is encouraged by the removal of basic taxation, administrative and planning constraints. Firms in such zones do not pay rates or development land tax. There are simplified planning procedures and customs facilities. Such zones are often in inner cities like the London Docklands area and the Salford Docks in Greater Manchester, or towns with special problems like Corby. Where an enterprise zone lies within an area for expansion those incentives still apply.

All of the case studies discussed earlier in this chapter have some connection with this list of Government incentives. Fords, for example, opened a £200 million engine plant in Bridgend, South Wales with aid from the Government. Already mentioned was the fact that BP were given Government aid with their Baglan Bay chemical factory. Daventry was not in a designated area to receive aid whereas Corby now is, which may well effect their ability to attract new firms.

Regional unemployment has been a problem since the 1930s and recognised as such by the Government. Various aid and incentive programmes have been run by all Governments but the sad fact remains that there is still greater unemployment in certain regions of our country than others.

CASE STUDY

The Nissan Car Assembly Plant

In February 1984 it was announced that Nissan, the second largest Japanese vehicles group, was going to build a £50 million 'pilot' assembly plant in the UK to produce 24 000 cars a year from kits imported from Japan. If this pilot scheme is a success the company has plans to expand to produce 100 000 cars by 1991 using between 60% and 80% EEC components.

Where was Nissan to site this new plant? The following factors had to be considered:

- a large site (800 acres) to allow for the planned expansion
- an area of high unemployment to qualify for Government regional development grants
- close to docks to allow for the easy importation of 'kits' from Japan

The company looked at many different sites suggested by the UK Government but concentrated upon 2:

Washington New Town (Tyne and Wear)
Shotton on Deeside (North Wales)

Both of these areas would secure the company grants under the Government's regional policy as they are in assisted areas. In addition an extra 10% grant of selective assistance was promised.

This pilot project will create between 400–500 new jobs but the second phase would mean 2 700 new jobs. The Nissan company has agreed that these 24 000 cars will count as imports and form part of the agreed 11% maximum share of the UK new car market for all Japanese cars.

The actual site chosen was announced in March 1984. It is Washington New Town with male unemployment running at 30%. We can therefore see that the Government, by offering grants, influenced the choice of site, in order to create jobs in areas of very high unemployment not only within the country, but also between countries. (Nissan could have built this factory anywhere in Europe or indeed in Japan!)

Exercise

UK Car Production 1983

BL	473 341
Ford	318 674
General Motors (Vauxhall)	126 524
Talbot (UK)	120 503
Total (incl smaller producers)	1 044 597
Nissan 1986	24 000
Nissan 1991	100 000

Source: Financial Times, 2 February 1984

1 If all other UK car manufacturers maintain their 1983 production, what approximate percentage of total UK car output will the Nissan UK operation represent in 1986?

a 10%   *c* 2½%
b 5%   *d* 1¼%

and in 1991?

a 19%   *c* 4½%
b 9%   *d* 2¼%

2 What approximate percentage of total UK output in 1983 was produced by **British owned** car manufacturing plants?

a 55%   *c* 35%
b 45%   *d* 25%

3 The Transport and General Workers Union welcomed the Nissan plant deal. Why do you think this was?
4 The AEUW–Tass (the white collar engineering union) with over 25 000 motor industry members condemned the project as 'a body-blow to British Leyland.' Can you think why and explain this difference of opinion between 2 unions?
5 Mr Norman Tebbit, the Secretary of State for Trade and Industry at the time, said: 'The project would make a significant long-term contribution to the UK economy.' Why should he think this?

ASSIGNMENT

With the use of a map write a short newspaper article explaining the choice of the Nissan site, where and why it was chosen and why it will or will not be good for the area and the UK as a whole.

SUMMARY EXERCISE

Answer *all* of the following questions in complete sentences as fully as possible.
1 For what products are the following areas famous:

a Sheffield
b Coventry/Midlands
c Stoke-on-Trent

2 What areas are famous for these products:

a Coal mining
b Ship building
c Textiles

3 The answers to questions **1** and **2** above give examples of industries which are carried out in just a few areas. These are called **concentrated** or **localised** industries. Can you think of one or 2 more examples?
4 The opposite to a concentrated industry is called a **dispersed** or **scattered industry**. These industries are carried out all over the country. Can you think of 3 examples?
5 Give an example of an industry which would need to be close to a good transport system and an example of an industry where this would not matter.
6 There are 3 types of industry which need to be close to their market. These are often called **market orientated** industries—give an example of each type.
7 A **weight-losing** industry such as pig iron manufacturing is usually located close to at least one of its raw materials. Can you explain why?
8 An industry may well continue producing in an area even though the reasons which made it move there in the first place have long since gone. This is called **industrial inertia**. Why does the industry remain there?
9 Take any one of your answers to question **2** and question **4** and explain why one industry is **concentrated** and the other is **scattered**.
10 Why, when trying to solve the problem of regional unemployment, does the Government not give grants to people to help them move to areas with employment?

ASSIGNMENT

1 Describe clearly the location of a factory that you have studied giving at least 4 factors which influenced the choice of this site.

2 Why are some industries said to be **scattered** whilst others highly **localised** or **concentrated**? What problems do you think can arise for *a* the country and *b* the area from the concentration of some industries?

3 Describe how the Government is trying to cure the problem of regional unemployment.

9 International Trade and Payments

If you look at your family's weekly shopping to see where the goods were made or grown you will soon notice that a great deal of what we buy is not made in this country. Look at your school car park and you will see cars from Japan, Germany, Sweden and France as well as the UK.

The UK exports 29% of all that is produced in a year and imports about the same value of goods. This chapter examines why countries trade with each other and how this benefits a country. It also looks at British trade in detail and asks how this trade is financed.

Why countries trade with each other

Countries trade with other countries for a variety of reasons:

- There are goods which some countries cannot make or grow in commercial quantities. For example the UK cannot grow citrus fruits.

- If a country produces far more of a product than the home market requires the industry might be able to enjoy economies of scale and so produce that product more efficiently and sell it at a lower price. For example, wheat from the USA.

- Some countries have a natural advantage in producing a product such as raw materials, climate etc, or they have acquired an advantage over time and now have an experienced labour force and special machines and equipment. This will mean that such countries can produce goods and services more cheaply than others. They therefore **specialise** in certain products. For example, Brazil and coffee or the UK and insurance.

- By importing goods which they *can* produce a country can enjoy greater choice and variety. The people are able to benefit from research and development undertaken in different countries in such things as cars, televisions, new drugs, and even films and television.

Exercises

1 There are some goods the UK *cannot* produce in commercial quantities; citrus fruit for example. List 10 examples of products which must be imported into this country.

2 List as many goods as you can that are produced in Britain of which a large percentage are exported.

3 Some countries have a natural advantage in producing goods and have specialised in producing them. Can you match these products with the following countries?

Kuwait	Sugar
New Zealand	Tea
Denmark	Oil
Australia	Bacon
Sri Lanka	Lamb
Mauritius	Butter

4 Give 2 further examples of countries which have specialised in the production of a product, stating the product *and* country.

5 List 10 goods currently imported into this country in large numbers but which we could produce ourselves.

ASSIGNMENT

To see just how much this country imports of a certain product, conduct a survey using the motor car industry. Make a note of the different cars in your staff car park or ask the pupils in your school what car(s) their families own. Produce a list which could then be converted into a pie chart. Remember your survey is very limited and could be distorted. A school in Dagenham might find very different results to one in Luton. Why? Think about your results and write a conclusion including your ideas on possible distortions.

Specialisation in Trade

In Chapter 2 we saw that people have different abilities, and likes and that the economy gains if people specialise in those jobs in which they have natural ability. The same applies to countries and the gain from specialisation and trade can be demonstrated very easily with a simple hypothetical example or model.

Model to Demonstrate the Gains from Specialisation and Trade

In this model it is assumed there are 2 islands close to each other. They both produce 2 crops, sugar and tea. To produce anything the factors of production—human, natural and man-made are needed. For the purpose of this exercise it is assumed that each island has the same amount of resources.

Before specialisation and trade each island devotes half of their resources to each crop with the following results:

Position before specialisation and trade	Sugar output ('000 tonnes per annum)	Tea output
Island **A**	500	50
Island **B**	300	200

If each island specialised in the product in which it has an advantage then it could devote all of its resources to this product and double production as follows:

Position after specialisation	Sugar output ('000 tonnes per annum)	Tea output
Island **A**	1 000	—
Island **B**	—	400

If they were now to trade at a rate of exchange of one tonne of tea for 5 tonnes of sugar and Island **A** were to buy 100 000 tonnes from Island **B** it would 'cost' 500 000 tonnes of sugar:

Position after trade	Sugar consumption ('000 tonnes per annum)	Tea consumption
Island **A**	500 (1000)	100 (—)
Island **B**	500 (—)	300 (400)

Compare this with the original position without specialisation and it can be seen that both countries have gained from specialisation and trade. Island **A** has now gained 50 000 tonnes of tea per annum and Island **B** 200 000 tonnes of sugar and a further 100 000 tonnes of tea per annum. How much each country will gain depends upon the agreed rate of exchange.

Work through the above example but with an exchange rate of one tonne of tea to 3 tonnes of sugar. If Island **A** sells 300 000 tonnes of sugar, what is the gain to each country?

A country therefore can gain from specialisation and trade. In Chapter 8 you were asked to pick out countries which have, to a certain extent, specialised in a product. It is rare to find a country which is totally dependent upon one product. When people specialise there are dangers of boredom and the risk of unemployment. These are also problems for a country as the following case study shows.

CASE STUDY

Sweet and Sour

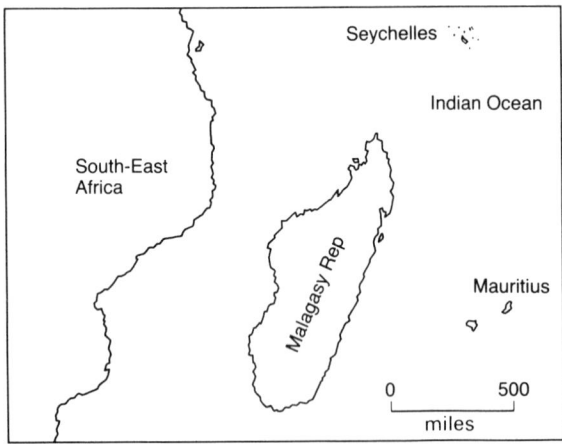

Mauritius, a member of the Commonwealth, is a small island in the Indian Ocean as you can see from the map. It is about 130 times smaller than the UK with a population of just 940 000. Although the island was known of before the 10th century it was not inhabited until Dutch explorers settled on the island in 1598.

During the 18th century it was occupied by the French who used it as a staging post for their ships on route to attack the British in India. The British captured the island in 1810 and it remained under British control until independence in 1968.

Mauritius is a volcanic island, or rather what is left after volcanic activity. It is shaped like a saucer with plains in the north and a plateau in the centre of the island bordered by mountains (all that remains of the volcanoes). The soil is composed of finely ground igneous rock (produced from the volcanoes), fairly fertile although rocky. The climate, known to geographers as 'maritime subtropical' has 2 seasons. Between May and October it is cool (25°C). For the rest of the year it remains hot (31°C). Rainfall is high averaging from 900 millimetres per annum on the west coast to over 1 500 millimetres per annum on the south coast. The air is humid with strong winds blowing most of the year and with

the risk of cyclones during the hot periods. The British changed the nature of the country from being a staging post to a plantation colony. Using slave labour from East Africa they built sugar cane plantations to take advantage of the climate. With the liberation of slaves in 1835 Indian workers were employed on these plantations. Today Mauritius is an example of a **monoculture economy**. The island has specialised to a great extent in the production of just one product—sugar—and in spite of efforts since the war to change things the country is still dependent upon this one cash crop as can be seen from the chart opposite.

Mauritius remains poor, however, with income per head being only £645 as compared to £4 851 in the UK. A country dominated by one product finds that the fortunes of that product determine the fortunes of the whole economy. If sugar prices are as high as they were during 1970–76, Mauritius prospers but if the world price of sugar falls or if the crops are ruined by cyclones as they were in 1980 then the whole country suffers. Much of the sugar is now refined from beet which can be grown in more temperate climates like Britain. Also many other countries grow the cane. Mauritius is forced therefore to take whatever price it can get. Being a member of the Commonwealth used to mean special agreements with Britain to buy sugar—now the country has an agreement with the EEC which buys 500 000 tonnes a year at a fixed price (above world prices). Even so, the income from sugar has not risen as quickly as the prices of essential imports like oil. This has led to major problems as you can see:

Mauritius trade 1982

	$ million
Exports	363.3
Imports	393.1
Trade balance	−29.8

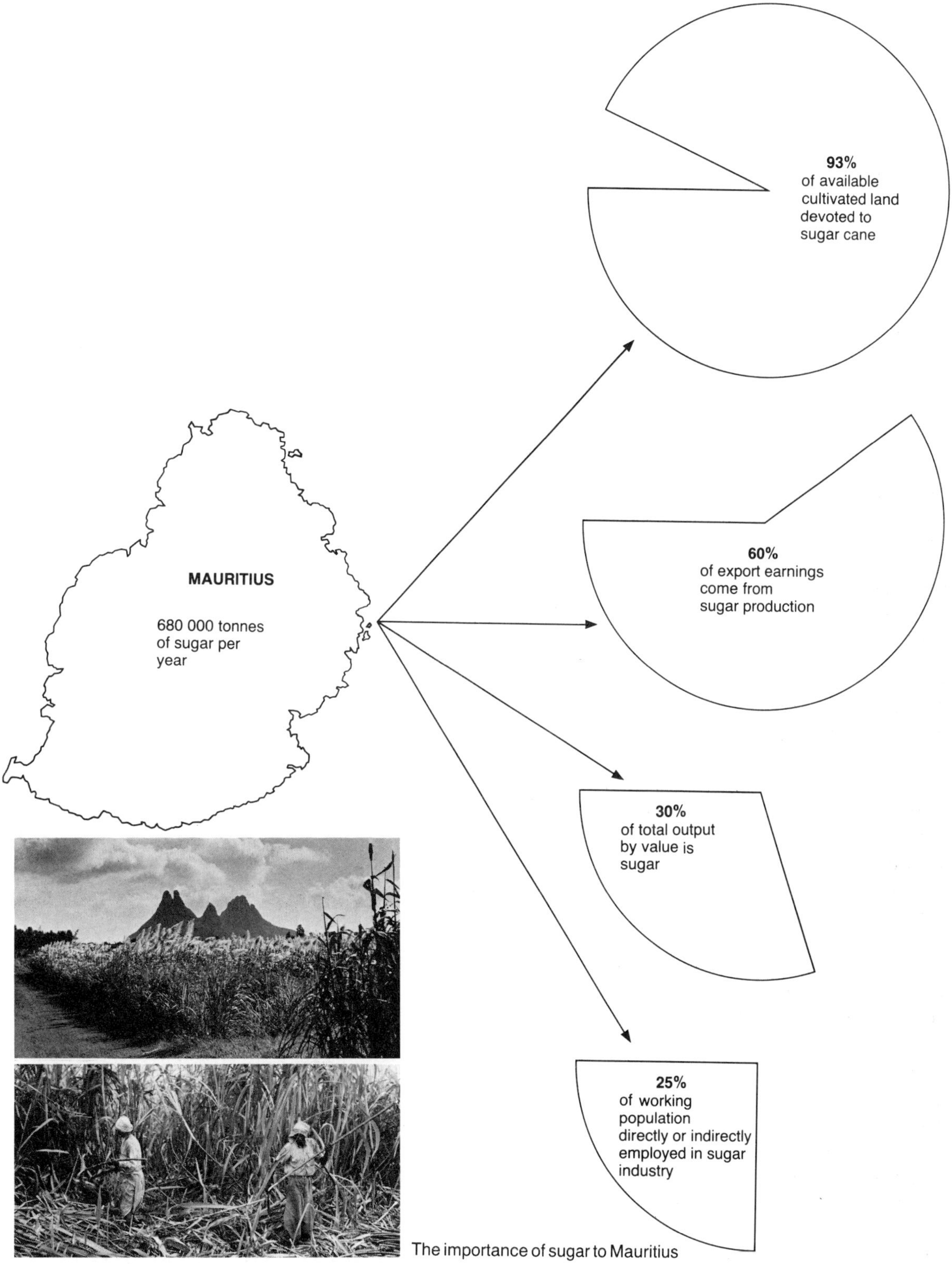

93%
of available
cultivated land
devoted to
sugar cane

MAURITIUS

680 000 tonnes
of sugar per
year

60%
of export earnings
come from
sugar production

30%
of total output
by value is
sugar

25%
of working
population
directly or indirectly
employed in sugar
industry

The importance of sugar to Mauritius

A typical year was 1982. The country bought more from abroad than it was able to sell. This meant they were forced to borrow from the International Monetary Fund (IMF).

The people of Mauritius are only too well aware of the problems and have tried to find a solution to the problem. They have tried to diversify (introduce new and different industries). Some have aimed at reducing imports. Vegetables are planted between the rows of sugar cane and in this way the island can produce 70% of their requirements. Also brewing, plastics, paint and packaging industries have been formed. The residue left after the sugar cane has been milled, (called bagasse), is already used to produce half of the electricity for the island. A further new power station is to be opened in 1984.

Tourism has been encouraged also, with the building of a new airport and the Government has introduced an export processing zone, with tax incentives for new exporting industries such as knitwear, diamond cutting and electronics.

Being dependent upon one crop left Mauritius extremely vulnerable. If this dependence can be reduced changes in the world price of sugar or bad weather will not affect the economy so badly.

Exercise

1 What natural resources first encouraged the British to turn Mauritius into a sugar plantation economy?
2 What agreement about sugar exports has Mauritius with the EEC and what do you think would happen to the Mauritius economy if this agreement was to be discontinued?
3 If the Mauritius people were able to produce more sugar would they necessarily prosper? If not, why?
4 What disadvantages from specialisation in one product does this example illustrate?
5 What disadvantages would you find from living in a country dependent upon one product?

For the reasons shown in the Mauritius example and others, countries do not specialise in the production of just one product but a range of products.

It would be ridiculous for any country to concentrate, say, on the production of housing bricks since however cheaply they could be produced the cost of transporting them to another country would make them far too expensive. For this reason most countries produce bricks.

A country like the UK can produce a limited quantity of agricultural products very efficiently. The UK could not specialise in these products because it does not have the land available to do so. It might be unwise also for a country to become too dependent upon supplies of vital goods from a foreign country in case of war or political disagreement. (South Africa for example distils oil for petrol from coal in a very expensive process because other countries will not sell her crude oil.)

We have learnt why countries trade with each other and also why they try not to overspecialise and the consequences of this, but some countries try to deliberately reduce or even stop some trade by creating barriers.

The barriers to trade

There are several ways in which a country can reduce or even prevent trade with other countries:

Tariffs One way of reducing imports is to impose a tax or tariff on imported goods as they enter the country. The importer has to pay the tax before he can sell the goods and therefore is likely to charge more for the goods in order to reclaim the tax. The imported goods therefore are offered to the public at a higher price and this hopefully deters them from buying them. As a member of the EEC the UK has no tariffs between itself and all of the other members but it has a small tariff, as do the other member countries, which applies to all other non-EEC countries. This **common external tariff** as it is called at present stands at 8.2%.

Subsidies The opposite way of reducing imports to tariffs would be to try and make home produced goods cheaper. To do this a country can give a grant to a home industry so that the goods produced by that industry cost less which encourages people to buy them in preference to dearer imports. This grant is called **a subsidy**. Many would argue that help given to British Leyland and the British ship building industry in recent years would fall into this category.

Quota agreements By this method the price of imports is not altered but the quantity of imports is limited to a certain number per year or month.

Other methods Some goods are considered to be dangerous like drugs and these are strictly controlled and in some circumstances trade with another country is made illegal. This is called an **embargo** and is used as a political weapon.

CASE STUDY

Japanese Video Tape Recorders (VTRs)

In February 1983 Japan agreed to restrict the number of VTRs exported to the EEC. At that time Japanese VTRs were being produced and sold at lower prices than European VTRs. For this reason European manufacturers were operating at below their full capacity. (1.2 million units per annum instead of 1.4 million.) The Japanese agreed to limit video exports to the EEC to 4.55 million units in 1983 and to charge higher European prices on those sets. The reason behind this agreement was to allow the 3 European manufacturers of VTRs, Grundig, Philips and Thopson-Brandt, an opportunity to increase production so that they could obtain the economies of scale enjoyed by their Japanese competitors, and as a result reduce their prices to compete on an equal footing with the larger Japanese companies. This seemed unlikely however, since the total estimated market for VTRs in 1983 was thought to be well below 5 million. Also several Japanese companies had assembly plants in Europe which received VTRs in kits from Japan and then assembled them in Europe allowing them to stamp 'made in EEC' on them. Since these plants put another 600 000 sets a year on the market there seems little room for a European manufacturer anyway. The same agreement also limited the number of large colour television tubes Japan would export to the EEC in 1983 to 900 000. This again might at first have looked like a good thing for EEC industries but within 3 months it had caused problems. Many firms, including British firms such as Thorn–EMI rely upon Japanese large tubes as their only source of supply. Faced with this restriction they announced the scrapping of expansion plans!

Exercise

1 What type of trade restriction does this case study illustrate?
2 What argument was used to justify it?
3 Why was it unlikely to help EEC industry?
4 How would it have been possible to make sure it helped EEC industry?
5 Why did the restriction of colour tubes stop planned expansion in the UK?

WHY COUNTRIES TRY TO RESTRICT TRADE

Many reasons are given for the reduction of trade by the imposition of barriers. Here are a few:

1 **To protect a young, growing industry** As seen in the case study a small firm that has just started production cannot enjoy the same economies of scale as an older, larger, well established firm in another country. For this reason the young firm will need to charge higher prices.

If there is a cheaper foreign alternative people will choose it and the firm will never survive. If the cheaper foreign alternatives are kept artificially high while the smaller firm grows then it will be able to compete fairly.

2   To allow an old, declining industry to do so slowly   A country may well be flooded by cheap foreign goods which will lead to the collapse of a traditional industry. This will cause unemployment. To allow time for workers to find new jobs the flood of cheap foreign goods could be slowed by some form of restriction.

3   To prevent dumping   *Dumping* is a term used to describe foreign goods sold in a country at below the cost of production. Here a home industry could be ruined by ridiculously cheap imports and they can be prevented by some form of restriction.

4   To help with a temporary balance of payments problem   Sometimes a country will import too much, more than they can really afford (as we saw with Mauritius). Restrictions on imports can help to reduce these imports so long as other countries do not retaliate and restrict their imports!

International Trade and the United Kingdom

THE COMPOSITION OF THE UNITED KINGDOM'S IMPORTS AND EXPORTS

As we have discussed, a country will specialise in producing those goods in which it has an advantage and will import those things it lacks or cannot produce commercially. In most cases it should be possible to predict the composition of the imports and exports of any country.

Exercise

Copy out the following table and complete for the United Kingdom.

	Those resources we have in abundance	*Those resources we lack*
Natural	coal	copper
Human	large skilled	large cheap unskilled
Man-made	factories	computer controlled machines

From the above exercise you ought to reach some conclusions about imports and exports to and from the UK.

The composition of UK trade is shown opposite.

EXPORTS

As I am sure you predicted the UK exports manufactured goods, chemicals, machinery and vehicles (being most important). Looking at the figures for just one year, however, does not let us see the whole picture. Certainly, since the industrial revolution the UK has imported raw materials and turned them into manufactured goods which have been exported but the type of manufactured good has changed considerably. Just before World War II, for example, textiles represented nearly 25% of all UK exports; today as you can see it is less than 3%. Iron and steel is another product which has fallen as a percentage of our exports. These have been replaced by machinery and the other high technology products mentioned above. A further change can be seen in the non-manufactures. Fuels have increased to 13.6% of exports because of the growing importance of North Sea oil. The UK still imports crude oil but today in value terms is a net exporter of oil. In the past the UK exported coal.

IMPORTS

This is a little more difficult to predict. Looking at what this country has and has not got one would expect imports in the main to be raw materials and foodstuffs. This is true up to a point. Over one third of UK imports are in this category but surprisingly the rest are manufactured goods, products which could be manufactured here. Since the war, as the country has grown in prosperity people have not wanted more and more food, but better manufactured goods with more choice and greater variety. This has meant that much of the growth in world trade has been in manufactured goods.

Just as there are plenty of British motorists who believe that you cannot buy a better car than a Renault—there are just as many French motorists who love to drive a BL Metro. The UK still imports a lot of foodstuffs (although British farms have become more efficient) but the growth of imports of manufactures has been very dramatic and leaves food as a smaller percentage of the total than before the war.

INVISIBLE TRADE

The trade considered latterly is known as **visible trade**—that is trade which can actually be seen (goods being loaded onto and off ships and planes etc). The UK earns much foreign currency by selling services to other countries. We call this **invisible trade**. Gross earnings from invisible exports are usually equal to about half the earnings from visible exports but, unlike visible trade, the UK always earns a surplus on invisible trade.

Figure 27 divides invisible trade into 3 groups. **Services; interest, profits and dividends** and **transfers**.

Britain's Invisible Transactions 1981

£ million

	Credits	Debits	Balance
Services:	16 754	12 779	+ 3 975
Private sector and public corporations of which,	16 290	11 540	+ 4 750
Sea transport	3 772	3 870	− 98
Civil aviation	2 359	1 922	+ 437
Travel	2 999	3 285	− 286
Financial services	1 954	—	+ 1,954
Other	5 206	2 463	+ 2 743
General government	464	1 239	− 775
Interest, profits and dividends:	10 082	9 078	+ 1 004
Private sector and public corporations	9 142	7 458	+ 1 684
General government	940	1 620	− 680
Transfers:	2 502	4 458	− 1 956
Private	844	1 119	− 275
General government	1 658	3 339	− 1 681
Total invisible transactions	29 338	26 315	+ 3 023

Fig 27 Source: United Kingdom Balance of Payments 1982 edition, HMSO

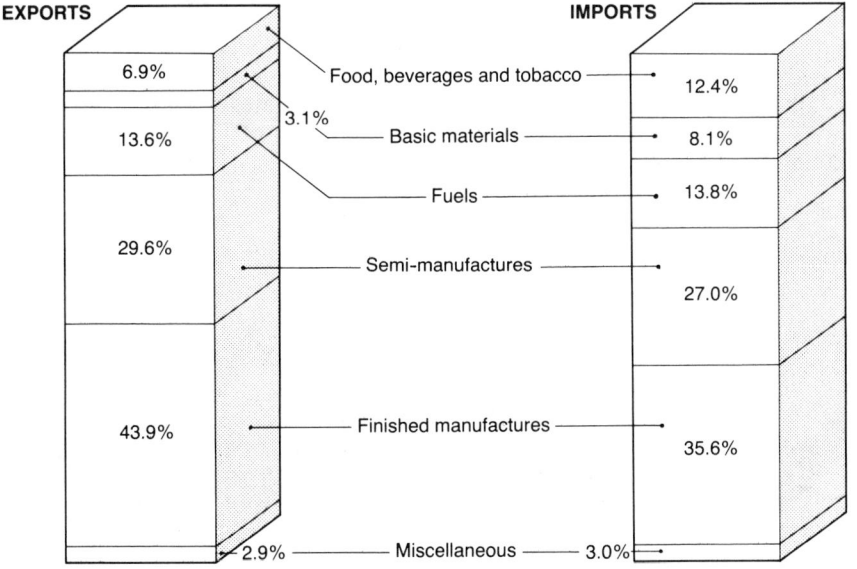

EXPORTS / IMPORTS

EXPORTS		IMPORTS
6.9%	Food, beverages and tobacco	12.4%
3.1%	Basic materials	8.1%
13.6%	Fuels	13.8%
29.6%	Semi-manufactures	27.0%
43.9%	Finished manufactures	35.6%
2.9%	Miscellaneous	3.0%

The **services** are a large positive item and are just what they sound like. For example, if a German flies to America on a British Airways Concorde it appears as a positive earning under civil aviation. If, on the other hand, a British firm imports some grain on a Greek ship the freight charge would appear as a negative payment under sea transport. The largest earning is that of financial and other services carried out by our banks and insurance companies in the City of London. General government refers to the costs of keeping embassy staff abroad. Transfers refer to direct transfers of money abroad. For individuals such transfers might arise due to emigration but for the Government they include membership fees paid to such organisations as the EEC and aid given to under-developed countries. **Interest, profits and dividends** refers to the earnings from money lent to foreign firms or reward for owning foreign shares. In 1981 it was a large positive item.

THE DIRECTION OF UK TRADE

It is not surprising that the chief market for UK exports and source of imports are her trading partners in the EEC. Over half of UK exports and well over half of her imports are with European countries. This has not always been the case. Just before World War II European countries only accounted for about 25% of UK trade. Nearly half was with Commonwealth countries, that is countries which in the past had formed the British Empire but now, although retaining links with the UK have their independence, countries such as Australia, New Zealand as well as India and many developing countries. The reasons for this change in the direction of UK trade and the relative importance of these different trading partners has already been seen. It is because of the growth in the post-war period of trade in manufactured goods. Since the war the developed countries have traded in finished manufactured goods and semi-manufactures and although the UK still purchases raw materials from developing countries and of course manufactured goods from countries like Hong Kong and Singapore, the main growth in trade has been with European countries like Germany, which is now the most important exporter to this country with over a 10% share. North America (which includes Canada) is still an important market for the UK and supplies important imports such as cereals, tobacco and metal ore as well as modern machinery like computer technology.

The pie chart singles out the oil exporting

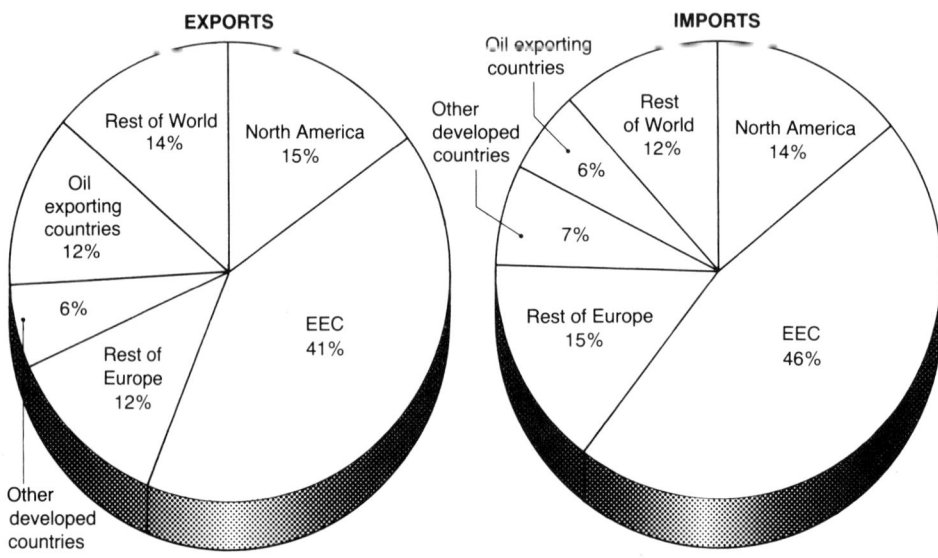

Source: Monthly Review of External Trade Statistics, Issue No 88, HMSO

countries. These developing countries, like Kuwait, Saudi Arabia, Nigeria and Libya, became important during the early 1970s when they increased the price of oil rapidly. For several years this meant that since the UK had no oil at that time, she had to purchase the same quantity of oil at these higher prices. This meant the UK imported far more (from these countries) than she exported to them and now with North Sea oil and export drives to these countries the chart shows that the UK exports more to these countries than she imports in oil from them.

THE MEASUREMENT OF TRADE: THE BALANCE OF PAYMENTS

The **balance of payments** statistics are a record, kept by the Government, of all movements of money into and out of this country. It is split into 2 main sections: current account; investment and capital transfer and official financing.

The **current account** (opposite) shows all monetary payments arising out of trade usually split into visible trade and invisible trade. If the UK exports goods and services then money to pay for them comes into the country and is shown as a positive figure, but if she imports goods and services and money is paid out for them, these are shown as negative figures.

Balance of Payments Current Account of the UK 1979/81 (£s million)

	1979	1980	1981
Visible exports	+40 678	+47 389	+51 100
Visible imports	−44 136	−46 211	−48 087
Visible trade balance (balance of trade)	−3 548	+1 178	+3 013
Invisible exports	+23 694	+25 764	+29 338
Invisible imports	−21 099	−23 736	−26 315
Invisible trade balance	+2 595	+2 028	+3 023
Current balance	−863	+3 206	+6 036

The invisible balance is usually positive but the visible trade balance is sometimes negative, as in 1979, or positive as in 1981. What these figures actually tell us is that in 1981 the UK exported goods and services to the value of £6 036m more than it imported. This is not the only reason for money moving into or out of a country.

To this we must add **investment and other capital transactions**. If a UK resident or company invests in a foreign company by, for example, buying shares, then money will leave this country and it will be shown in the balance of payments figures as negative. If a foreign person or company invests in this country—a Japanese car firm opens a plant here for example—then it is shown as positive.

Selected Investment and other Capital Transactions from UK Balance of Payments 1979/81 (£s million)

	1979	1980	1981
Overseas investment in UK:			
Public sector	+902	+589	+188
Private sector	+3 405	+4 676	+2 743
UK investment overseas			
Private	−6 555	−8 039	−11 171
Long-term government	−401	−91	−335
Other capital transactions	+4 774	+971	+466
Total investment and capital transactions	+2 125	−1 894	−8 109

Source: Annual abstract of statistics, HMSO

For the 3 years shown here private investment abroad was much greater than private investment in the UK by foreign private investors. In 1981, for example, UK residents and companies invested £11 billion abroad whereas only £2.7 billion was invested here. This is because in 1979 the Government removed all restrictions on capital movements abroad. It must be remembered that these net outflows of capital will result in large invisible earnings into the UK in the future (which will show as a gain under interest, profits and dividends).

The last section of the balance of payments is that which shows movements of money undertaken by the Government and this section is called **official financing**. The Government can add to or draw on its reserves (or savings). It can borrow or pay back loans to the International Monetary Fund (an international bank to which most western nations belong and can borrow from when in difficulties). The Government can also borrow or pay back loans to other countries.

UK Official Financing (£s millions)

	1979	1980	1981
Net transactions with overseas monetary authorities	−596	−140	−145
Foreign currency borrowing (net)	−250	−941	−1587
Official reserves (+ drawings on, − additions to)	−1059	−291	+2419
Total official financing	−1905	−1372	+687

Thus in 1981 the UK monetary authorities were paying back loans to both the IMF and other countries *and* drawing upon their reserves, whereas in the previous 2 years not only were loans paid back but reserves were increased.

Exercise

For each of the following state where on the UK balance of payments statistics they would occur and whether they are visible or invisible, export or import, current account or capital transfer etc.

For example, if a German flies to America on British Airways Concorde this would be:

Invisible Export—on the current account

Try to categorise the following:

a A French farmer buys a Ford tractor manufactured at the British Basildon plant.
b The UK Government repays a loan to the IMF.
c The British Post Office pension fund managers buy shares in an American computer manufacturing firm.
d British troops, stationed in Germany, take their wives out for a meal in a German restaurant.
e A friend's father purchases a brand new Japanese motor car.
f An Arab businessman buys all of the shares in an ailing British company.
g An American airline company insures a new Boeing 747 with British insurance underwriters based at Lloyds in London.
h The UK Government makes its contribution to the EEC funds for the year.
i British Leyland purchase German computer controlled 'robot' welding machinery.
j British Leyland send a number of technicians to Germany to learn how to service the robots they have just bought.

As we can see it would be very surprising for the value of a country's imports to be exactly the same as exports, that is for the current account balance to be zero. After all, decisions to import are made by a different set of people than decisions to export. A country cannot keep on importing more than it is able to export. To do so would require heavy borrowing from organisations like the IMF. We saw in our case study that Mauritius was in this position. When a country has a series of current account deficits it is often referred to as a **balance of payments deficit** or **balance of payments crisis**. To try and cure such problems a Government might undertake a number of measures:

Deflation If the Government increases taxes and makes it difficult for people to borrow they will be forced to reduce their spending. This will mean less imports and more goods produced at home available for export. The problem with such measures is that if they last for any length of time they tend to increase unemployment.

Trade barriers A Government could increase tariffs to reduce imports and as we have already seen encourage exports by the use of subsidies. As the UK is a signatory to the *General Agreement on Tariffs and Trade* which aims to reduce trade barriers, we could not use such policies for long, although in the short run other members of GATT might be sympathetic.

Currency deflation The example below shows that the price of imports and exports depends upon the value of a nation's currency. When you go abroad you have to buy foreign currency to spend in the shops. If a UK importer wishes to buy Japanese cars he must pay for them in yen which have to be bought. If the value of a country's currency falls, foreign currency will cost more and the price of imports rise. Since a foreigner can now purchase more of that

country's currency for the same amount our exports appear to cost less.

In this simplified example the prices in the USA and UK of a product produced in the UK—whisky—and a product produced in the USA—wheat are analysed. It is assumed that a case of whisky costs £48 in the UK where it is manufactured and a tonne of wheat costs $100 in the USA where it is grown. Ignoring *all* taxes, import duties and transport costs the effects of changes in the exchange rate on prices of these 2 goods can be shown.

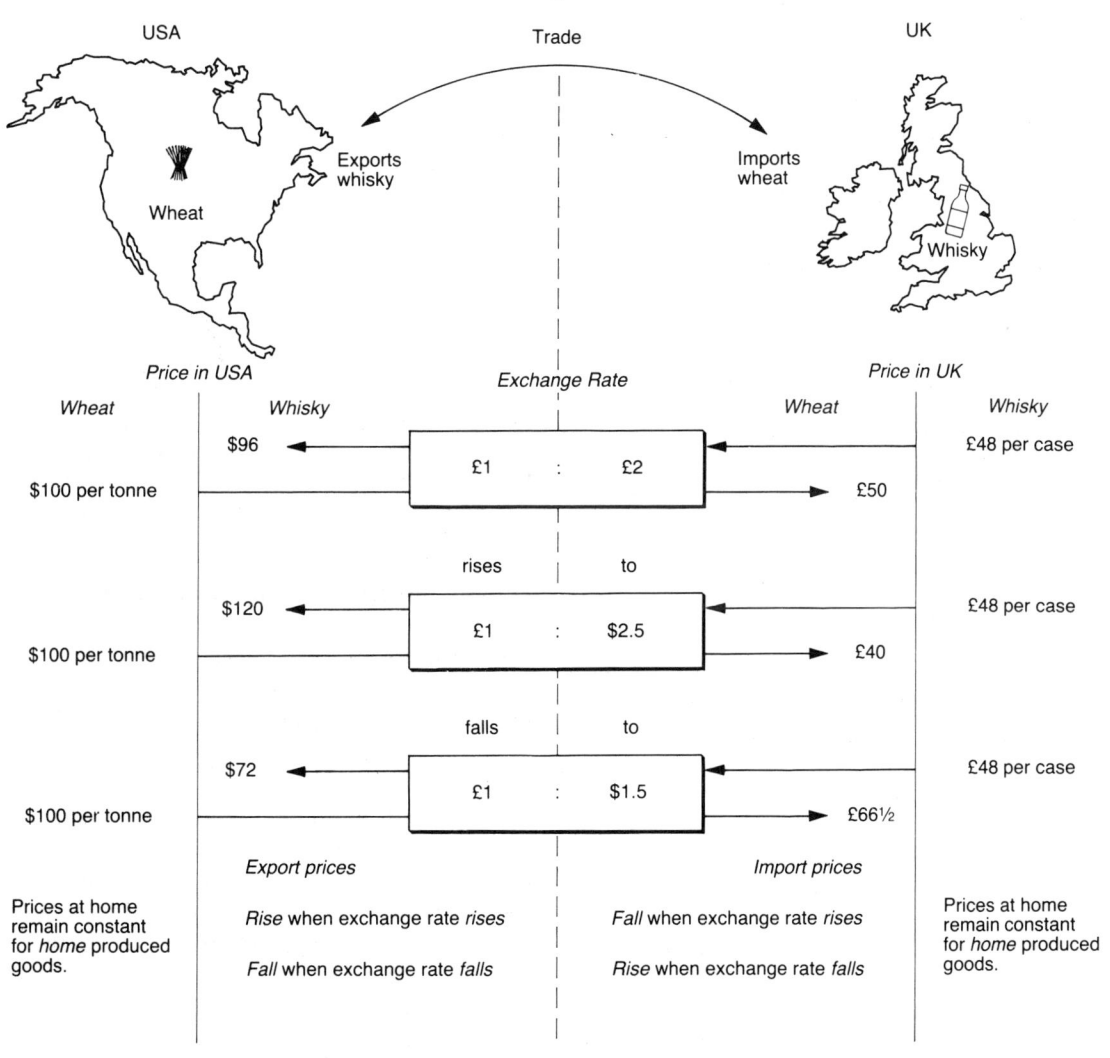

If the exchange rate were £1 to $2, then to buy a case of whisky an American would need to convert dollars into pounds. Since it costs $2 for every £1 it will cost $96 to buy £48. On the other hand for the British importer of wheat he will need $100 which will cost £50.

If the exchange rate were to rise to £1 to $2.50, the American has to pay $2.50 for every £1. So to buy £48 would now cost $120. However, the British importer of wheat receives $2.50 for every £1 so now it only takes £40 to buy $100. A rise in the exchange rate therefore causes the price of the UK import of wheat to fall but the price of the UK export to rise.

If the exchange rate were to fall to £1 to $1.50, then the American only has to pay $1.50 for every £1. So to buy £48 would now cost $72. The British importer of wheat however, receives only $1.50 for every £1 so now it takes £66.50 to buy $100. A fall in the exchange rate causes the price of the UK import of wheat to rise but the price of the UK export—whisky—to fall.

Whether or not a fall in the value of a currency will reduce a deficit on the current account of the balance of payments will depend very much upon how sensitive consumers are to changes in the price of that country's imports and exports.

In the past exchange rates have been fixed but now they are allowed to fluctuate on the exchange markets. If people want to hold a currency its price will rise. This solution is to a certain extent automatic since a deficit on the current account of the balance of payments would mean that less people required that currency than wanted to sell it. The price or exchange rate would tend to fall therefore and exports would become cheaper.

Exercise

1   Three British tourists travel abroad for their holidays. One goes to France, a second to Holland and a third to Norway.

A three course meal costs the following in each country:

45 Guilders (in Holland)
96 Francs (in France)
110 Kroner (in Norway)

Who is buying the cheapest meal if the exchange rates are as follows?

£1 to 4.5 Guilder
£1 to 12 Franc
£1 to 11 Kroner

2   If the exchange rate for the French Franc were to fall to £1 to 10 Francs would your answer be the same?
3   Under which heading on the UK balance of payments would meals bought abroad by tourists from this country appear?

The European Economic Community (EEC)

The European Economic Community (or Common Market) is an organisation to which many European countries, including the UK belong. Originally it was a group of 6 countries: France, West Germany, Italy, Belgium, Holland and Luxemburg. Following the success of an earlier agreement between these countries on the price and output of coal and steel they negotiated the terms of a far more comprehensive agreement called the **Treaty of Rome** which they all signed in March 1957. This established the EEC which started to operate from 1 January 1958. It is an organisation of cooperation with regard to

Currency deflation and a current account deficit

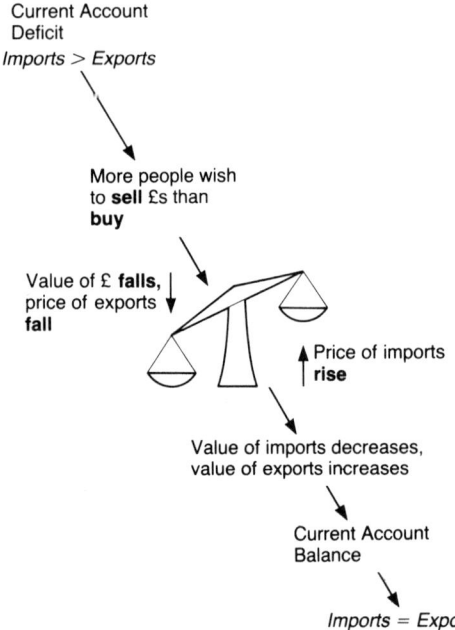

Current Account Deficit
Imports > Exports

More people wish to **sell** £s than **buy**

Value of £ **falls**, price of exports **fall**

Price of imports **rise**

Value of imports decreases, value of exports increases

Current Account Balance

Imports = Exports

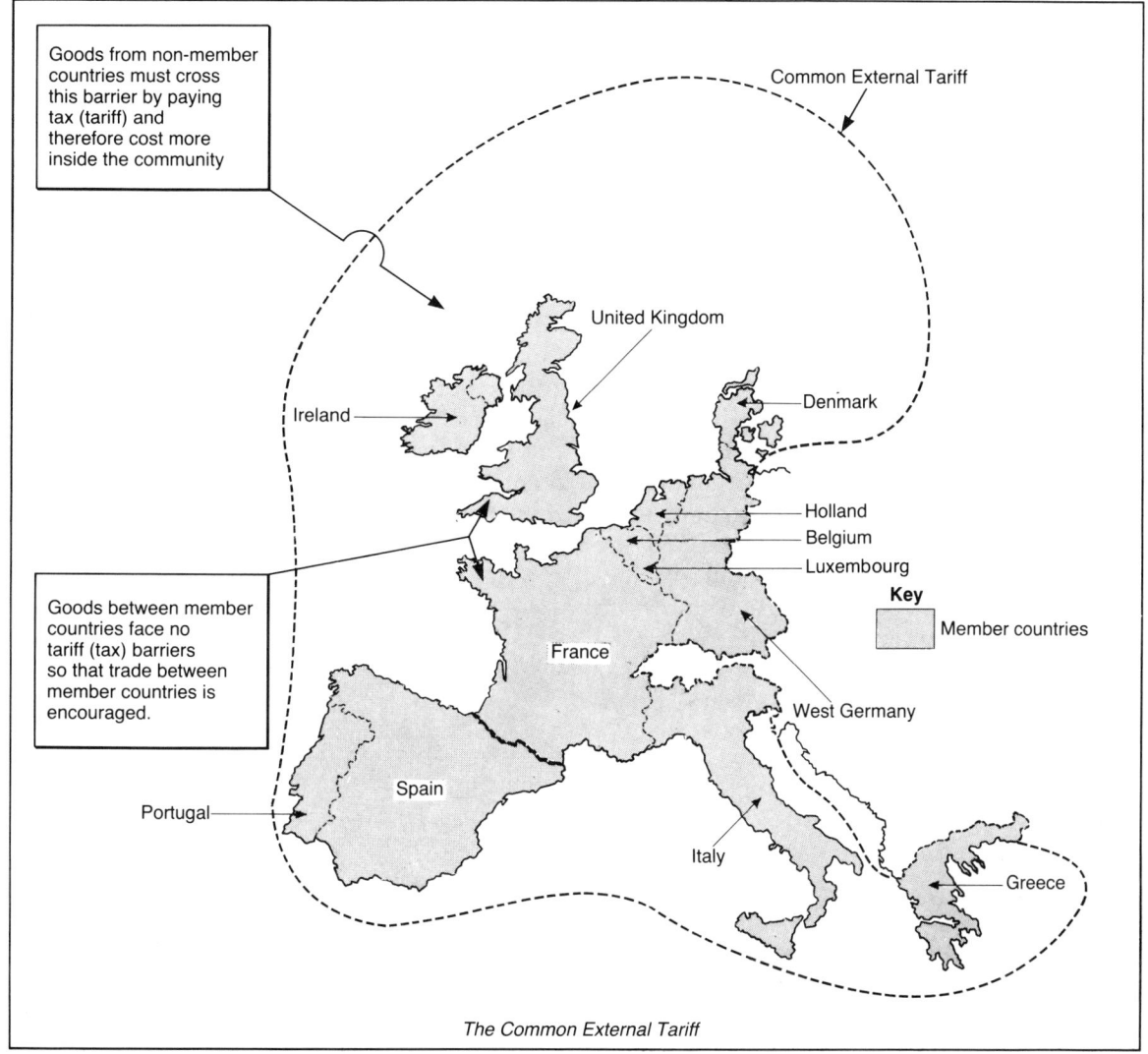

Goods from non-member countries must cross this barrier by paying tax (tariff) and therefore cost more inside the community

Common External Tariff

United Kingdom

Ireland

Denmark

Holland
Belgium
Luxembourg

Key

Member countries

France

West Germany

Goods between member countries face no tariff (tax) barriers so that trade between member countries is encouraged.

Spain

Portugal

Italy

Greece

The Common External Tariff

The common external tariff

trade between the member nations. Within 10 years of establishment all tariffs and other barriers to trade between member countries had been removed and a common external tariff of 9.3% (later reduced to 8.2%) had been established around them all. Any good arriving from a non-member country faces this common external tariff but any goods bought and sold between member countries do not. This should encourage trade and growth between member countries.

From the very beginning the EEC was far more than the customs union just described. The 6 countries meet regularly to discuss economic and social problems they share and to come to agreement upon how to jointly solve them. They have, therefore, common policies on agriculture, transport, regional development, energy and foreign trade.

The organisation has its own administrative centre called the European Commission which employs over 10 000 civil servants to help put these common policies into practice. Each member country contributes money to a common fund which the Commission spends on these common policies. The members aim to allow a free movement not only of goods and services between themselves but also the free movement of people who wish to work in other member countries and entrepreneurs who wish to establish businesses in other member countries.

At first the UK did not wish to belong to the EEC since much of her trade was with the Commonwealth—countries like Australia from whom we bought butter and New Zealand from whom we bought lamb. We had special agreements with these countries dating back to the 1930s called the **Commonwealth Preferential Trading Agreements** where the UK guaranteed not to prevent imports from the Commonwealth by use of barriers like tariffs. During the 1960s the UK made a similar agreement, to reduce certain tariffs, with a further 8 European countries to create the **European Free Trade Area**. This was purely a trading arrangement which left member countries free to retain their own existing additional agreements with non-member countries.

During this period UK trade developed far more with European countries many of whom were members of the EEC. Also the original 6 members of the EEC were growing faster than the UK and had less inflation and unemployment so that many people in the UK felt that we had made a mistake in not joining. So, after one unsuccessful attempt in 1962 the UK became a full member of the EEC on 1 January 1973 together with Ireland and Denmark.

Our membership of the EEC meant many changes. To be a member we agreed to accept all of the common policies and put them into practice. The major one was the **Common Agricultural Policy (CAP)** which was a very different system to ours. Until we joined the prices of agricultural produce were kept low since we imported so much from the Commonwealth. To help UK farmers the Government gave them a grant to bring the price they received up to a price it was agreed they needed to stay in business. Under CAP, higher prices are maintained for the European farmer by placing tariffs on

cheaper imported foodstuffs and buying excess production from the Community funds. You may have heard of the 'butter mountain' which refers to butter bought by the Community in order to keep prices high. (Some has been sold cheaply to Eastern European countries.) The EEC has continued to grow; in 1981 Greece joined and talks are currently being conducted with both Spain and Portugal.

Higher food prices, little sign of the expected growth, and high net contributions to the Community budget (see Fig 28) has led to some criticism of our membership. It must be remembered, however, that Germany and France, 2 of the most important markets for UK exports are members. If the UK were to leave the market then these goods would face the Common External Tariff.

Net Contributions To (−) and Receipts from (+) the Allocated Community Budget

	Millions ecus*		
	1979	1980	1981
Denmark	380	327	285
Germany	−1430	−1526	−1750
France	−78	431	597
Netherlands	288	454	191
Belgium/Luxemburg	610	439	568
UK	−849	−1512	−1422
Italy	534	737	778
Ireland	545	650	586
Greece	—	—	167

* ecu = European currency unit
   value: 1979 ecu = £0.646
              1980 ecu = £0.598
              1981 ecu = £0.553

Fig 28

The UK is a significant net contributor to the community budget together with Germany. (These figures do not include the budget refunds negotiated by the Government.)

In 1979 the **European Parliament** became the first internationally elected body. It sounds very grand but has limited powers.

The European Parliament can dismiss the Commission with a two thirds majority. It can

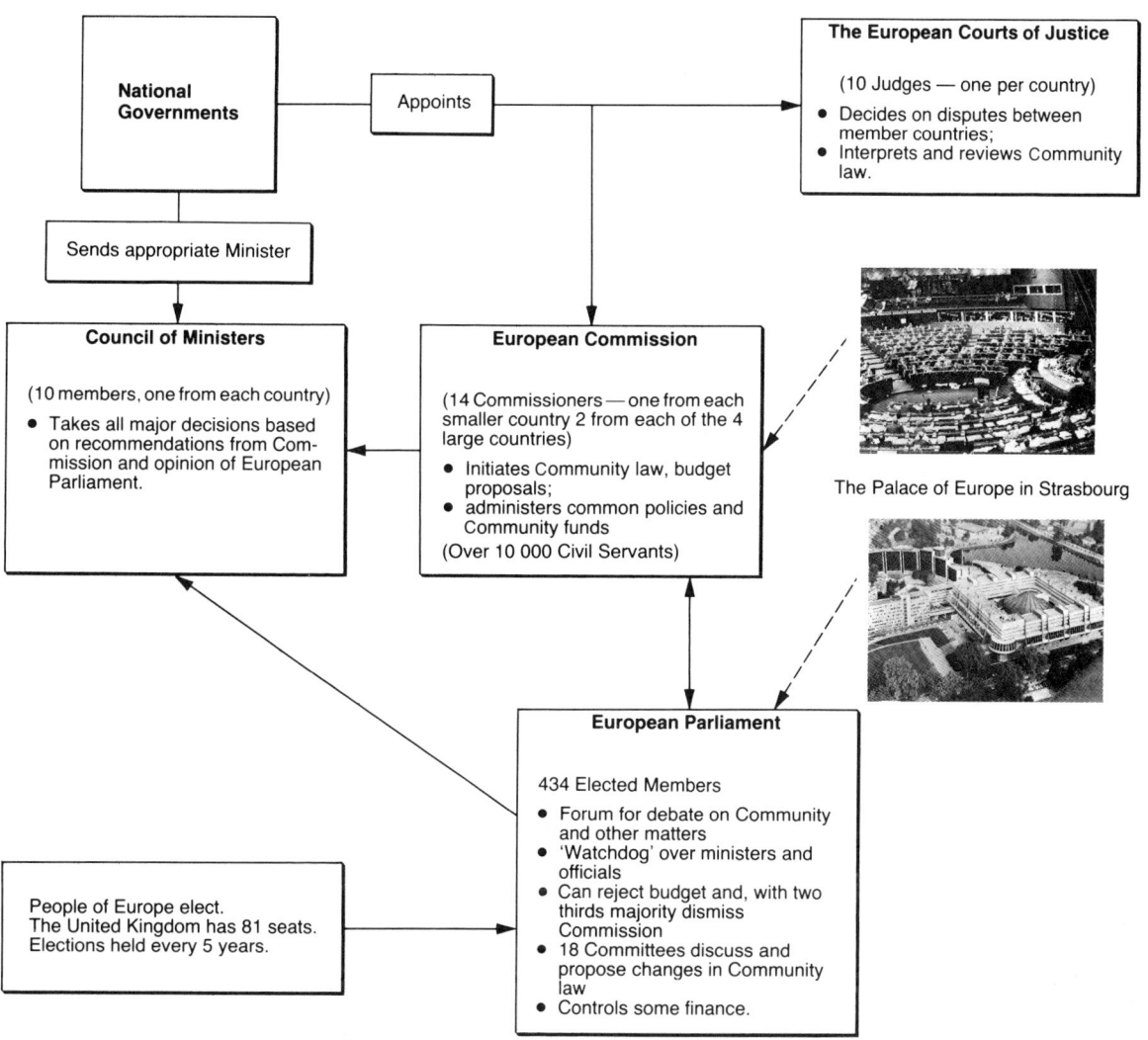

The Palace of Europe in Strasbourg

also reject the Community Budget (its spending plans for the coming year) as well as being consulted in the process of Community law-making. As you can see above, however, the most impor-tant decision-making body is the **Council of Ministers**. This is where the appropriate Minister from each member country's Government meets to agree policy put forward by the

Commission. The **Commission** is run by 14 Commissioners, one from each of the smaller countries and 2 from the 4 larger countries (including the UK).

This is the main administrative body for the EEC. The 10 000 civil servants who work for the Commission not only have the task of putting into practice all of the agreed Community policies but are also responsible for suggesting new laws and budget proposals each year. The Commission consults with the European Parliamentry Committees who scrutinise proposed Community law and suggest alterations and improvements.

Each member country appoints a Judge to sit on the **European Court of Justice** to interpret Community law and settle disputes between member countries.

SUMMARY EXERCISE

1 The UK depends upon international trade. Can you list 4 benefits we gain as a country by such trade?

2 Give 3 reasons why countries do not specialise totally in the production of just one product.

3 Name 3 types of **barriers to trade** currently used by the UK.

4 Give one reason given by countries to justify the use of **trade barriers**.

5 What is the difference between **visible** and **invisible** trade?

6 Give an example of an **invisible import** that you or your family might undertake.

7 Which 2 countries joined the EEC with the UK in 1973?

8 The UK often has a **balance of trade deficit**. What is meant by this statement?

9 Which body takes the major decisions in the EEC?

10 Give one power that the European Parliament has.

ASSIGNMENT

1 'It is important for Britain to trade with other countries.'

a By mentioning at least 2 of the advantages of international trade show why the statement is true.

'In spite of these advantages Governments still set up barriers which reduce or even prevent trade.'

b Take 3 of these barriers and say what each one is called and state why and how they reduce or prevent international trade in each case.

2 Many people own a foreign car; perhaps you own or will soon own a foreign motor bike. Both are examples of visible imports into this country.

a Explain the difference between **invisible** and **visible imports** using your own examples.

b Give 4 types of invisible exports from this country, with examples of each.

c In what ways might a country try to prevent foreign imports from entering the country?

10 The Means of Exchange

If you were to empty all your pockets you would probably find some cash; coins and banknotes which we all know as **money**. In this chapter this strange idea of money will be considered.

This chapter is entitled 'the means of exchange' as this is one of the most important functions of money. It provides a mechanism for changing what people have into what they want. Your teacher sells his talents to the local education department in order to buy those goods and services he desires. Although, if asked, we would all probably admit to wanting more money it would not be the actual notes and coins we desired but those extra goods and services for which this money could be exchanged. Imagine a bank robber who obtains £1 million from his crime and flies away in a light aeroplane to avoid capture. If the plane were to crash land on a desert island although he may be very rich in terms of cash he would probably starve since you cannot eat banknotes and coins.

Legal Tender

Exercise

Here are pictures of 2 coins worth one pound. One is an ordinary one pound coin, the other fits a car wash machine at a garage and we shall assume costs one pound.

Copy this table into your book filling in the gaps. For some of the answers you will have to make an intelligent guess.

		£1 coin	Car wash token
1	Manufactured by?	The Royal Mint	
2	Manufactured from?	Cupro nickel (cheap hard wearing metal alloy)	
3	Cost of manufacture?		A few pence
4	Distinguishing features?		Groove which fits machine and prevents copies
5	Available where?	From Bank of England through banks	
6	Exchangeable for?		One car wash

Now answer these 2 questions:

1 Which of these 2 coins would you prefer to be given and why?
2 If the price of a car wash were to increase to £2 which of these 2 coins would you prefer to be given and why?

From the above exercise we can see that these two coins are not that different. They both are made cheaply from a hard-wearing metal alloy. They are about the same size and have special markings to prevent forgery and are a standard weight to operate machines. Most people would probably prefer to be given a £1 coin, however, because this coin is 'money' and can be exchanged for anything priced at £1. The car wash token can only be exchanged for one car wash and is *not*, therefore, money.

Many different commodities over the years and in different societies, have been recognised as money. Such objects as shells, sharks teeth, cattle, salt and of course gold and silver. They all have at least one thing in common. When they were used as money they were generally accepted, that is most people in that society would accept them in payment for goods and services.

Today our cash, the notes and coins, have no value in themselves. They are almost worthless but by law people must accept them in payment for goods and services because they are **legal tender**. Legal tender is any means of payment which must be accepted by law in settlement of a debt. In this country Bank of England notes and Royal Mint coins are legal tender. Although anyone selling goods and services must accept these notes and coins in payment they can insist on the exact money and they are protected from being given large quantities of small change since coins are only legal tender up to these amounts:

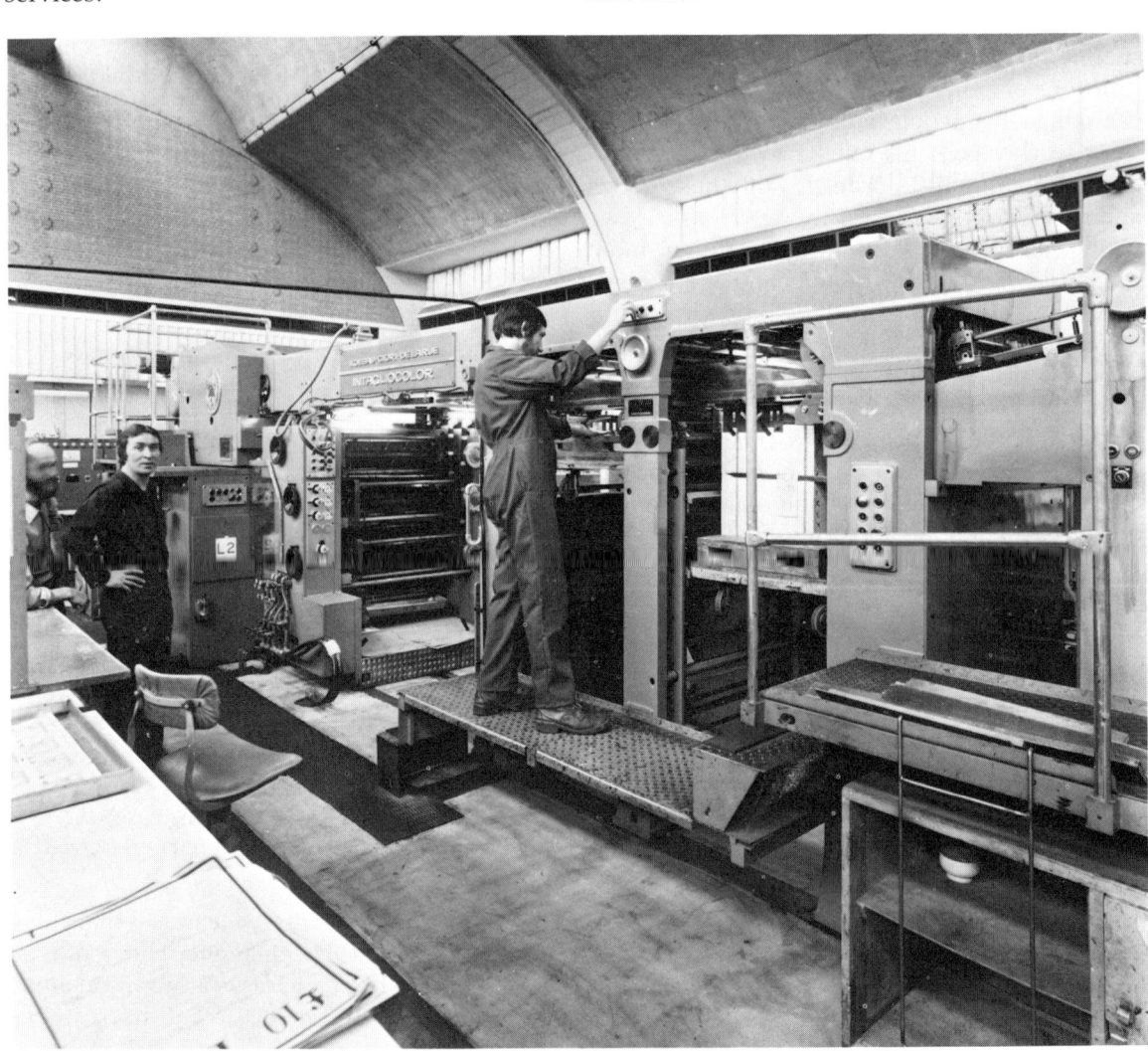

A printing press used to print £10, £20 and £50 notes

Bronze coins (1p and 2p) up to 20p
Cupro nickel coins (5p and 10p) up to £5
50p coins and 20p coins up to £10
£1 coins up to any amount
Banknotes (£1, £5, £10, £20, £50) up to any amount

Exercise

All of the following can be used to buy certain goods and services but only 3 are legal tender. Can you pick out which?

a A book token
b A postal order
c A cheque
d A money-off voucher from a newspaper.
e A commemorative Crown
f A 16½p stamp
g Trading stamps
h A 10 pound note
i A one pound coin
j An old silver sixpence

Which of the 3 you picked are you unlikely to spend and why?

Bank Deposits

Most of the money we use in a modern society is not in the form of notes and coins. Many people have **bank accounts**. Often wages are paid straight into a bank account. Rather than going to the bank every time you wish to buy something and drawing out your money you can use this money to buy goods and services without drawing it out, in fact you can do so hundreds of miles from the bank. As we shall see in the next case study it is becoming easier to use these deposits as if they were cash.

In December 1983 the Bank of England published these figures:

	£bn
Notes and coins in circulation	12.1 (28%)
Private sector bank deposits	31.5 (72%)
Total money supply	43.6

We consider bank deposits as money since they are generally accepted in payment for goods and services. As you can see they represent nearly three quarters of the money held by private individuals.

CASE STUDY

A Cashless Society?

It was reported in *The Times* on 28 February 1984 that British Telecom and IBM were joining together to design an electronic money transfer system to be used by retailers all over the country. The major high street banks set up a study group 7 years ago to look at such schemes.

The idea is that the cash register at the checkout of large shops would be replaced by a specially designed computer terminal. This is already being called **an electronic point-of-sale** (EPOS). The customer would give the sales assistant a plastic card, similar to those already in use for cash dispensers (common sights outside banks today). Just as with these cash dispenser cards the customer would type in a code number known only to him or her and within a few seconds an approval message from the card issuer's computer would be received. The sales assistant would type in the price of goods bought, or even simply run the goods over a special laser beam or wand that would read the bar code on the goods. The shop's computer would note the sale and instruct the computer at the customer's bank to deduct the amount of the sale from their account and at the same time instruct the computer at the shop's bank to add the amount of the sale to the shop's account. A record of each transfer from one bank to another could be kept and at the end of each day the net amount owed by one bank to another calculated. Since all banks keep accounts with the Bank of England this net amount could be added to one bank's account and deducted from the others.

Such a system would be simple, efficient, quick and cheap.

Cheques

Today the most common way of using bank deposits as money is the cheque. In 1983 about 2 500 000 000 cheques were written and each cheque costs about 50 pence to process.

A cheque is a written instruction to your bank asking them to transfer money from your account to the account of someone else. It must be remembered that the cheque is not money or legal tender. It is merely a formal letter to a bank asking them to transfer money from one account to another. The *money* is the bank deposit. Figure 29 shows a correctly completed cheque. At the top is the address of the bank and the date. It asks the bank to **pay** the person whose name appears in the space *or* do anything they **order** the bank to do. There is space for the amount to be written in words and figures to avoid confusion and a space to sign. The numbers identify the cheque, the branch and the account and can be read by electronic sorting machines. The 2 vertical parallel lines mean that the cheque is crossed and must therefore be paid into the account of the person named on the cheque. It is possible to have uncrossed or open cheques which can be exchanged for cash at the branch upon which they are drawn. An open cheque is clearly not very safe since it could be lost and cashed by anyone who finds it. A crossed cheque is very safe since it can only be paid into an account.

Most banks give their customers a **cheque card**. This encourages shops to accept cheques written by such people. If someone writing a cheque has a valid cheque card which has the same signature as the cheque and the same bank number as the cheque, then anyone accepting such a cheque can simply write the cheque card number on the back and the bank promises to pay any amount up to £50—even if the customer does not have £50 in their account! A cheque can be written on any scrap of paper. In the past people have written cheques on hens eggs, the side of a cow and even on a shark! Banks have to deal with so many cheques each day, however, it helps them if we all use a standard form, so customers are given a cheque book containing blank cheques whenever they need them.

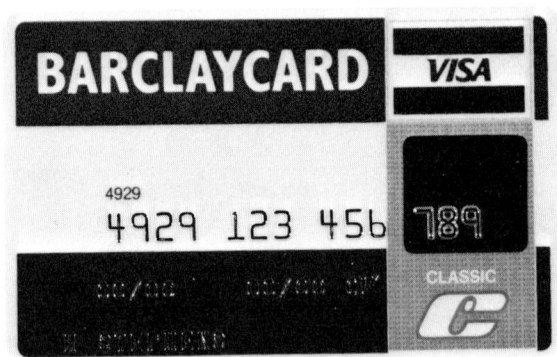

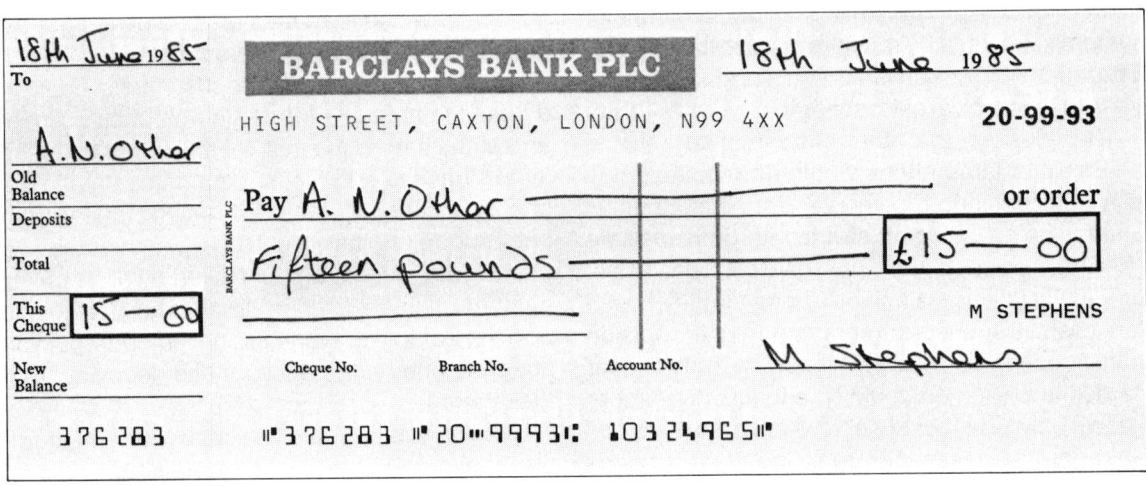

Fig 29 A cheque

CASE STUDY

The amazing 3 day journey of a cheque

Peter Griffiths has a bank account with National Westminster Bank at South Woodford. His wages are paid straight into his account each month and he uses the cash dispensing machine once a week to draw out any cash he needs for buying small things. This week after drawing out his cash he has a balance left in his account of £189.90.

On Saturday he travels to Central London to do some shopping. In a sale he notices a jacket he likes at a price too low to miss—£46.75. He has only a few pounds on him but he does have his cheque book and cheque card. The shop accepts the cheque Peter writes and he leaves for home. The story of his cheque is only just beginning.

The shop has an account with Lloyds Bank. Peter's cheque asks his bank to take £46.75 from his account and give it to Lloyds Bank so that they can add this amount to the shop's account. This is how it happens. It is called the **cheque clearing system**.

Step 1 The shop pays Peter's cheque into their bank—probably on Monday morning.

Step 2 Lloyds Bank instruct their computer, which keeps records of all accounts, to add £46.75 from Peter's account, along with all other cheques paid in by the shop, to the shop's account. This it will do but this money cannot be spent since it has not yet been received. The amount—£46.75—will be printed by a special machine along the bottom edge of the cheque in magnetic ink so it can be automatically read.

Step 3 At the end of that day all the cheques paid into that branch of Lloyds Bank would be sent to Lloyds Bank head office in London and sorted into different banks. Peter's would be in the National Westminster pile along with hundreds of others.

Step 4 On Tuesday morning Lloyds head office would have received piles of cheques from all of their many branches. These piles would be put together. Now Peter's cheque would be one of thousands and their combined total would represent the total amount owed that day by National Westminster Bank customers to Lloyds Bank customers.

Step 5 During Tuesday, Lloyds Bank representatives will take all these cheques to the **Bankers' Clearing House**. This is a building owned jointly by all of the high street banks where they can present each other with the various piles of cheques. The Lloyds Bank representatives will pass over the piles of National Westminster Bank cheques and in effect say this is what your customers owe our customers. At the same time the National Westminster Bank representatives will have similar piles of Lloyds Bank cheques which in total will show how much Lloyds Bank customers owe National Westminster Bank customers.

By subtracting one amount from the other it is possible to find the net amount owed by one bank to the other.

Step 6 Peter's cheque, along with all the other cheques picked up at the clearing house, would be taken back to the head office of National Westminster Bank and electronically sorted into different branches and at the same time the amount of each cheque and the account from which it must be taken is stored in the memory of the bank's computer. The cheques are then sent to their branches. (Peter's to South Woodford.)

Step 7 Peter's cheque would arrive in South Woodford on Wednesday and, along with other cheques, would be checked. A clerk would make sure it was not a stolen cheque and had been properly completed. If all was in order it would be stamped 'paid'. (Any improper cheques would be stopped and the bank's computer, via the branch terminal, would be instructed not to deduct the amount. The cheque would be sent back to the person to whom it was paid with a reason for it not being paid. Since it goes straight back to the person who paid it in it is said to **bounce**. They would have their account deducted by this amount.) Peter's account would automatically be reduced by £46.75 leaving him a balance of £143.15. The shop, having not been advised that the cheque was to be stopped, would be able to use this £46.75. Also on that day the net amount owed by Lloyds to National Westminster or vice-versa from Tuesday's exchange of cheques would be made by a simple adjustment of each bank's account at the Bank of England.

We have followed just one cheque through the system. Remember this is just one of 4 million cheques which pass through this incredible system every day. People can use the money they have in their bank accounts without having to draw it out in the form of cash.

On 9 February 1984 the clearing banks launched a new fully automated electronic same-day payments system called CHAPS (Clearing House Automated Payment System). This was designed for companies and individuals who need to transfer money very quickly. Peter's cheque took several days to complete its journey and therefore transfer the money. Using computers the CHAPS system allows a customer to contact his bank and ask for money to be trans-ferred that same day to any other bank account. This replaces the old 'town clearing' which used cheques (which had to be drawn on banks in the City of London) and was operated in a similar way to the general clearing but much faster. It is hoped that the system will be expanded to cover more payments.

Exercise

Using your own example draw a flow diagram to show a 3-day journey of a cheque. Look carefully at the **steps** in the case study.

The Functions of Money

There are various functions money can carry out:

- It helps people **exchange** what they have into what they want. It is sometimes called **a medium of exchange**.
- It is a convenient way to **store wealth**. It is possible to save money in a bank account which is safe and to a certain extent a good way of maintaining its value.
- It can be used as a standard **unit to measure value**. Money places a value upon objects which everybody understands. If we describe an object as being worth £10 then auto-matically we can compare it to other objects worth £10 and have a real idea of its value.
- It enables people to **borrow, lend** and **pay for things later**. If people relied upon bartering, that is directly swapping objects, it would be impossible to pay for things in the future. You could not, for example, swap a pig for a goat if you did not have the pig; since quality and size etc could vary. One could, however, buy a goat for £50 by offering £15 now and £5 a week for the next 7 weeks. The seller would know that the quality and value of the money would be constant.

Money in developed economies therefore has no value in itself. It is only a token, but it is made generally acceptable in exchange for goods and services by the weight of law. Most of our money is kept not in the form of cash (notes and coins) but in bank deposits which can be used to settle debts by the use of various methods to transfer amounts from one bank account to another. The most popular current method is the cheque, although technology will soon change this!

Exercise

1 The direct swapping or exchanging of goods without the use of money is called **barter**. Suppose you live in a society which has no money and you are asked to swap a pig for a plough at the local market. Write down 2 problems you might encounter.

2 The BBC ran a television programme for children on Saturday mornings called *Swap Shop*, perhaps you remember it. Amongst other things children were encouraged to take toys they had outgrown or didn't want to an outside broadcast location where they could swap them. Very little swapping ever appeared to take place. Write down why you think this was so.

3 Why are the banks, British Telecom and IBM spending so much money on inventing a new way of spending bank deposits? What is wrong with the cheque clearing system?

ASSIGNMENT

Look carefully at the 2 groups of advertisements. Copy out and fill in the following table:

	Old Price	New Price	% Increase or Decrease	Quality better/ worse/ same as today
Gents Watch				
Radio	£34			

Now answer these questions:

1 Which of the items increased by the greatest amount over the 30 or so years?
2 Which of the items fell in price? Can you think why?

THE P53

WILL

CALL

AT

ALL

STATIONS

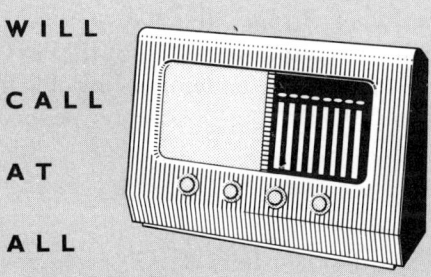

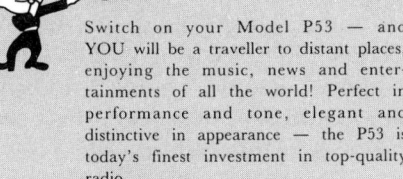

Switch on your Model P53 — and YOU will be a traveller to distant places, enjoying the music, news and entertainments of all the world! Perfect in performance and tone, elegant and distinctive in appearance — the P53 is today's finest investment in top-quality radio.
Ask your Dealer
for a demonstration!
MODEL P53
5-valve, 8-waveband bandspread superhet for A.C. Mains.
£34 *TAX PAID*

News Chronicle, 1951

Precision with Elegance

5 YEARS' WRITTEN GUARANTEE

   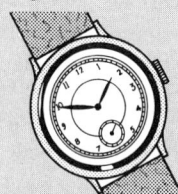

416
No. 416.
Gents' model in 9-ct. gold case. Plain dial, £15.19.6 *inc. postage. Luminious dial 5/- extra.*

414
No. 414.
Ladies' model in 9-ct. gold case. Plain dial, £14.2.6 *inc. postage. Luminious dial 5/- extra.*

846
No. 846.
Gents' model in 9-ct. gold case. Plain or, luminous dial, £20.15.0 *inc. postage.*

Each watch shown has a 15-jewelled, Swiss lever, bench-tested, movement.

To secure any of the watches illustrated write your name, address and the model number required on a postcard. Further supplies will be available shortly, but as stocks will be limited, order now. Do not send any money until you are advised that your watch is ready for dispatch. A limited variety of other models is also available, send 1d. for illustrated leaflet.

Woman, 1945

£33·99

£22·99

£35·00

1984 advertisements

4   We define **money** as 'any kind of material or object that has come to be accepted within society as a normal means by which people pay for their purchases'. Before our token money and bank deposits people used gold and silver coins. Before this societies used real commodities like cattle as money. In this chapter, 4 others have been mentioned. Write down 2 further commodities which have been used as money and, for each, state at least one problem such money might have.

5   Which of the 4 functions of money is being fulfilled in each of the following examples:

a James puts £100 into a Building Society account.
b Mrs Bright buys a washing machine on hire-purchase.
c Jane buys a record.
d Mr Smith calculates the value of his house contents for insurance purposes.

The Value of Money

The value of money, the number of goods and services we can buy with a certain unit of currency, does not remain the same. Prices change. If there is a general increase in prices then we can buy less with the same amount of money. This is called **inflation** where prices have risen and the value of money fallen. The trouble is that although prices change they do not all change by the same amount nor even in the same direction as the previous case study showed.

In general, prices rise over time and the UK has been through a prolonged period of rapid price rises. Between 1963 and 1983 prices rose on average by 625%. Put another way you needed £6.25 to buy roughly the same basket of goods in 1983 as £1 would buy in 1963.

Some prices such as for fuel, light, housing and eating out rose more sharply than the 625%. Others such as clothing and household goods rose less sharply. Since prices change for different goods at different rates it is very difficult to measure these price changes accurately. It is only possible to estimate the rate of inflation. This is done using the calculation known as the **retail price index**.

Each month 130 000 separate prices on 600 different goods and services are collected by the Department of Employment. These are turned into an average increase in prices which is quoted in the newspapers and on television. It is not a straightforward average of the 130 000 prices however. Some price increases are more important to the average family than others and these are given greater importance by a statistical operation called **weighting**.

INFLATION AND EARNINGS

Prices rose by over 6 fold between 1963 and 1983. Fortunately for the average family wages during the same period rose by more than this.

In 1963 the average weekly take-home pay (earnings less tax and national insurance) for a married couple with one wage earner and no children was just £15. Prices, as we have seen, were considerably lower in 1963. To buy the same amount of goods in 1983 as £15 would have bought 20 years earlier, that same average family would have required a take-home pay of at least £121 per week. In fact, the average take-home pay for such a couple in 1983 was £151 per week. The 1983 family were better off being able to buy a further £30 worth of goods and services (or 25% more!).

THE PROBLEMS OF INFLATION

From the previous paragraphs it could be assumed that inflation is not a problem. If wages and prices increase at the same rate nobody seems to suffer. This is not quite true however. Some people did not fare as well as the average couple above. People on fixed incomes, for example, would see their spending power fall. Also, if prices in this country rise more rapidly than those in other countries it might make it difficult to sell our exports and lead to a balance of trade deficit.

Governments try to prevent prices from rising too rapidly. Sometimes they will try to stop wages from rising by agreement with the trade union movement and even pass laws to prevent prices from rising. This is called a **prices and incomes policy**. Other governments have tried to reduce the rate of growth of our money. If people cannot borrow money they are unable to spend, less goods are sold so producers are only able to sell goods by reducing their price. It is a very complicated problem.

Exercise

For 20 years the Ford Cortina proved to be one of the most popular cars in Britain. Durings its history it sold 4 279 079 cars and had 4 different body shapes.

These four body shapes are shown here. Beside each picture is the year of introduction and the price of the most basic model.

Mark I Cortina 1962–66

September 1962
1200cc basic
£639

Mark II Cortina 1966–70

October 1966
1300cc basic
£669

Mark III Cortina 1970–76

August 1970
1300cc basic
£909

Mark IV Cortina 1976–82

September 1976
1300cc basic
£1 950

Using the graph on page 134 showing the average wage for manual workers calculate how many weeks' wages would be needed for the average manual worker to be able to buy the basic Cortina in each of the 4 years. This would be best undertaken in a table:

Model	Year	Price	Average Weekly Manual Wage	Price ÷ wage	No of weeks
Mk I	1962	£639	£15.86	40.29	40
Mk II	1966	£669	£20'30$\frac{1}{2}$	—	—
Mk III	1970	£909	—	—	—
Mk IV	—	—	—	—	—

1 By how much did the price of the basic Cortina increase from September 1962 to September 1976?
2 Did the ability to buy the basic Cortina for the average manual worker increase or decrease from 1962–1976?
3 Did the quality/size/performance of the Cortina improve or deteriorate between 1962–1976?
4 What evidence is there to suggest that the standard of living for the average manual worker improved during the 1960s and 70s?
5 Which group of people might not have enjoyed this improvement in standard of living?

Banks

When considering money in this chapter banks have been mentioned many times since the deposits or accounts that are kept with the high street banks are money. For the next few pages we look in detail at these banks.

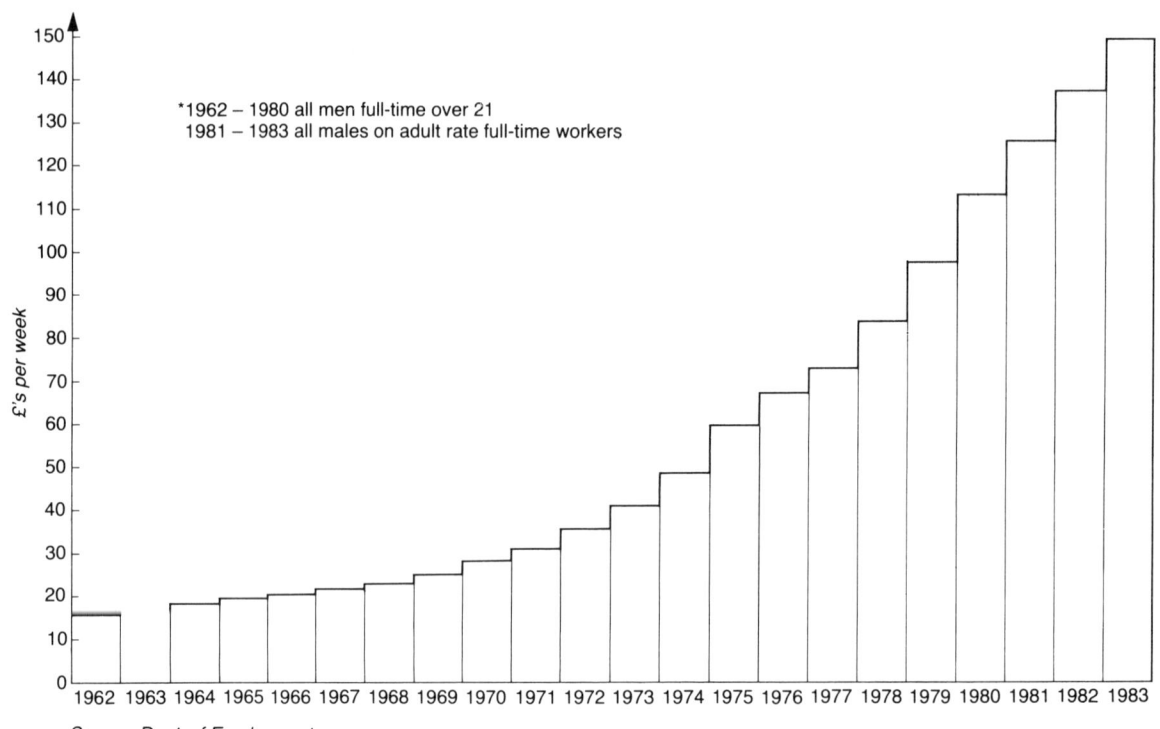

*1962 – 1980 all men full-time over 21
1981 – 1983 all males on adult rate full-time workers

Source: Dept of Employment

CASE STUDY

Simon and Michelle

Simon and Michelle are married. Simon, who is 22 years old, has worked as a trainee manager for a large food retailing chain since leaving school at 18. Michelle is 2 years younger and left school at 16. After several jobs she took a post as secretary at the same store as Simon. Last year they were married and live in a rented flat near the store. At about this time Simon completed his training and was made assistant manager. This meant that he became part of the salaried staff and, instead of receiving a weekly pay packet with cash, he received a monthly pay cheque. It was a crossed cheque so he needed to open a bank account. After talking to his manager he discovered that he could have his wage paid straight into a bank account every month and just receive a pay slip telling him how much he had been given.

Simon and Michelle chose a bank close to the store; it happened to be a branch of the National Westminster Bank. Opening an account was very easy. Simon and Michelle filled in a form, paid in £10 to open the account and gave the name of their manager at work to act as a referee (that is confirm that they were who they said they were). They decided to open a **joint current account**. This meant they would both receive cheque books and be able to spend their money this way. Soon Simon and Michelle's wages were both being paid straight into their account and they both had cheque books. Simon and Michelle have both been surprised at just how many services their bank will undertake for them and most of them free of charge! In just a few months they have used all of these:

1 On the wall of their bank is a 24 hour money dispensing machine called a **service till**. Simon and Michelle have a plastic card and secret code number which enables them to draw out money whenever they need it. Recently they had a weekend in France as a sort of late honeymoon. They returned on Easter Sunday and had no cash (having spent more than they anticipated on duty free drink and perfume). The bank did not open again until Tuesday but the service till allowed them to draw out all the cash they needed. This

machine also lets them order a new cheque book and statement (a sheet showing how much they have in their account and what they have spent).

2 Regular bills like rent, rates, electricity and gas are now paid automatically by the bank. Simon and Michelle just completed and signed a form for each. Where the amount and frequency of payment remains unchanged they use a **standing order**. They order the bank for example to pay their landlord the rent for the flat on the 26th of every month. Where the amount varies they use a **direct debit** which instructs the bank to allow certain organisations, like the local authority who collect the rates, to ask for payment which the bank will then make—unless Simon or Michelle instruct the bank not to.

3 When they were planning their weekend in Paris, Simon and Michelle were able to order all the **foreign currency** (in this case French Francs) from the bank. Next year they plan a holiday in Spain but they will take travellers' cheques which again they will order through their bank. These are much safer than cash. When they collect them at the bank they sign them. Then, whilst abroad, they will be able to exchange as many as they wish when they wish into foreign currency at the hotel or in shops, garages or banks. If they have them stolen they will be able to claim the money back.

4 Simon and Michelle do not want to live in rented accommodation all of their married lives. Recently they went to see the bank manager about buying a house. He was very helpful and explained that they would need to borrow a large sum of money over as many as 30 years paying back a small amount each month plus interest. This is called a **mortgage**. At National Westminster they have a special scheme where young couples like Simon and Michelle can open an account called a **mortgage saver account**. They agreed to put £150 per month from their current account into this special account. They have no cheque book for this account and will not spend the money they save, but the bank will pay them interest which will be added to their account. In 2 years they will have saved £3 600 plus interest and will be able to borrow up to £30 000 to buy a house or flat. Both Michelle and Simon were surprised that the bank manager could talk about lending them so much money without batting an eyelid.

5 This month Simon and Michelle were able to open an **access account.** They were sent a card like the one opposite. With this they can pay bills very simply. A special form, together with the access card, is put in an imprinter machine, and Michelle or Simon sign the completed form. At the end of each month they receive an account from Access which shows how much they have spent in this way and they can either settle at once by sending one cheque or send a small amount and pay off the rest in future months. If they only pay a small amount they will have to pay interest. Simon and Michelle are planning to buy a video in this way next month.

This couple have certainly used their bank since opening an account. These are just a few of the hundreds of services that large banks, like National Westminster, can offer their account holders.

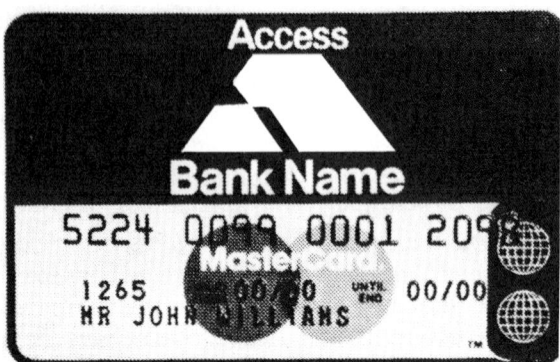

Exercise

1 Why did Simon and Michelle open a **joint current account?**
2 Name 3 ways in which the bank enables Simon and Michelle to pay bills without using cash.
3 In what 2 ways do Simon and Michelle hope to borrow money from the bank?
4 In what way did the bank help Simon and Michelle by giving advice?
5 Why do you think the manager seemed happy to lend Simon and Michelle money?

Some people think that a bank is an expensive way of holding money or paying bills. At Simon and Michelle's bank this is not so. As long as they keep at least £100 in their joint current account or £500 in their savings account they do not pay bank charges. This means that the cheques, standing orders, direct debits etc are free. If they were to fall below this amount then the charges are very low. Cheques only cost 29p each and direct debits only 12p each. The annual charge for keeping the account is only £12. Most people who hold bank accounts do not pay charges because they have more than the minimum sum of £100. There are special schemes for students and young couples which allow them free banking.

Banks like the National Westminster are public limited companies. This means they are owned by shareholders and are in business to make a profit. How can they manage to do this if they do so much for nothing? The clue to this is contained in your answer to question **5** of the last exercise. Banks make a profit by lending out the money that customers deposit with them to other customers who need to borrow. Banks are careful and will only lend to people who they are sure can afford to pay back the loan and the interest charged. In this way they are able to make a profit. The more money people and companies deposit with them the more they can lend out, and so the larger the profit they can make. For this reason each bank tries to offer a large range of useful services for their customers so as to attract as many customers and accounts as possible.

SUMMARY OF BANK FUNCTIONS

Banks carry out many functions but, above all, remember, banks are in business and their aim is to make profits.

1 Accept deposits Individuals and companies can deposit money with a bank by opening an account. There are many different types of account. **Current** or **cheque accounts** offer the customer the ability to pay bills using cheques and other devices (soon electronic) but they do not in general reward the customer with interest and if the balance (amount in account) falls below a certain minimum they may have to pay charges. **Deposit** and **savings accounts** do not allow the customer to pay bills. They are not given a cheque book for example. They are rewarded with interest which is a certain percentage of the amount held in the account paid every 6 months. In general, the harder it is to take the money out, for example if the customer agrees to leave it in the account for 2 years as Simon and Michelle did, then the higher the interest the bank will pay.

2 Agents of payment For customers with current accounts banks will pay those people or companies to whom the customer owes money. This is done by transferring money from one account to another on the instruction of the customer using a cheque, standing order, direct debit mandate etc.

3 Lenders of money Banks lend money in several ways but they all cost the customer who borrows. They must pay back the loan with interest (a percentage of the loan added to the amount borrowed) and it is in this manner that banks make a profit. There are various types of loans:

a An overdraft Here a customer is allowed to write cheques for more than they have in their current account. They only pay interest on the amount they are overdrawn which can be any amount up to an agreed minimum. They can be overdrawn for just a few days or many months. It is a flexible way of borrowing. Very useful for a small businessman.

b Personal loan Account holders, over 18 and who can demonstrate their ability to pay back are able to borrow a lump sum for such large items as a new car, house repairs and improvements, holidays and expensive household items like televisions. Most banks make it very easy to borrow in this way and it probably means just a form to fill in. The sum borrowed is fixed as is the length of time. The interest is added on and monthly repayments made. It is not as flexible as an overdraft but in general a little cheaper.

c Credit card Access and Barclaycards allow customers to pay for items at the end of the month with one cheque and simply using one plastic card when shopping. They also allow the customer instant credit since when the account is

The Role of the Banks

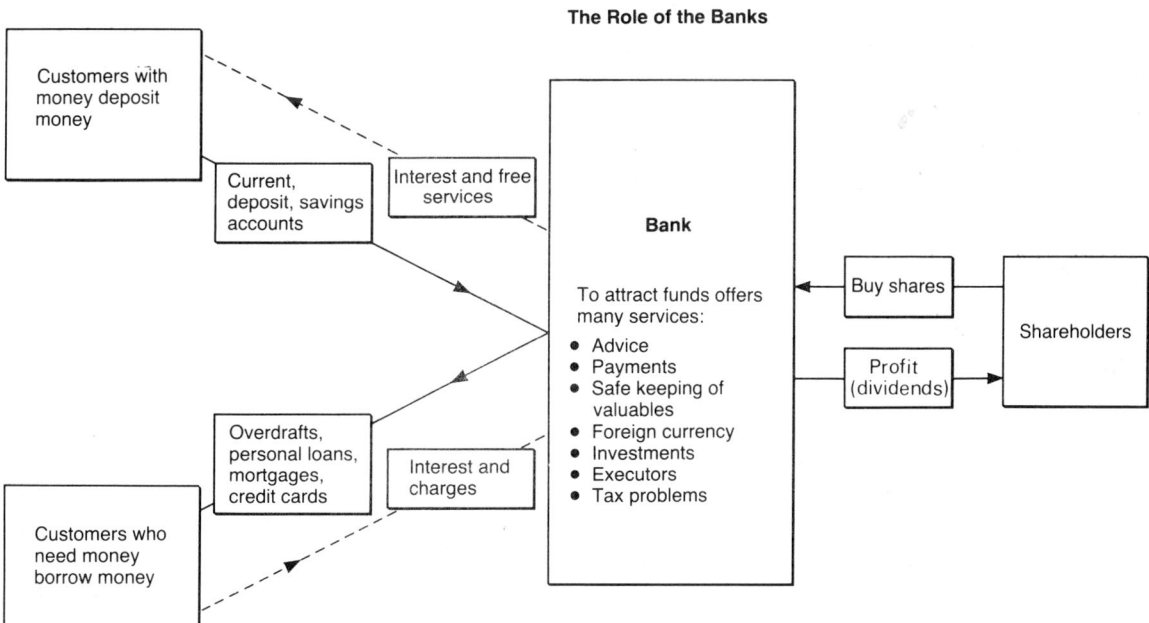

sent at the end of each month the card holder does not have to settle in full. They can pay a small minimum amount and then the rest over a period of time. This is perfect for those last minute decisions where there is not enough time to negotiate a loan. They are expensive however, with a much higher rate of interest.

d Mortgage This is a special form of long-term loan given to people who wish to buy a house. The sum borrowed is so large that the house being bought remains the property of the bank until the payments are complete. A monthly repayment is made which contains the interest and part of the sum borrowed.

e Loans to businesses Banks also lend millions of pounds per year to businesses. They have special schemes such as the National Westminster Business Development Loans which lends £2 000 to £100 000 for 1–10 years, or Farm Development Loans where up to £250 000 can be borrowed for up to 25 years. Large businesses and small one-man operations can also borrow. There are even special schemes for students who have long expensive training like medical, law and dental students.

Looking at the functions of banks like this it can be seen that the services offered by banks attract customers so that they will deposit money which can be lent out at a high rate of interest.

As shown in the advertisement, banks are quick to point out the range of services open to their customers.

'From the manager's office you can dip into the resources of Britain's biggest banking system.'

Here are a few more of the services on offer at a typical bank:

- **Income tax advice**
- **Investment management**—look after investments in stocks and shares, normally for amounts of more than £20 000
- **Stockbroking services**—will arrange for the buying or sale of shares
- **Insurance advice**
- **Unit trusts**—scheme to buy shares for large numbers of small savers.
- **Safeguarding valuables**—safe deposit boxes

to lock up valuable documents or jewellery
- **Night safes**—shopkeepers or owners of expensive items can drop money or valuables into a special safe using a door in the bank wall to which they have a key
- **Executors and trustees**—can appoint the bank in your will to carry out your wishes after you die
- **General financial advice**
- **Many special services for business customers**—For example, up-to-date profiles of foreign countries to help exporters from this country. (Much of the information in the Mauritius case study came from a National Westminster country fact sheet.)

ASSIGNMENT

1 Visit a local bank and find out the rate of interest they pay for:

deposit accounts
savings accounts

Also find out how much they will charge in interest for:

a personal loan
an overdraft

2 Using the information you have gathered explain how banks make a profit.
3 You have a family member who runs a small business but does not believe in banks. Write a letter using the information above trying to convince them to open a bank account.

Finance Companies

One of the most common ways of borrowing is to buy goods on HP—**hire purchase**. When a person buys a car or washing machine over a number of months they have in fact borrowed from a special type of bank called a **finance company** (or **finance house**).

With a hire purchase agreement the purchaser is hiring a good while they pay for it. Of course

Your local NatWest branch is bigger than it seems.

Walk into your local NatWest branch and you enter one of the top ten banks in the world.

From the manager's office you can dip into all the resources of Britain's biggest banking system.

You can make use of one of the country's leading factoring organisations or computer-service bureaux, or one of the largest foreign-exchange dealing rooms in the world.

You can lease an entire vehicle fleet, or raise funds to acquire property or equipment with a multi-million-pound price tag.

You can even save yourself a trip abroad by calling on the local know-how of any of our 193 offices overseas.

No matter what financial help your business needs, talk to your local NatWest manager.

He'll do more than just lend a sympathetic ear. He'll act.

NatWest.
The Action Bank.

they are able to use that good from the beginning of the agreement but it is not legally theirs until it is fully paid for. Until the last instalment has been paid the good belongs to the finance company which has paid the retailer and now collects the repayments. These repayments will include the interest and part of the original price of the article. Towards the end of a hire purchase agreement the purchaser might well be paying a very high rate of interest. This is because the rate of interest is often a fixed amount per month but by the end of the agreement the amount owed is very small since so much has been paid back. For this reason the **Consumer Credit Act (1974)** requires that all agreements over £30 should specify the **Annual Percentage Rate** of interest (APR). It will be found that in most cases hire purchase is a very expensive way of borrowing.

Building Societies

Since 1 January 1987 most Building Societies have been able to offer a full range of services similar to those of banks (pages 137–8). They remain the chief source of loans for house purchase, however (page 187).

Example

If a person took out a hire purchase agreement to buy a motorbike at £1 000 and the rate of interest was 10% and repayment period 2 years he would need to repay:

£1 000 (loan) + £200 (interest 10% × £1 000 × 2)
= £1 200 or £50 per month

After the first year this person would have repaid £600 or £500 (half) of the loan plus £100 interest. In the following year they would pay:

£500 (loan) + £100 (interest)

The interest is now 20%, this percentage growing as the months pass.

If a person cannot keep up with repayments the finance company can reclaim the goods if they have a court order but will often extend the terms if someone is in trouble. It is illegal to sell goods which are being bought on hire purchase.

The finance company lends out money which

savers have deposited. Normally only large amounts for long periods of time are accepted by the finance company which pays a high rate of interest to the saver.

Banking Services at the Post Office

The **National Girobank** was established some 20 years ago to offer a cheap banking service through the Post Office. Anyone over 15 can open a Giro account with just £1. The Girobank offers some of the services of the high street banks but not all. It is cheaper than the high street bank in that no charges are made as long as an account is in credit. Here are the main services:

- Cheque book and card (for those over 18)
- Standing orders/direct debit
- Free statement
- Deposit accounts
- Personal loans
- Thomas Cook travellers' cheques and foreign currency

There are post offices in most villages (20 000) and they are open longer hours than banks.

Exercise

Compare a current account at a high street bank with the National Girobank cheque account.

For what sort of customer would a Giro account be preferable to a bank account and for what sort of person would the opposite be true?

The Bank of England

The **Bank of England** was formed in 1694 although in the early days it was just like any other bank. In those days it did lend a large amount to the Government and this started a long association with the Government which led to control by Parliament and eventual nationalisation. Today the Bank of England is a very special bank, called the **Central Bank**. It is in control of the money system of this country.

Today the functions of the Bank of England include:

Note issue All banknotes are printed in Debden in Essex and circulated through the Bank of England.

Government's banker All taxes are paid into the Government's accounts and all Government spending passes through the accounts at the Bank of England. Our Government borrows vast sums of money and the Bank of England is responsible for this debt.

Bankers' bank All banks keep at least 1% of their deposits in their accounts at the Bank of England. At the end of each day if one bank owes another bank money due to the cheque clearing system the debt is settled by a transfer of funds from one account to another.

International cooperation The Bank of England represents the UK on such international monetary bodies as the IMF.

Government monetary policy If the Government wishes to reduce the money in circulation—to control inflation—it is the Bank of

England that is responsible for putting this policy into effect.

SUMMARY EXERCISE

1 Explain clearly what is meant by **barter** and **commodity money**. Give 2 disadvantages of both as a system of exchange.

2 We have in this country a token money system where our cash is worthless. Why then do people readily accept this in payment for goods and services?

3 'A cheque is *not* money but a **bank account** is.' Explain this statement.

4 If a country experiences a period of rapid inflation what happens to the value of its currency?

5 For what reasons is **inflation** often considered a bad thing for the economy of a country?

6 Explain in detail the difference between a

personal bank loan and an **overdraft facility**.

7   The high street banks offer most of their services freely to customers. How then do they make such large profits for their shareholders?

8   Name one service offered by the high street banks but *not* offered by the National Girobanks.

9   Give one advantage of holding a National Girobank account rather than a high street bank account.

10   The high street banks all have accounts with the Bank of England which holds about 1% of their total deposits in these accounts. How do these accounts help in the operation of the cheque clearing system?

ASSIGNMENTS

1   You discover that an old relative keeps all of her money in a shoe box under the bed because she does not like banks. Write down all the points which you would mention to her in order to change her opinion of banks. Be sure to include the different types of account and all the standard banking services which would be of use to her.

2   Some people have odd notions about banks. Those who have never been inside one tend to look upon them as cold, aloof and mysterious. Nothing could be further from the truth. Banks are friendly places, staffed by men and women whose desire is to help. Other people talk scathingly of banks—as scathingly as Mark Twain who claimed that 'a banker is a fellow who lends you his umbrella when the sun is shining and asks for it back the minute it starts to rain'. These people forget that a banker is handling other people's money and has to be just as careful with it as if it were his own.

Source   BIS Booklet No 1, Page 1

a List 4 services provided by banks for their customers which convince you that they are indeed '... friendly places staffed by men and women whose desire is to help'.

b Mark Twain obviously thought of banks as places which do not like lending money to people. Of course banks do like to lend ... they have to—why?

c Describe 2 ways in which banks lend money so as to show the difference between these 2 ways.

3   There are said to be 4 main functions of money in a modern society. Take each one of these functions in turn and with examples show how they are performed.

4   You probably have a few coins in your pocket or purse at the moment. If you lived in a primitive society you might not use money to trade. You might still **barter**. Describe what is meant by **bartering** and show why it is no good as a system of exchange in our highly developed society.

11 Prices and Incomes

The main source of 'money' for most people is the reward they receive for making a contribution to production, their **wages**. In Chapter 1 we learnt about the circular flow of income.

People specialise in a certain occupation or job and are paid a wage in the form of money. Some people, known as entrepreneurs, undertake a very special type of work. They bring together other types of resource and create businesses, produce goods and services and satisfy wants. These individuals, either acting alone or in groups, receive **profit**.

Once individuals have money they are able to exchange it for goods and services by spending. This we call **consumption**. It is also possible for an individual to keep some of this money to be spent at a later date. This is known as **saving**.

Once individuals have earnt money they are faced with several choices—to spend, save, where to spend etc.

Since most people do not have enough money to be able to satisfy all of their wants they are faced with these choices. If they are to act sensibly they must consider the opportunity costs of using their scarce money in one particular way rather than another. If the individual decides to spend some money on shoes they might not be able to buy a coat.

Wages

When someone finds paid employment they receive a **wage**. This can sometimes be paid weekly

	Gross pay	A person's **earnings**
	less	
Collected by the employer for the Government	Income Tax	— Money taken by the Government to provide public and merit goods
	less	
	National Insurance	— Money taken by the Government to provide a State pension and benefits
	less	
Collected by the employer for the worker	Pension Contributions	— Money taken by the firm in order to provide a larger pension than the state
	less	
	Voluntary Payments	— Money taken at persons request to pay for trade union membership, or to save for holiday etc
	equals	
	Net pay	A person's take-home pay

in the form of cash or a cheque or it might be paid monthly with a simple transfer from the firm's account to the workers account. This monthly pay is often called a **salary**. However they receive their pay people do not take home all the wage they earn. A person's earnings are called their **gross pay** but from this certain deductions are made (see previous page).

All workers are given a statement each week which itemises each deduction and addition. This is called a **wage slip** or **pay advice** (below).

WAGE RATE/EARNINGS

Each job has an agreed rate of pay. This could be expressed hourly, weekly, monthly, or even as an annual figure:

Example

An annual salary of £9 100, for a 35 hour week could be expressed as:

£5	per hour
£175	per week
£758.33	per month
£9 100	per year

In some occupations it is possible to earn more than this basic rate for the job. This can be achieved by working for more than the agreed number of hours: **overtime**. It is usual for the hourly rate for overtime to be more than the basic hourly rate. Some firms pay a bonus on top of the basic rate if production targets are met or if difficult or dirty work has been undertaken. Bonuses are also paid for night work.

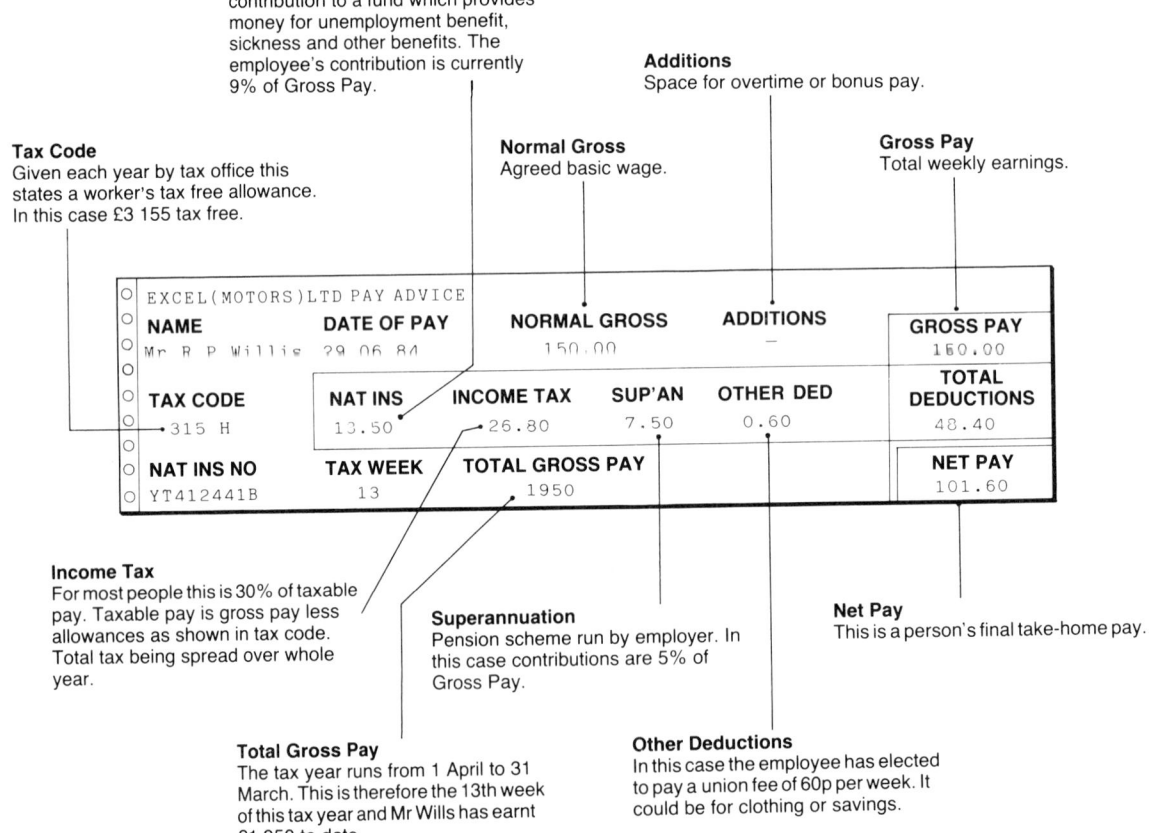

National Insurance
Employees and employers make a contribution to a fund which provides money for unemployment benefit, sickness and other benefits. The employee's contribution is currently 9% of Gross Pay.

Additions
Space for overtime or bonus pay.

Tax Code
Given each year by tax office this states a worker's tax free allowance. In this case £3 155 tax free.

Normal Gross
Agreed basic wage.

Gross Pay
Total weekly earnings.

Income Tax
For most people this is 30% of taxable pay. Taxable pay is gross pay less allowances as shown in tax code. Total tax being spread over whole year.

Superannuation
Pension scheme run by employer. In this case contributions are 5% of Gross Pay.

Net Pay
This is a person's final take-home pay.

Total Gross Pay
The tax year runs from 1 April to 31 March. This is therefore the 13th week of this tax year and Mr Wills has earnt £1 950 to date.

Other Deductions
In this case the employee has elected to pay a union fee of 60p per week. It could be for clothing or savings.

Pay advice

In some businesses profit sharing schemes operate. Here workers are given a share of the profits as part of their wage. It is therefore quite common for a person's **earnings** (what they actually earn as their **gross wage**) to be much higher than the **wage rate** (the agreed rate for the minimum number of hours worked).

PIECE RATE/TIME RATE

It is possible not to pay workers by the number of hours they work: **time rate**, but instead by the amount they produce: **piece rate**. With piece rate a worker is encouraged to work faster and produce as many items as possible, to be as conscientious and to waste as little time as possible. This has obvious advantages for the owners of the factory and for those workers who can work quickly. It is, however, not always possible to pay people a piece rate. A teacher or doctor would not necessarily be more efficient if they dealt with more people. A bus driver could become very unsafe if he were to rush his job. Often jobs are collective, a group of people are involved. In these circumstances the individual's contribution to production is difficult to determine.

Exercise

1 Draw up a list of 3 advantages and 3 disadvantages of **piece rate** and **time rates** (saying clearly whether the advantage or disadvantage is to the employer or employee).
2 Which method of payment already mentioned combines many of the advantages of both piece and time rate?

WAGE DIFFERENCES

CASE STUDY

The Weekly Wage Ladder

Study the wages information in the diagram overleaf. It is clear from the evidence that there is considerable variation in the level of pay between different occupations. An extreme example would be that which exists between the Chairman of British Oxygen and his hairdresser. Both work, both have a skill, but one earns considerably more than the other. This evidence shows that there are 2 differences in wages. The first is that which exists between different occupations, the second is that which exists between different sexes. Male nurses have an average wage of £136.4 per week but their female colleagues have an average wage of £115.1 per week. If we consider secondary school teachers again male teachers have an average wage of £188.5 but female teachers only £163.1 per week.

Exercise

Look at the information on the weekly wages ladder overleaf.

1 List the 4 top paid male occupations with their weekly pay as shown on the ladder.
2 List the 3 bottom paid male occupations with their weekly pay as shown on the ladder.
3 List 2 things the highest paid occupations have in common.

4 List 2 things the lowest paid occupations have in common.
5 Write down the average weekly pay for both male and female nurses.
6 Give one other occupation in which male workers earn on average more than female?
7 In both nursing and your answer to question **6** workers receive equal pay. Can you think why their average income is different?

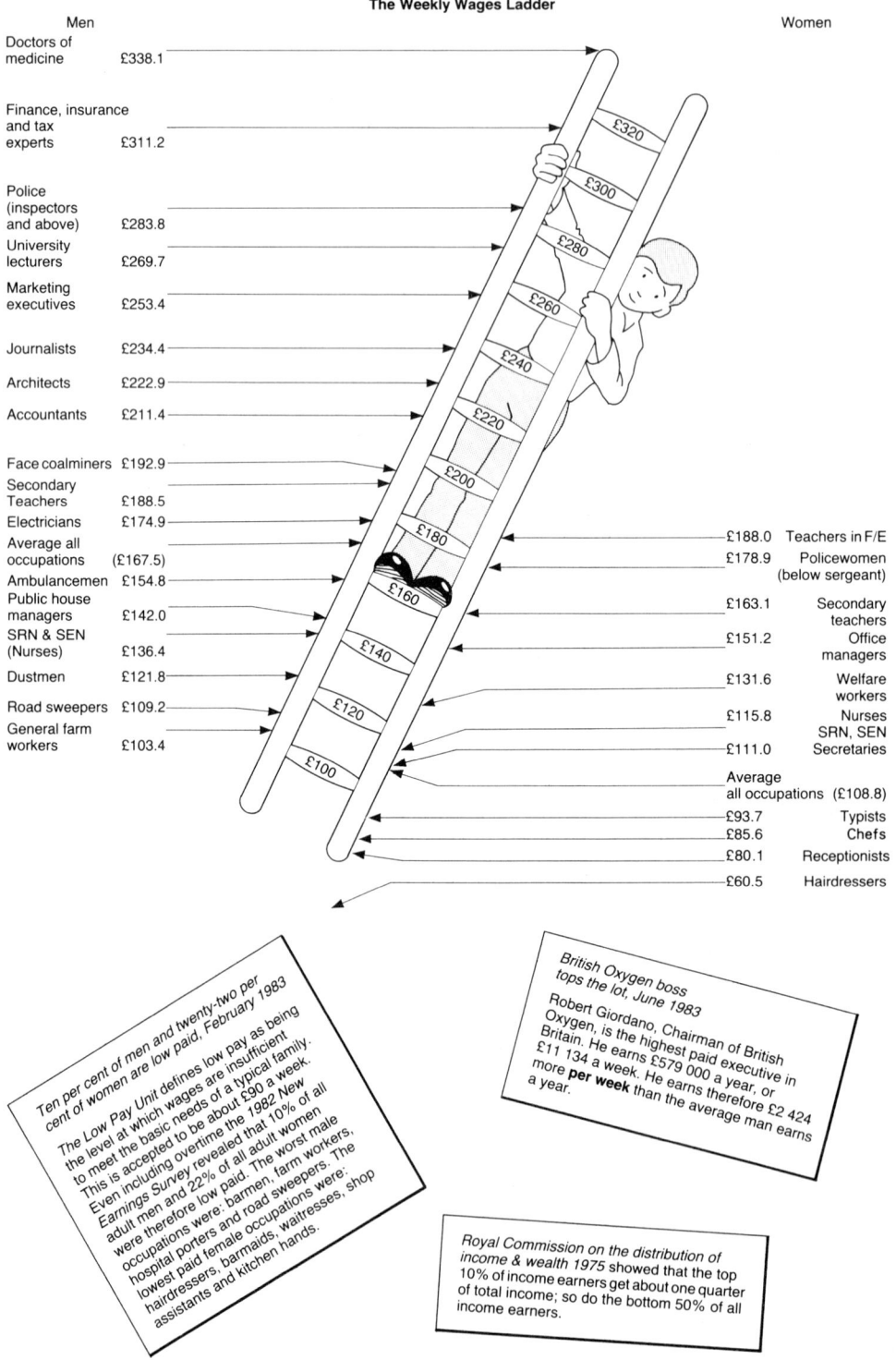

The Weekly Wages Ladder

Men

Doctors of medicine	£338.1
Finance, insurance and tax experts	£311.2
Police (inspectors and above)	£283.8
University lecturers	£269.7
Marketing executives	£253.4
Journalists	£234.4
Architects	£222.9
Accountants	£211.4
Face coalminers	£192.9
Secondary Teachers	£188.5
Electricians	£174.9
Average all occupations	(£167.5)
Ambulancemen	£154.8
Public house managers	£142.0
SRN & SEN (Nurses)	£136.4
Dustmen	£121.8
Road sweepers	£109.2
General farm workers	£103.4

Women

£320	
£300	
£280	
£260	
£240	
£220	
£200	
£180	
£188.0	Teachers in F/E
£178.9	Policewomen (below sergeant)
£163.1	Secondary teachers
£151.2	Office managers
£131.6	Welfare workers
£115.8	Nurses SRN, SEN
£111.0	Secretaries
Average all occupations	(£108.8)
£93.7	Typists
£85.6	Chefs
£80.1	Receptionists
£60.5	Hairdressers

Ten per cent of men and twenty-two per cent of women are low paid, February 1983

The Low Pay Unit defines low pay as being the level at which wages are insufficient to meet the basic needs of a typical family. This is accepted to be about £90 a week. Even including overtime the 1982 New Earnings Survey revealed that 10% of all adult men and 22% of all adult women were therefore low paid. The worst male occupations were: barmen, farm workers, hospital porters and road sweepers. The lowest paid female occupations were: hairdressers, barmaids, waitresses, shop assistants and kitchen hands.

British Oxygen boss tops the lot, June 1983

Robert Giordano, Chairman of British Oxygen, is the highest paid executive in Britain. He earns £579 000 a year, or £11 134 a week. He earns therefore £2 424 more **per week** than the average man earns a year.

Royal Commission on the distribution of income & wealth 1975 showed that the top 10% of income earners get about one quarter of total income; so do the bottom 50% of all income earners.

April '83 average gross weekly wages for selected occupations, New Earning Survey Department of Employment HMSO

This case study shows that there are 2 differences in pay in this country. Different occupations receive different rates of pay and different sexes on average receive different rates of pay. Twenty-two per cent of women workers are defined as being low paid whilst only 10% of men workers are. Women in the same occupation earn on average less than men. The highest paid 10% of workers share the same amount of total income as the lowest paid 50%.

The reasons for this are complicated. Your answers to the questions in the case study help us to see why but there is no one satisfactory answer.

WAGE DIFFERENCES BETWEEN OCCUPATIONS

The case study shows that the 4 top male wages were all for occupations which required long training, high abilities and skills. The lowest incomes were earnt in occupations where the training was short and ability rather low. It is obvious that in order to attract people of high ability to certain jobs and to encourage them to train for many years they would need to be offered a higher wage.

The demand for the product the worker produces will also have an effect. Workers are not wanted by the entrepreneur for their own sake but for the particular skill they have in helping to produce a good or service. If the good or service is wanted very much by consumers who have the money to pay for it, then this might help wages to rise. For example, if a garage owner finds that he has queues of customers with cars needing servicing but has to turn them away because he has only one mechanic he would advertise for a new mechanic. If he found that no one applied for the job he might advertise again but at a higher wage.

A job might not only require a high wage because of the long training. There might also be other barriers which prevent people from taking the job unless there were high wages (see diagram overleaf).

People would not travel to the inhospitable North Sea to work in unpleasant surroundings, away from their families, often risking their lives, if the wages were not very high. Some professions and unions manage to keep the numbers entering the occupation low so that wages are kept high. For example, barristers and print workers. Pop stars are unique and can charge very high fees because no other person sounds quite like them and they are irreplaceable.

It is not quite so straightforward as this however, as one can find examples which do not fit our model. Nurses, for example, need dedication, work very long hours including nights, often have to undertake dirty tasks and have 3 years of training. One would expect them to be paid high wages, but they are not and earn much less, for example, than women police constables whose job description is very similar. This is perhaps due to the attractiveness of the job. Nurses are not very well paid, especially when compared with other countries but in spite of this being a well-known fact nursing schools still have no shortage of applications. School leavers are attracted to nursing since they see it as a job with responsibility, variety and a sense of achievement. Perhaps such jobs do not need to offer high wages.

In some occupations the trade unions are powerful. A large percentage of the workforce are members and are united. They are prepared to take strike action to secure higher wages. In occupations where workers are spread out in small workshops, such as the clothing trade, or where there are many non-union members or even where the workers feel that they cannot strike, (such as nurses again) then wages tend to be lower. In industries where there is little or no union and owner organisation the Government establishes wages councils to set minimum wages for that occupation. These often become the normal wage and are very low.

SEX DIFFERENCES

Under the **Equal Pay Act, 1970**, women in the UK are entitled to equal pay with men, when undertaking work which is the same or broadly similar. The **Sex Discrimination Act, 1975**, makes it illegal to discriminate, on grounds of

Determination of wage rates

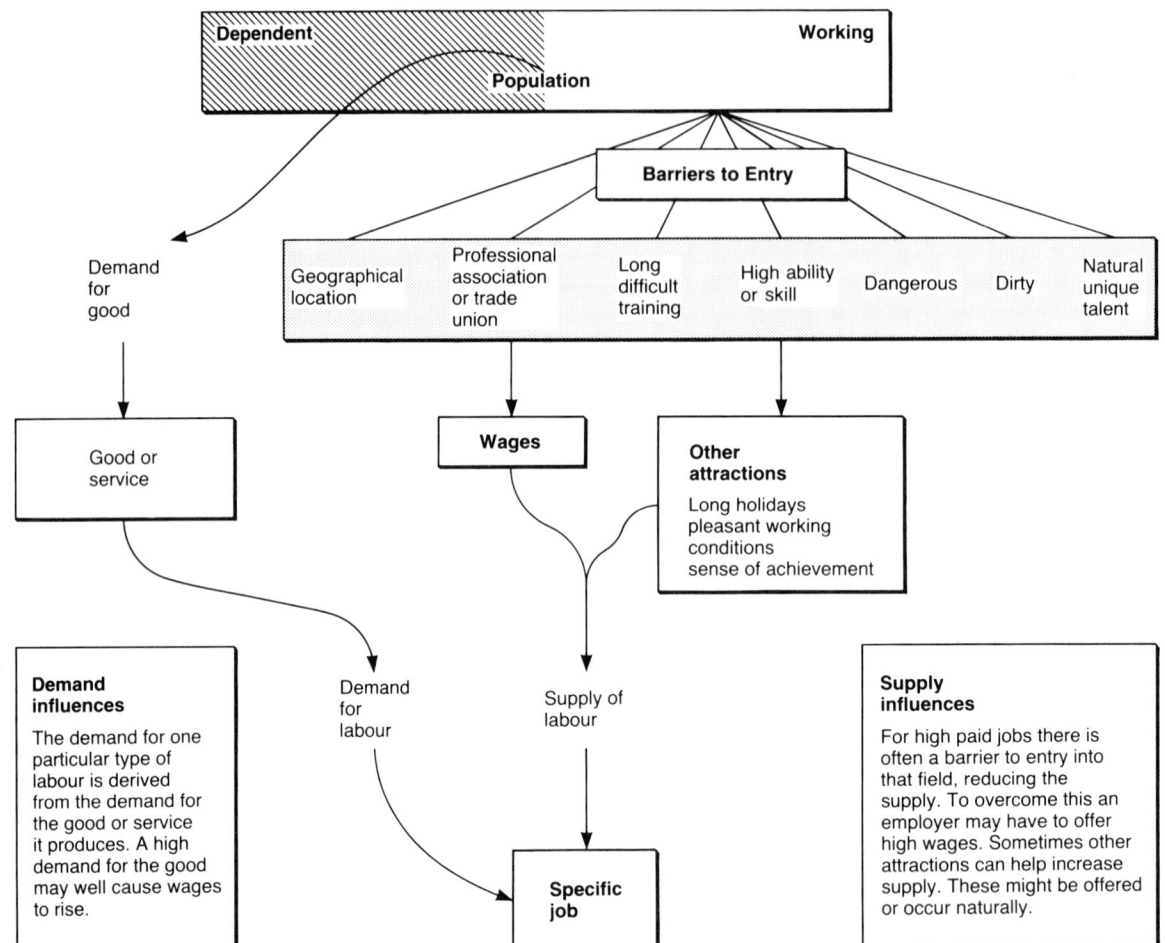

3ex, in the recruitment, training, or promotion of staff except where there exists a genuine reason such as midwifery—reserved for women, and coalmining—reserved for men. Advertisements might read 'attractive bar staff required' but cannot read 'attractive barmaids required'. This legislation ought to mean that in most occupations women are paid the same as their male colleagues. Our case study shows the opposite. In teaching and nursing the average wage for women is lower than that for men.

One explanation is that women do not gain posts of responsibility and therefore higher pay as often as men because they break their careers to have a family. This need not be necessarily so. **The Employment Protection Act, 1978,** gave women the right to maternity leave for 29 weeks,

with 6 weeks' pay and the right to return to their old job. This is only a right and many women choose not to exercise that right. This could be due to the lack of day-care nursery facilities in this country. If they do return to work women are often unable to work overtime since they might have to rush back home to feed and look after their family. This would explain some differences between men and women but not the very large number who are earning low wages.

Where trade unions are weak and workers spread out over many small establishments the Government has set up **wages councils** who set a legally enforceable minimum wage for those industries covered. Very often this becomes the wage and in most cases it is very low. Women are very much more likely to receive the minimum in wages council industries but most significantly about 75% of wages council employees are women. Women are concentrated into occupations which are traditionally poorly paid and the wages councils, although preventing them from being exploited, tend to set the wage they will receive which is a 'minimum' figure. These industries include clothing (manufacture, ie machine operators in jean manufacturers), hairdressing, barworkers, hotel and catering, retail trade. In many areas such as secretarial work women are the only workers. Very few men are employed in such tasks so that the equal pay legislation made little effect and left these women in traditional 'female' employment low paid.

Exercise

1 'Workers can choose how to spend their net pay but not their gross pay.' To what extent is this true?

2 Write down 2 advantages of a **profit sharing scheme**; one for a worker and one for the employer.

3 Male secondary school teachers are, on average, paid more than their female colleagues. Explain why this can be so given the *Equal Pay Act, 1970*.

4 Why might a pop star earn more than a brain surgeon?

5 What might happen to the wages of car workers if people bought less cars?

ASSIGNMENT

Gather as many different wage rates as you can. Either visit the local jobcentre, or look at advertisements in your local paper. Make a list in order of wage size and try to explain the differences you notice.

Consumption

PRICES

CASE STUDY EXERCISE

Mr Higgins owns a small farm in the West Midlands. Most of his land is devoted to wheat and other cereals but over the last few years he has been experimenting with a couple of fields of strawberries. He sells these on a 'pick-your-own' basis. By displaying boards on the main road he is able to attract passing motorists. He has made a small car park and constructed a shed in which customers can weigh the strawberries they have picked and pay his son who sits and takes the money. He has calculated that to make about the same profit from a field of strawberries as a field of wheat he must sell them at about 20p per pound.

Strawberries have a very short season depending upon the weather. The first few strawberries are ready in early June but within a few weeks all the fruit is ready for picking. This year he found that when the first few strawberries were ripe by setting the price at 35p per pound only a few motorists were stopping and some fruit was being wasted by becoming over-ripe. He dropped the price after a few days to 30p a pound and found that many more people stopped to pick. After one further week of very hot, sunny weather most of his field was ready for picking but not enough customers were coming. He dropped the price still further to 25p per pound and found that now most of the strawberries were being picked.

By the end of the season he found that he had made a healthy profit.

Exercise

1 Why did Mr Higgins find that more people stopped to pick his strawberries as he dropped his price?

2 In a poor year, with little or no sun, less fruit would ripen. Do you think that the price charged by Mr Higgins would be higher or lower than 25p per pound?

3 Local farmers, neighbours of Mr Higgins, envious of his new car bought with the profits from his strawberries, decide to plant their own strawberries. Within a couple of years many farms along the same main road will have pick-your-own strawberry signs. How do you think this will effect the price of strawberries?

4 Mr Higgins tried to increase his custom by reducing price. What other methods might he have used?

5 If Mr Higgins found that the only way he could sell all of his crop was to lower the price to 15p per pound and in this way clear his fields what would he do next year?

6 If an authoritative report showed that strawberries were definitely a strong aphrodisiac (a substance which is supposed to increase sexual desire), what do you think would happen to the number of people wanting to pick Mr Higgins' strawberries and what do you think he would do to his price?

This hypothetical example illustrates some important economic principles. In general, more of a good or service will be bought at lower prices. Mr Higgins was able to sell more strawberries at 25p per pound than 35p per pound. Mr Higgins set the price to clear his fields. When there is little fruit, such as in a poor year for sunshine, he charges more but if several farmers in the same area were all selling strawberries he might be forced to sell for less. If the price at which he could clear his fields proved to be so low that he could make more profit growing a different crop he would clearly switch crops, but if he found that people were queuing to buy his fruit at 40p per pound he might plant more.

In general the price charged for a good or service will be that which enables all of the items produced to be sold. If this price is not sufficient to produce a satisfactory profit the entrepreneur will leave the scene, either by giving up or changing to another product. The price charged will depend therefore upon the desire consumers have to buy a product, or **demand**, and the amount of that product available, the **supply**. If either of these change the price might well be affected as our case study has shown.

CASE STUDY

The Marine Aquarium

Andrew, a sixth form student at West Hatch High School, has recently set up his own, small tropical fish importing business. He calls it 'The Marine Aquarium'.

Andrew had worked part-time for several years in a shop selling tropical fish. He noticed that only one business in the London area imported certain rare types of salt-water fish into the country from places like Hawaii. On holiday in America Andrew was able to contact the divers who caught these tropical fish and found that many were prepared to send fish to him. Special containers to keep the fish warm were needed and the only transport method fast enough was air freight.

Andrew made a few 'test imports' and was surprised to find that he could sell fish far cheaper than his rival and still make a profit. There were problems. He had to pay for the fish and the transport in advance—before he had sold them. This meant that he needed some cash or **working capital** and since he had very little money saved he needed to borrow. Also more tanks to keep his fish in and special equipment to filter and oxygenate the water had to be purchased. He needed a van to deliver the goods, collect them from the airport and to collect food and equipment. He found that he could insure the fish whilst in transit.

Faced with such problems many would have given up but Andrew went to an accountant and drew up a plan. Together they decided that he would need to borrow £10 000, but, if things went well he could expect to make a healthy profit.

One of the most important decisions Andrew had to make was what price to charge for the fish he imported. He knew that he would need to cover his **costs**. These were of 2 types:

Variable costs The fish had to be bought in Hawaii and transported to London. The more he imported the higher these costs would be (if he imported more fish he paid higher bills). Look at the example of variable costs; the cost of importing a box of Yellow Tang.

VARIABLE COSTS

The Yellow Tang—Hawaii

Cost per box—assuming 10 boxes in consignment, average weight—35 lb per box

	$	£
Cost of fish (1 box, 30 fish)	60.00	
Freight	96.60	
Packing	7.50	
Import duty (15%)	24.61	
TOTAL	188.71	134.80 (£1 = $1.4)
Handling charge (Heathrow) (£35 per consignment)		3.50
Transport to Barking (£15 per consignment)		1.50
*TOTAL (28.5 fish)		139.80
COST PER FISH (÷ 28.5)		4.90

*(Average 5% loss)

If Andrew were to charge £4.90 for each Yellow Tang he would cover these variable costs—the costs of importing the fish into the country, but, he would not cover his **overheads** or **fixed costs**.

Fixed costs These are those costs Andrew will have to cover however many fish he manages to sell. Expenses such as interest repayments on his loan, advertising, insurance, certain of the costs of running a van (road tax and insurance) and his own wages will occur and have to be paid even if he sells no fish. Andrew was also advised to set aside some money each year in order to replace his equipment after a few years. This is called **depreciation** and would also count as a fixed cost. As can be seen in the following table this came to £13 637 in his first year. Andrew was lucky to have won a competition run by the Abbey National Building Society called 'Head Start for Business' which gave him free accommodation for a year. If he had to pay for this it would add to fixed costs.

FIXED COSTS

	£
Van	3 185
Insurance	450
Interest	1 452
Depreciation	1 550
Wages	2 600
Advertising	800
Others	3 600
TOTAL	13 637

These costs had to be spread over the number of fish Andrew could sell; the price of each containing an element to cover **fixed** costs as well as the **variable** costs calculated above. The amount to be added to variable costs, in each case, to cover fixed costs would depend upon how many fish Andrew could sell. If he only sold one fish he would need to charge the variable cost *plus* £13 637. Andrew and his accountant estimated that he could expect to import 34 shipments in the first year each costing him (variable cost) £1 200. If these were sold for £2 000 (a 40% mark-up) a profit could be made:

ESTIMATED PROFIT (34 shipments)

	Expenses £	Income £
Sale of fish (34 shipments @ £2 000)		68 000
Variable costs		
Purchase of fish (34 shipments @ £1 200)	40 800	
Fixed costs	13 637	
TOTAL COSTS	54 437	
NET PROFIT (Income—total costs)		13 563

The 40% mark-up means that the **final selling price** £68 000 would split 60% to cover variable costs and 40% to cover fixed and profit. (It is calculated by multiplying £40 800 by 100 and dividing by 60.)

If this 40% mark-up is applied to individual fish Andrew is able to calculate the price list.

The Yellow Tang had a variable cost of £4.90 which with a mark-up would equal:

$$\frac{£4.90 \times 100}{60} = £8.17 \text{ (Andrew charges £8 for ease)}$$

This is how it is made up:

Variable costs. Cost of fish in Hawaii	20%
Freight and duty	40%

Fixed cost: Overheads (comprising van, interest, *wages, depreciation and others) — 20%

Profit: — 20%

Note Wages are sometimes considered to be **variable costs** since in large concerns they can alter with output. More can be produced, for example, if workers undertake overtime. Other workers will be paid the same however much is produced and are unlikely to be sacked if there is a temporary drop in production—such wages are therefore **fixed costs**. In this case Andrew expects to reward his efforts with £50 per week (£2 600 per year) however many fish he imports and in this sense represents a **fixed cost**.

Exercise

1 If low orders or poor weather in Hawaii prevent Andrew from reducing his target number of shipments he will make less profit if he keeps the same mark-up. **Calculate** using the table Andrew's net profit if he only manages to import 17 shipments each costing £1 200 in his first year, assuming all other costs remain unchanged.

	Expenses £	Income £
Estimated profit (17 shipments)		
Sale of fish (17 shipments @ £2 000)		

Variable costs: Purchase of fish
 (17 shipments @ £1 200)
Fixed costs
Total costs
Net profit (Income—total costs)

2 Using a suitable table calculate Andrew's expected profit if he manages to import only 13 shipments in his first year.

3 Using similar axes to those below complete a line graph to show profit or loss for different numbers of shipment:

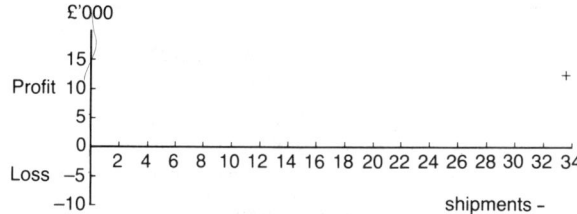

£'000

Profit 15 10 5 0

Loss −5 −10

2 4 6 8 10 12 14 16 18 20 22 24 26 28 30 32 34

+

shipments −

4 If Andrew found himself unable to cover his costs he would be making a loss. Since he must pay back his loan he might be tempted to increase the price of his fish. Why might this be a mistake?

5 Some large fish, for example the 'Naso Tang' have a much higher mark-up. A Naso Tang costs Andrew £10 per fish to import into the country but he can sell one for as much as £35. Give one reason for this higher mark-up.

6 In the 'Yellow Tang' example the air freight charge is $96.60 ($2.76 per pound) because Andrew imported 10 boxes at 35 lb per box—a total shipment weight of 350 lb.

Pan-Am Freight Charges Hawaii—Heathrow

Total shipment weight	Cost per lb $
100–219 lb	3.44
220–659 lb	2.76
660–1 099 lb	2.10
1 100 lb and over	1.69

If Andrew were to import 35 boxes (35 lb per box) of Yellow Tang in one shipment use the information above to calculate the **variable cost** of a single Yellow Tang.

	Cost per box (35 boxes average weight 35 lb)	
	$	£
Cost of fish (1 box 30 fish)	60.00	
Air freight		
Packing	7.50	
Import duty (15%)	____	____
TOTAL	÷ 1.4	
	____	____
Handling charge (£35 per shipment)		1.00
Transport to Barking (£15 per shipment)		.50
TOTAL PER BOX		____
COST PER FISH (÷ 28.5)		____

7 Andrew's only competitor in the London area imports very large quantities of fish—far more than Andrew will at first. This competitor would not only pay the lower air freight charges but with a larger van and storage facilities will buy in bulk and therefore probably pay less for the fish and feed etc. It is surprising that this competitor charges similar prices to Andrew. What do you conclude about this competitor's mark-up and profit?

8 Andrew is tempted to charge lower prices than his only rival in the London area, but had heard that this rival would like to see Andrew out of business. If Andrew did lower his prices:

a What would be the likely response of Andrew's rival?
b Would this help tropical fish collectors?
c What would happen to Andrew's profit?
d What else could Andrew do with his borrowed capital?

9 If the rate of exchange of £1 to dollars were to **fall** to £1 = $1.2 what would be the effect on Andrew's **variable costs**?

10 If the rate of exchange of £1 to dollars were to **rise** to £1 = $1.6 what would be the effect on Andrew's **variable costs**?

SUMMARY

1 Andrew must charge a price which covers *all* of his costs. Fixed costs remain constant but variable costs increase as Andrew imports more. For Andrew although variable costs increase as orders increase they do so at a falling rate. The variable cost per fish *falls* as Andrew imports more fish since air freight charges are less per pound for large orders and some handling charges are fixed. Large orders result in Andrew using his capital more efficiently and enable him to make a higher profit.

2 When deciding upon a price Andrew must cover all costs but he must also be aware of his competitor's price. If Andrew charges more than this competitor he will probably sell fewer fish.

3 A rare fish can sell with a much higher mark-up. Collectors are prepared to pay these very high prices. The fish are so rare that the divers do not find them very often—or offer them to Andrew very often.

4   Whilst his trade is small Andrew cannot afford to undercut his competitor. If Andrew were to charge a very low price for fish this competitor would do the same and both businesses would receive lower profits. The competitor with large shipments and more equipment enjoys economies of large scale operation and would be able to force Andrew out of business.

5   If Andrew is unable to make a profit he must look for an alternative use for his capital and expertise; perhaps he could specialise in importing crustacea (crabs).

6   Changes in the exchange rate of the pound to the dollar will be a major influence upon Andrew's variable costs. A fall in the exchange rate will mean that he has to pay more pounds for the same number of dollars and will therefore cause a rise in variable costs. A rise in the exchange rate will mean that he is able to buy more dollars for the number of pounds and therefore cause the variable costs to fall. The cost of the fish in Hawaii remains the same but the value of the pound has changed. This outside influence will affect *all* fish importers and not just Andrew.

POSTSCRIPT

Andrew was unable to borrow the £10 000 he needed to make this business work. Although most of the banks and Government agencies he contacted all agreed that these figures were correct and that he could make a profit and perhaps in a few years have a firm which employed several people he had one problem—his age. At 17 it is very difficult to borrow money for any purpose since 18 is the legal age at which people become adults.

Andrew did not give up and has, through various contacts, managed to arrange an overdraft facility for £5 000 at the National Westminster Bank. He has been promised a further £1 000 from a charitable trust. This has meant a reduction in plans. He has not got the cash to order large shipments from abroad to sell and he is short of working capital. But he still trades as this recent advertisement in a specialist magazine shows.

The advertisement mentions 'consolidation'. This means acting as an importing agent for a number of customers—in this case shops. Each shop does not require a full order or have the expertise to arrange a shipment. Andrew will undertake the paperwork required for a number of shops adding their small orders together to make one large worthwhile shipment. The shops pay him in advance for the cost of the fish they require plus a commission to cover Andrew's costs and provide him with a profit. This is not what Andrew wants and the profits are much less but he does not need so much working capital and it suits him until he is 18 and can start importing on a large scale.

SUMMARY EXERCISE

1   What are **wages councils**? Why are some industries' wages covered by them and not others?

2   Why in some industries are **earnings** higher than **wage rates**?

3   Name one low paid occupation for which there is a long and difficult training and one highly paid job that most people could perform. Why does this situation exist?

4   Name 3 deductions which are made from **gross pay**.

5   How can trade unions influence wage rates?

6   Give one example of a fixed cost faced by an entrepreneur and one example of a variable cost.

7   As output increases do fixed costs represent an increasing or decreasing proportion of total costs?

8   What would be the likely effect on the price of coffee if bad frosts in South America damaged the coffee crops?

9 Which of the following goods might sell as many even if the price increased.

a Tomatoes
b Cigarettes
c Caviare

10 What might happen to the price of petrol if vast oil fields were discovered in Wales?

ASSIGNMENT

1 Choose one perishable good such as tomatoes. Conduct a price survey over a period of 6 months taking the price every week from the same shop. Draw a graph to show price fluctuations and explain the results.
2 Surveys of incomes show that in the UK there exist great differences in wage rates for different occupations. For example an electricity power worker earns more than twice as much as a trained nurse. With examples explain why such differences occur, and why some people think that such differences are important.
3 After 4 weeks' work we are told in their advertisment on London Weekend Television that an unskilled worker at Fords Dagenham can earn £72 per week. If you were to take such a job you would not take home £72 per week, you would take home much less. Under the following headings list what you would expect to lose and what each deduction is for:

a Taxes
b National Insurance
c Pension
d Voluntary Payments

12 Distribution

Transporting finished products to the customer from the producer is an important part of satisfying wants. It is therefore a part of the production process. People 'want' goods and services close to their homes, not 200 miles away in a factory. This last element of production is known as **distribution**.

Traditionally distribution is split into 2 steps:

1 Manufacturers deliver large loads of their one product to a **wholesaler**.
2 The wholesaler delivers consignments of many types of goods from many different manufacturers to the shops or **retailers**.

The Wholesaler

The **wholesaler** is sometimes called the middleman—he stands between the producer and retailer. At first it would seem possible and even desirable to do away with the wholesaler since as businesses in their own right they must make a profit and therefore charge more for the goods they sell to the retailer than that they pay the producer. When we consider what they do it becomes clear that the wholesaler performs a number of useful services.

THE FUNCTIONS OF THE WHOLESALER

1 Breaking bulk By taking large loads from the producer and dividing them into smaller consignments we say that the wholesaler is **breaking bulk**. This provides a service for both the producer and retailer. The producer does not want the trouble of selling many small loads and the retailer does not want the bother of contacting many producers so as to provide a choice for his customers. It also saves money since having a middleman is more efficient.

2 Warehousing Retailers have little room for storing goods—they require maximum space for selling. Producers do not wish to fill their factories with finished goods as they will take up the space needed for production. The wholesaler allows the retailer space to sell and the producer room to produce by storing goods in bulk. In doing so they take a risk. If the goods they hold go out of fashion retailers will not buy them and the wholesaler will make a loss.

3 Finance The wholesaler will often give the retailer time to pay or credit. This is particularly useful for small businesses that might need time to sell goods before paying for them. The producer needs payment immediately, however, in order to be able to pay wages and buy raw materials. The wholesaler will pay for the goods soon after delivery.

4 Specialist services Wholesalers employ expert buyers and can give expert advice. They also package items often putting them on to cards which hang in the retailer's shop. Wine wholesalers bottle and blend.

Some wholesalers like Nerdin and Peacock offer **cash and carry** services to the small retailer or caterer. They look like huge supermarkets and customers, either retailers or caterers, buy items for sale or bulk catering packs for use. They pay by **cash** and then **carry** their purchases away in their own vans. This reduces the cost since they do not have to pay delivery charges. It also gives them choice since it presents them with a range of products on show.

Large supermarket chains such as Sainsbury

or the Coop and voluntary groups like Londis must still have a wholesaling operation but they undertake this themselves thus keeping the profits within one firm or organisation. It would be incorrect to think that the wholesaling function had been removed. Such organisations will still have central depots or warehouses to which bulk orders are delivered and from where smaller multi-product deliveries are made to branches. The wholesaler as a separate business unit may well have been removed but not the function.

Retailers

Retailers or shops provide a valuable service to the customer. They are the last link in the chain of production and provide a range of goods locally thus saving the customer time and trouble as well as providing a choice of products, specialist help and advice and after sales service. Think of a consumer who wants a video recorder. By going to one shop he can look at many models, some produced in other countries. He can try them and ask an expert about the qualities of each. He can have the machine he purchases serviced and repaired at the same shop and be given advice on how best to look after it. The shop will sell him blank tapes and even sell or rent him pre-recorded ones.

CASE STUDY

'Open all hours'

Study the following 2 shop profiles and then answer the questions.

Profile 1 **Universal Stores**

OPENING HOURS

Mon	8.00—20.00
Tue	8.00—20.00
Wed	8.00—20.00
Thur	8.00—20.00
Fri	8.00—20.30
Sat	8.00—18.00
Sun	9.30—12.00

Ownership Sole proprietor—one family, Mr Reynolds, aged 40, and his wife aged 38.

Location Main road in suburban area. Opposite factory and close to railway station. A bus stop is quite close and the shop is surrounded by terraced and semi-detached housing. A new housing estate is being built opposite, next to the factory.

Type of Shop Converted front room of terraced house. Counter service but limited range of groceries, cigarettes and frozen food only. Will serve any amount of unwrapped food—even one slice of bacon.

Car parking Difficult—main road but side streets quite close.

Staff Mr Reynolds and his wife only. Very

friendly, always a laugh and joke, especially with regulars.

Prices Expensive compared with super-markets:

Five Price Survey (Feb 1984)

1 pt Homogenised milk	20½p
50 g Nescafé coffee	67p
1 kg Granulated sugar	49p
540 ml Fairy washing-up liquid	50p
Johnson Glade Air Machine	50p
Total	**£2.36½**

Profile 2 **Starbuy Supermarket Ltd**

OPENING HOURS

Mon	9.00—18.00
Tue	8.30—20.00
Wed	8.30—20.00
Thur	8.30—20.00
Fri	8.30—20.00
Sat	8.30—17.00
Sun	CLOSED

Ownership Public joint stock company—thousands of shareholders, many of whom are customers or employees. The majority of shares, however, are owned by institutions like pension funds or banks.

Location Centre of large town shopping precinct purpose built by council and Starbuy Supermarkets Ltd 7 years ago. All bus routes from neighbouring villages run to the centre. It would cost 30p each way from the bus stop outside Universal Stores.

Type of shop Modern supermarket selling all lines from groceries, fresh fruit and vegetables, toiletries, household goods, some clothes, beer, wines and spirits, cigarettes. It has a delicatessen, hot bread shop, fresh meat and wet fish counters. All self-service with trollies and baskets.

Car parking The centre has 2 multi-storey car parks with lifts to all shops. Cost 35p flat rate. (Open-air car parks surround the centre with pay and display at 25p but they are a good half mile from the shops.)

Staff Starbuy employs nearly 100 staff throughout the week—many working flexi-time. Specialist managers run the major departments—all have been trained.

Prices Much cheaper than Universal. Many 'own brand' items cheaper still. In our Five Item Survey we compared the same brands. It must be remembered that a cheaper 'own brand' often existed which we did not buy.

Five Price Survey (Feb 1984)

1 pt Homogenised milk	20p
50 g Nescafé coffee	60p
1 kg Granulated sugar	47½p
540 ml Fairy washing-up liquid	39p
Johnson Glade Air Machine	46p
Total	**£2.12½**

Exercise

1 Universal Stores are at least 10% more expensive than Starbuy on all items. If a shopper lived close to Universal, approximately how much would they need to spend to make it worthwhile travelling into the town centre if:

a they had a car and
b they did not have a car?

2 Why might a young couple, with a car, prefer to shop in Starbuy even if they plan only to spend a few pounds?

3 Why might an old age pensioner prefer to do her weekly shop at Universal.

4 What would be the likely effect on Universal's trade if the Council reduced bus fares and car parking charges?

5 Give 3 advantages Starbuy has for the customer over Universal other than price and location.

6 Give 3 advantages Universal has for the customer over Starbuy.

7 Write 2 sentences describing the typical customer at Universal.

8 Write 2 sentences describing the typical customer at Starbuy.

9 Give 2 reasons which might explain why Universal prices are higher than Starbuy.

Types of Shop

Independent, single outlet retailer Universal is an example of an independently owned shop. The owners, in this case Mr and Mrs Reynolds, only have one shop from which to sell goods. Such small establishments like Universal in our case study are to be found in residential areas where they survive by providing a service because they are convenient and open unusual hours. They can be found in villages again proving far more convenient than a long trip into town. Some small shops offer a specialist service selling unusual products and giving expert advice.

Multiple retailers Public companies like Tesco and J Sainsbury have opened hundreds of similar outlets all over the country. They have a chain of stores and are therefore often called **chain stores**. They can buy large quantities of the goods they wish to sell at lower prices. As we saw in the Tesco case study it became worthwhile for Tesco to produce its own brands—indeed Tesco Tea was the product which started Jack Cohen on the road to success.

Customers become familiar with these chain stores and stay loyal to them even when they move.

Retail cooperatives also fall into the above category (see Chapter 4).

Supermarkets Most chain stores are organised as supermarkets. This means that goods are laid out on shelves and the customers serve them-

selves. They are very large and carry many different products. Prices are kept low because they sell so much to so many customers that they can afford to make a little profit from each cus-

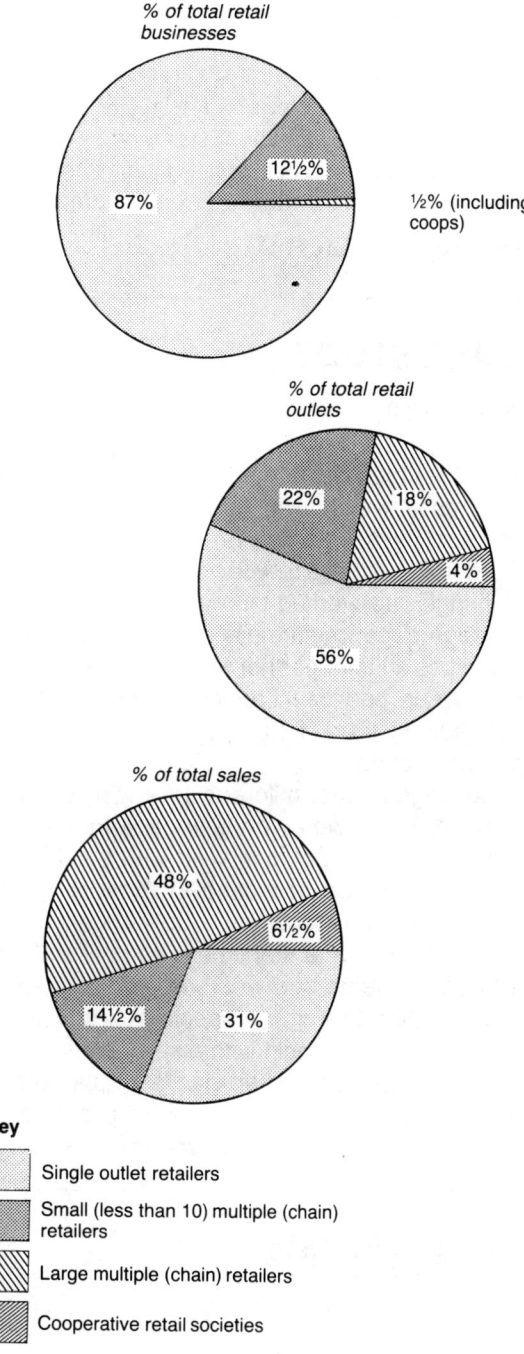

% of total retail businesses

% of total retail outlets

% of total sales

Key

Single outlet retailers

Small (less than 10) multiple (chain) retailers

Large multiple (chain) retailers

Cooperative retail societies

Retail trade in Great Britain, 1980, Annual Abstract of Statistics 1984, HMSO

tomer. Fewer staff are required since the customer does much of the work and, as we have seen, they are able to undertake their own wholesaling cutting out the middleman's profit. They also produce their own products cutting out the manufacturer's profit.

As we can see from the chart on page 159, although single outlet retailers represent a very large percentage of all businesses involved in retailing when it comes to total sales the larger chain stores have by far the largest share.

Department stores A department store is a large shop which can cater for all of a shopper's needs under one roof. The store is really several specialist shops in one. It is organised into many different departments such as electrical goods, food, mens clothing etc. Each will offer a wide range of goods and trained staff to advise and assist the customer. Within the building, which is often extremely luxurious, many services are offered. Such stores often rent out sales space to well-known chain stores, for example the Sketchley Dry Cleaning Centre in Selfridges.

CASE STUDY

Selfridges

The Selfridges department store, perhaps one of the most well-known and largest stores in London, was opened in 1909 by Mr Harry Gordon Selfridge, a 52 year old American. Gordon Selfridge had worked his way up to the top in a Chicago department store called Marshall Field. He left as a junior partner feeling that many of his best ideas had been rejected and it was on a subsequent tour of Europe that he decided to build his London store.

Selfridges was different to most shops in London. There were very few department stores and goods were not displayed with the flare that Gordon Selfridge had used in America. Conditions for the customer were better than in most shops in London at that time. The new store had 130 departments and was carpeted throughout. Mr Selfridge brought a specialist from his old American store to help with display work—it was the first time that a shop had a display department. At that time it was usual to pile as many goods as possible into the windows. Selfridges introduced such ideas as an annual sale and the bargain basement.

In order to generate custom Selfridges staged 'events' such as the exhibition of Bleriot's aeroplane; the first to fly the Channel. By the time he died at the age of 90 Gordon Selfridge had seen his Oxford Street shop more than double in size.

Today it is a landmark and institution with numerous departments and services for the customer. Some of these services includes men's and ladies' hairdressers; Lloyds Bank cashpoint and foreign exchange counter, ear-piercing, electric chavor oorvioc ocntrc, 24 hour film service, a fur store, Interflora, jewellery and watch repair, picture framing, opticians, photographer, 6 restaurants, safe deposit facilities, photocopying, key cutting, heel bar, theatre ticket booking service, formal dress hire and even an underground garage with a 'valet service'. Selfridges is now part of Sears Holdings but is run as a separate unit with its own board of directors.

Buying without Shops

It is possible to buy goods and services without going to a shop.

Mail order About 9% of all non-food retail sales is made through mail order. One family in 2 will buy something from a mail order catalogue this year. Perhaps your family has such a catalogue. People are able to choose in the comfort of their own home from a wide range of goods and order them on a special form. Goods are sent direct from a warehouse by post to the customer who can keep them and pay or return them. Often credit is available so that the customer can pay so much per week. With some firms the person who keeps the catalogue is known as the **agent** and is given a small percentage of the value of all goods sold, as a commission. With other firms there is no agent and any shopper can have the catalogue.

Door-to-door selling Some products are traditionally brought to the door by the salesman. Most milk is delivered in this way, also papers and even bread. In country areas **mobile shops**, often converted vans or coaches, travel around from village to village taking the shop to the customers. The range of goods is limited and prices high but this is a valuable service to the old and handicapped who cannot get out.

Street markets In many areas traditional street markets are held on certain days of the week. Traders rent the space from the local council by paying a small fee. This space is known as **a pitch**. Most councils will only grant a limited number of pitches in order to control the number of traders. The only other cost to the trader is the price of a cheap stall and somewhere to store his goods. Overheads—that is all of the traders' costs—are much lower for the stall holder than small shopkeeper. For this reason prices are lower in a market. Many people enjoy the hustle and bustle of a market and the fact that they can pick and choose from many stalls. It is usually difficult to try clothes on or take goods back but markets flourish in most towns.

The structure of retail trade has been changing with a movement towards more supermarkets and chain stores and away from the traditional corner shop, independently run.

As the population has become better off spending patterns have changed. More families now have cars and can travel to large shops in town centres. More women work and only have time for one visit to a large shop where they can stock up on all the families needs. Many families now have a deep-freeze which enables bulk purchases of perishables. In the future we may all visit one huge shop called a **hypermarket**. This is a shop much larger than a supermarket selling not only food and clothes but furniture and household goods all in one building along self-service lines. These are very popular in America and Europe but not so much in the UK. They are usually situated outside the town centre where land is not so expensive.

Mail order has been expanding again due to the lack of shopping time. Soon it will be possible to view goods on our own television screen and order using a small computer terminal. Perhaps this will bring about a decline in shops as we know them.

Voluntary Groups

The small independent retailer faces several problems. Being unable to buy large quantities of goods he is forced to pay much higher prices than the large supermarket chains. He must therefore charge higher prices. Being small he will have less customers and need to make more profit on each item sold. The shopper does not recognise his shop since he cannot afford to advertise on television or in the national papers.

CASE STUDY

The Londis Group

Peter White bought a small shop (500 sq ft) in the Midlands about 5 years ago. The shop had a low turnover (value of goods sold) about £350 per

week and faced stiff opposition from nearby supermarkets selling goods at lower prices.

He heard of a group of independent grocers

who in the 1960s had joined together to buy goods in bulk. They now owned their own wholesaling operation. They all called their shops **Londis** so that they could advertise together although they still owned their own shops. Today they own 4 warehouses to which goods are delivered in bulk. Members receive a price list of items in stock every week and order from the closest depot. Goods are delivered within 48 hours and the member then has 7 days to credit his account at the head office. Fresh goods, like bread, are delivered straight to the member from the producer but charged through the Londis head office so that the member is charged cheaper bulk rates.

Each fortnight 20 popular brands are cut in price and bright posters sent to members. The company also organises advertising campaigns, competitions etc to encourage shoppers to use a Londis store. Each store has the same distinctive façade which members rent. The group also produces 150 own brands which are cheaper still.

The company is run by a board elected by members the majority of whom are retailers, although experts are also employed. A member can always receive help and advice.

Peter decided to join. He had to pay a fee and sign a membership agreement but within 5 years his turnover had increased to £9 000 a week and he had been able to increase the size of his shop. Being a member of a voluntary group gave him the independence he needed to make his own decisions coupled with the lower prices of bulk buying, brand loyalty and back-up usually only found in a large chain store.

Other voluntary groups such as VG and Spar operate on slightly different lines as the group is run by the wholesaler which is not owned by members. Other than this, however, the services they offer their members are similar to Londis.

1   Why are prices higher in a shop than a market stall?
2   Give one reason why a person might prefer a department store to a market stall.
3   Name 3 services any shop performs for its customers.
4   Give 2 disadvantages of using a small independent store for the customer.
5   If small independent stores have the disadvantages stated before give 2 reasons that help explain their survival.

ASSIGNMENT

Undertake your own shopping survey. Choose about 10 common products and visit a number of different types of shop in the same week recording the prices. Construct a graph to show the differences and then write an explanation of these differences.

Transport

The UK is a trading nation, exporting approximately one third of its total output and accounting for 5–6% of total world exports. It is one of the world's largest importers of agricultural products, raw materials and semi-manufactures. To be able to accomplish this and distribute goods efficiently throughout the country a modern, quick, relatively cheap integrated transport and communications system is required.

Firms often choose a certain location because of the proximity of a certain method of transport. In the early days of industrialisation water transport was the only efficient way of moving goods.

Firms would group around canals and navigable rivers. Today the lorry is the most important method of transporting goods and firms might be tempted to locate close to a motorway.

For high bulk/weight products, like slate, transport costs can account for 80% of the price. Even for everyday items the cost of transport can be a high percentage of the final price. Transport costs for example account for one third of the price of a pint of milk!

Exercise

1   Which methods of transport were influencing factors in the choice of site for the following plants already considered elsewhere in this book?

a   Fords, Dagenham
b   Fords, Daventry
c   BP Llandarcy refinery
d   BP Baglan Bay, chemicals
e   The Marine Aquarium, Barking

2   For which of the following 2 manufacturing processes would the transport costs be more important in determining the choice of location and why:

a   aluminium smelting
b   diamond cutting

OVERSEAS TRADE

Britain is an island which means that at some point all visible imports and exports must cross the sea. Air freight is impractical for heavy and bulky cargoes such as oils, cereals, iron ore or coffee since it is so expensive. For this reason the majority of international trading is undertaken by ships.

In 1980 95% of Britain's overseas trade by weight was transported on ships but in the same year 18% of Britain's overseas trade by value was transported by air.

This difference in the relative importance of air freight is explained by the fact the air transport is only suitable for goods with a high value-to-weight ratio where speed is essential. That is goods which are expensive but fairly light. Such items are precious stones, live animals, medicines and scientific instruments which are all transported using air.

Almost 64% of all passenger traffic in 1981 to and from this country was by air (nearly all of that using shipping was on cross-channel ferries). Businessmen fly all over the world selling British products since a firm cannot afford to have top executives wasting weeks on passenger ships.

CONTAINERISATION

During the last 20 years there has been a move towards greater containerisation. This is the packing of goods into large metal containers, either at the factory or in special depots. These specially designed containers can be moved from railways, to ships to lorries without the expensive, time wasting process of unloading each individual item. Special machinery in modern railway centres and ports can handle containers quickly and cheaply.

Lorries can drive straight from a factory in Britain onto a ferry and then on into Europe without unloading or waiting (this is known as a **'roll on'** system). In recent years money has been spent increasing the specialised facilities at British ports to accommodate the move towards containerisation (see opposite). Current developments include: £32 million spent on 2 deep-water container berths at Felixstowe (1981), £12 million spent on 2 roll on berths at Dover (1980) and a £15 million scheme at Portsmouth. This has caused the total volume of container and roll on traffic to more than double in the last 10 years.

INTERNAL TRANSPORT

The majority of goods transported in this country are moved by road. The other methods of transporting goods internally are water (canals, rivers and coastal traffic), rail and pipeline. Air freight for internal distribution is limited to those which are required very quickly—such as mail. In 1982 59% of all goods were transported by road; 26% by water; 9% by rail and 6% by pipeline.

ROAD TRANSPORT

Road transport or haulage is the most important

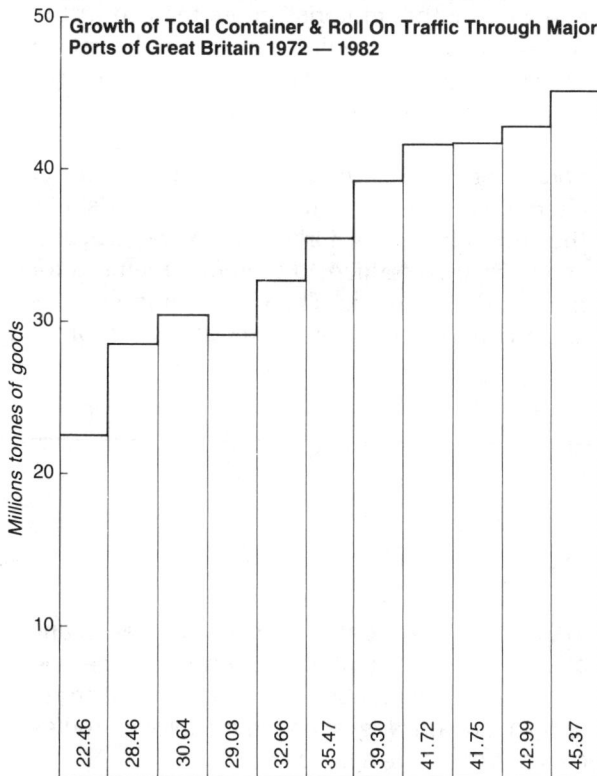

Growth of Total Container & Roll On Traffic Through Major Ports of Great Britain 1972 — 1982

Millions tonnes of goods

Year	1972	1973	1974	1975	1976	1977	1978	1979	1980	1981	1982
	22.46	28.46	30.64	29.08	32.66	35.47	39.30	41.72	41.75	42.99	45.37

Source: British Transport Statistics 1972–1982, HMSO

method for the internal movement of goods. If only weight and not a measure of weight/distance is used then 8 out of every 10 tonnes of freight is carried by road. This form of transport is more important for some industries rather than others. For example 99.7% of all food, drink and tobacco and 96.3% of all building materials and aggregates were moved by road in 1980. The road network links every village, town and city and for certain journeys, particularly short journeys, road transport is the only practical method

of moving goods. Over 60% of all lorry traffic in 1981 was over 50 kilometres (31 miles) or less.

For longer journeys road haulage can remove the need for expensive and time consuming unloading and reloading since the lorry can deliver from factory to customer direct.

The modern motorway network has increased the efficiency of road transport reducing costly delays. Gradually restrictions have been eased allowing larger more efficient lorries onto British roads. The larger lorries reduce the operating costs per tonne mile (the cost to move one tonne of goods one mile):

	Operating cost pence per mile	Operating cost pence per tonne mile
21.5 tonne lorry	81.0	3.77
27.5 tonne lorry	94.6	3.44

Today over 67% of traffic is carried in lorries of over 28 tonnes gross laden weight.

Lorries have several other advantages over rail traffic. They do not have to run to predetermined timetables and small vans can move small loads. Specially designed lorries can move many different types of goods.

The industry is privately owned. In 1981 there were 127 700 registered road haulage operators many of them one-man outfits with low overheads. Certainly it is therefore a highly competitive industry which helps to keep costs down. It has been stated that road haulage operators can charge lower prices because they do not have to bear the true costs in full of transporting goods by road. It is argued that although a road haulage operator has to pay for the lorry, petrol (which carries a high level of tax, see Chapter 14), and a licence this does not cover all of the costs. Some costs are paid by other tax payers, such as the costs of building and repairing roads. Other costs are born by society—social costs such as pollution and congestion, police and ambulance services.

The opposite view is held by the Road Haulage Association. In 1983/4 the total tax paid by the motor industry and motorist came to £10 175 million and it was estimated that the total road costs—construction and maintenance—was £2 990 million. It must be remembered that the majority of road users are private motorists (in 1981 of 277 700 vehicle–kilometres, cars and taxis accounted for 81%)—and therefore although it may be true that motorists more than cover the costs of road construction it might not be true to say that road haulage firms do. Also this does not take into account other social costs.

Many people are concerned at the growing volume of motor traffic and the gradual decline of alternative forms of transport. Better roads, like the new M25 London Orbital motorway, encourage more road traffic and therefore the need for more and more roads. This can become a vicious circle at the expense of rail and water transport.

CASE STUDY EXERCISE

'Ban the juggernauts?'

Each night over one quarter of a million Londoners are subjected to the almost constant noise of heavy lorries. Lorries deliver to the markets and shops of London and others cross through London on their way to the channel ports. The M25 London Orbital motorway is under construction to ease the problem. As the map opposite shows the M25 produces a much longer route than the old A roads. During the day many operators would probably choose to use the motorway to avoid costly delay and congestion but at night and on weekends the old through routes prove an attractive alternative.

In October 1981 the GLC appointed a panel of inquiry to investigate the social, economic and environmental effects of a ban on heavy lorries

Proposed night time and weekend ban on heavy lorries

Area of ban

- - - - Routes to be excluded from ban

in London. On 31 January 1986, after consultations with all interested parties, the following scheme came into operation:

The scheme

1 Lorries over 16.5 tonnes are banned from using most routes in London from 9 pm to 7 am on weekdays, after 1 pm on Saturdays and all day on Sundays.
2 Operators who can show a genuine need to use vehicles during the ban can apply for

exemption, providing they reduce noise (i.e. fit 'hush kit', better driver training).

3 Exempted lorries must display special plates. Lorries ignoring the ban risk a £400 fine.
4 Some roads, with little or no housing, leading to industrial areas are excluded from the ban. (See map.)

Benefits from the Ban

- Less disturbance to Londoners' sleep
- Reduction in vibration/physical damage to houses and roads

- Reduction in accidents and congestion at weekends—Londoners' more willing to use roads and facilities

Costs Resulting from Ban
- Operation costs would increase, and perhaps prices
- Firms might close or move from London—unemployment
- Companies could introduce smaller lorries—more congestion

Exercise

Suppose you live in London during the GLC consultation period. Using the evidence given in the 'Information sheet' below write a report to the GLC stating why you are in favour or against the lorry ban. (The GLC no longer exists but the ban is operated by the London Residuary Body for the time being until one London Borough takes over.)

Now answer these questions:

1 Give one of the social costs caused by heavy lorries using London roads at night.

2 The GLC ban excluded lorries fitted with 'hush kits'. These modifications have been available for some time. Why do most lorry operators not use these already?

3 It is stated that the lorry ban increases lorry operating costs. Give 2 reasons why operating costs have been increased by the ban.

4 The GLC estimated that it cost £700 000 for road signs and publicity alone to implement the ban. Who paid to implement the ban? Give one alternative way in which this money could be spent to reduce the social costs of heavy lorries using London roads. Why is this not suggested?

5 If costs increase, as predicted due to the ban, who will pay in the long-run?

6 If firms move out of London because of the ban some unemployment will result. Name one industry where the ban might *increase* employment.

INFORMATION SHEET

- A ban on heavy lorries could reduce traffic noise by up to one third. Heavy lorries over $16\frac{1}{2}$ tonnes are up to 22% noisier than those of $7\frac{1}{2}$ tonnes at speeds below 30 km per hour.

- An opinion poll conducted in London found that 83% of those questioned felt that heavy lorries were a major problem on London roads. In 1979 a 20 000 signature petition calling for a ban on heavy lorries was received by the GLC.

- Studies in Sweden have shown that lorry noise causes sleep disturbance and poor mental and physical recuperation. Young children in noise affected kindergartens, for example, were found to take on average 4 times as long to fall asleep and remained asleep for less time than those in quiet kindergartens.

- A survey in 1981 found that 29% of all lorries using London roads at night were over $16\frac{1}{2}$ tonnes and that 37% of these were making through journeys.

- Heavy goods vehicles are cheaper. Unit costs (the cost of transporting each item) are 45% higher using a 16 tonne lorry rather than a $32\frac{1}{2}$ tonne lorry and 175% higher using a $7\frac{1}{2}$ tonne lorry rather than a $32\frac{1}{2}$ tonne lorry.

- If firms are forced to use smaller lorries it could lead to as many as $2\frac{1}{2}$ times more lorries on London roads.

- Lorries that travel at night could be rescheduled to run during the day.

- 'Fifty Five' representative firms were asked how the proposed ban would affect their business. These were the answers given:

close down	1
move depots	15
buy smaller lorries	13
reschedule to day-time operation	15
reschedule and buy smaller lorries	4
not affected	7
Total	**55**

- A large supermarket chain estimates that the cost of operating smaller lorries and moving depots would add $7\frac{1}{2}$ pence in every pound to food prices.

RAIL TRANSPORT

Railways, as a means for moving freight, suffer from several disadvantages; particularly in a country as small as the UK. The service is forced to run to predetermined schedules on fixed routes. In the majority of cases lorries must be used to transport the goods from a rail terminal to a customer which, for short journeys, would make the use of rail pointless. Where customers have their own rail terminal (grants of up to 50% exist for firms to construct or modernise their own rail terminals) at least one lorry journey is eliminated. A firm, such as Fords, makes use of specially designed rolling stock to deliver cars manufactured in Dagenham to 7 points throughout the country from where they are taken to the customer.

The majority of rail freight is confined to 4 major products. All are bulky items and moved on special trains which carry just one type of good. Coal and coke are moved by rail from mines to power stations and are by far the most important product moved. It is interesting to note that three quarters of British Rail's freight is produced by other nationalised industries.

British Rail has recently introduced a new 'Speedlink' high speed freight service using larger wagons which are capable of higher speeds. This accounts for the drop in the number of freight wagons over the last few years.

Total freight carried for 1981 was 154 million tonnes. Coal and coke formed 62% of this figure; iron and steel formed 12%; earth and stones 8%; petroleum products 8%; and various other freight 10%.

Railway Statistics 1976—81

	1976	1981	% reduction 1976–81
Freight train traffic (millions tonnes)	176	154	12½
Freight train traffic (million net tonne miles)	12 794	10 877	15
Freight vehicles	187 000	87 955	53
Route miles open	11 189	10 831	3

Source   *Adapted from Britain: An Official Handbook, HMSO 1983*

Further time and costs have been saved by the introduction of a computer-based total operations processing system which monitors all consignments and has led to a more efficient use of rolling stock. This has led also to the scrapping of obsolete wagons.

The overall decline of the rail network is part of a continuing trend started in the early 1960s when the then Chairman of British Rail, Dr Beeching, produced a report which called for the drastic reduction in the number of route miles, stations and staff to make British Rail more profitable. Today it is an essential and integrated part of the internal transport system. Container trains link with major ports and heavy goods are moved long distances reasonably efficiently. The problem lies in the very high capital outlays necessary for modernisation. (Extending electrification to Ipswich, Norwich and Harwich cost £30 million.) Also the commuter passenger services need vast capital outlay but often lie idle for most of the day.

WATER TRANSPORT AND PIPELINES

Pipelines offer a very special form of transport for liquids and gases. Clearly a pipeline will cost a great deal of money to lay and can only be used for one product. Once down it proves an extremely efficient method of transport which has become very important with the discovery of North Sea oil and gas.

There has also been a revival in interest in inland waterways, mainly for recreation. Their advantage is the reduction in costs due to greater efficiency in the use of fuel. Canals are slow however and many of the older canals have fallen into disrepair. There are just under 1 000 miles of canals and rivers open to commercial freight carrying vessels with some improvements being made in the Rotherham area. Inland and coastal shipping accounted for 26% of internal freight movements in 1982, the vast majority of this (88%) being oil or petroleum products which were shipped around the coast from, or to, refineries. Inland waterways have a long way to go before they either recapture their early 19th Century predominance or equal the importance of such transport in the rest of Europe.

Exercise

1 Name 2 products which would be suitable for transport by air and state why. Why would it be impractical to transport a greater proportion of internal freight by air?
2 Give 2 facts which demonstrate economies of scale when applied to road transport.
3 Which **social costs** are not taken into account by road haulage operators? How could they be?
4 Why are railways more expensive to operate than roads?
5 Which group of workers would not benefit from containerisation?

Advertising

Most goods are advertised in one or more of a variety of ways. The aim of advertising is to both inform potential customers that a certain product is available and to persuade them to buy it. Advertising is not cheap—in 1981 it cost industry £2 880 million (or 1.4% of total output). A producer spends money on advertising to increase sales of his product and to make larger profits for the company.

Some advertisements are purely **informative**—they present only the basic facts about a product that is for sale and do not attempt to encourage people to buy it. In your local paper, for example, you may find a *Small Ads* section where people inform others that they have items for sale.

Most advertisements are tempting people into trying a product. We call this **persuasive advertising**. This can be done in many ways.

Sexy advertisements Many advertisements either feature physically attractive men and women or show a person who uses a certain product being attractive to the opposite sex.

Scientific advertisements Some advertisements concentrate upon the scientific advances made by the product, such as motor car manufacturers who might stress the petrol consumption figures or margarine makers who might stress market research findings.

Worrying advertisements Some advertisements ask worrying questions. Do my feet smell. Are my clothes as clean as they could be? By playing on our fears they cause us to change our buying habits.

Funny advertisements Radio and television advertisements are today often very humourous—you probably have your favourite. We remember the name of the product because we enjoy the advertisement.

Life-style advertisements Many advertisements show the product being used in a perfect setting. The implication is that the model modern home is not complete without that product.

Dream-world advertisements These present a fantasy world, perhaps of pink clouds or knights in shining armour well removed from reality.

Now try the assignment opposite.

ADVERTISING COSTS

In 1981 the Advertising Association estimated that £2 880 million was spent on advertising.

This was divided as follows:

Press	65%
Television	29%
Posters	4%
Radio	2%

The advertising industry (including those in market research) employs about 37 000 people.

The costs of the various methods of adver-

ASSIGNMENT

Collect advertisements from magazines which illustrate each of these methods of persuading consumers to buy. For each state which type it is and why you think it is or is not a good advertisement. When next you are watching commercial television or listening to commercial radio list all of the advertisements in one hour and for each say which type it is and why you think that it is or is not a good advertisement.

Which form of advertising is used here?

tising differ widely. The costs for an average television commercial are shown here:

North West Region, Saturday 1983

Time	Cost of 30 sec	Approximate number of homes viewing in '000's
ITV		
11.00–12.14	£980	147–203
12.50–16.01	£1 150	157–212
16.19–17.01	£2 600	231
17.23–22.17	£10 000	517–840
22.44–23.19	£2 920	471–821
23.43–00.28	£2 600	92–147
Channel 4		
14.49–01.41	£2 400	0–101

Advertising on radio is considerably cheaper as you can see:

LBC News Radio (Rates from 23 April 1984)

Time	Cost of 30 sec
Monday–Friday	
07.00–09.00	£545
06.30–12.00	£435
16.00–18.30	£215
06.00–06.30	
12.00–18.30	£172
21.00–24.00	£126
18.30–21.00	
00.00–01.00	£50
01.00–06.00	£8

Packages of different times and discounts for a run of several weeks are also offered.

National newspapers also prove expensive, yet do reach a very wide audience:

	Costs for unspecified whole page Spring 1984	Circulation (millions) 1982
Daily Mail	£13 100	1.9
Daily Star	£8 800	1.4
Daily Express	£15 300	2.1

There are many different methods of advertising. The most popular methods appear to be newspapers, magazines and of course the television.

Exercise

1 List 4 further ways goods are commonly promoted.
2 Why is it cheaper to advertise on television on ITV at 11.00 hrs than at 20.00 hrs?
3 Why is it cheaper to advertise on Channel 4 at 20.00 hrs than ITV at the same time on a Saturday night?
4 Why is it cheaper to advertise on commercial radio during the evening when it becomes more expensive to advertise on commercial television? What could change this?
5 Why is a full page advertisement more expensive in the Daily Mail than the Daily Star when the size and cost of printing would be the same?

THE ADVERTISING CAMPAIGN

Most companies do not undertake their own advertising. They employ the specialist services of an advertising agency. These agencies, for a fee, will put together an advertising campaign for a customer. The agency may well undertake market research to discover what customers attitudes are to a product and help to design an effective campaign. They will decide upon which types of advertisements to use and produce TV commercials, magazine advertisements etc. A company can either leave the whole exercise in the hands of the experts or retain some control.

ASSIGNMENT

You work for an advertising agency. One of your clients manufactures high quality fountain pens but their sales have been falling steadily over the years.

Your own market research shows that most people find fountain pens a bother to keep filling up and more likely to make a mess *but* readily concede that their own handwriting is better when they use a proper pen. The firm has limited funds but is prepared to make one last attempt to increase sales through an advertising campaign.

Your task is to:

a Think of a new name for the pens which retail for £15.
b Devise an original theme for an advertising campaign.
c Design posters and TV commercials deciding what type of advertising you will use.
d Decide which age group to sell to and when and where you will advertise.

CONTROL OF ADVERTISING

Advertising is controlled in 2 ways in this country. First, there are a number of laws which prevent certain types of advertising. It is, for example illegal under the **1968 Trade Descrip-**

tion Act for false claims to be made in an advertisement. This same act made it an offence for a trader to put false price reductions on items. If a price has been crossed out and a lower one written over it the original higher price must have been charged for that good in that shop for at least 28 consecutive days in the previous 6 months.

The advertising industry also enforces its own **Code of Practice** through 2 watch-dog organisations: **The Advertising Standards Authority** (ASA) which looks at all non-broadcast advertising (press, posters etc) and the **Independent Broadcasting Authority** (IBA) which watches television and radio advertising.

The ASA has a Council whose chairperson (and at least half of its members) has nothing to do with the advertising industry. This body tries to ensure that all advertisements are in line with the industry's own agreed codes of practice: **The British Code of Advertising Practice** and the **British Code of Sales and Promotion Practice**. These codes state that advertisements should be legal, decent, honest and truthful. They have specific rules about the running of competitions, the use of children and the advertising of medicinal and health products for example. If members of the public complain to the ASA they will investigate the complaint and publish their findings in a monthly case reports or even stop the advertisement from being published.

The IBA enforces the IBA **Code of Advertising Standards and Practice**. This states that all television and radio advertisements should be accurate and not misleading. It also has many other specific regulations. All advertisements are studied before they can appear on television. Members of the public are invited to write and complain if they find advertisements misleading or offensive. You may have seen their advertisements in the *TV Times*!

CASE STUDY

'I see no ships'

Kevin saw advertised a holiday break at an hotel in the South West. The advertisement said the hotel was 5 minutes from the sea and that you could see the sea from the bedrooms. Having 2 small children he thought this looked fine and booked up for a week.

When he arrived he was disappointed to discover that the hotel was in fact 5 miles from the sea and although you could just about see the sea from the bedroom it took a good half hour to walk to the beach—and much longer to walk back as it was all up hill! He complained to the Manager of the hotel who said that it must have been a misprint and that they meant 5 miles not 5 minutes.

When he returned home Kevin wrote to the Advertising Standards Authority who investigated the complaint. They wrote to the agency who had been responsible for the advertisement and gave them a reasonable time to investigate. The agency replied that the advertisement was not misleading since the hotel was only 5 minutes from the beach—if you used a car or the local bus.

Exercise

1   Do you think that Kevin was misled by the advertisement?
2   Do you think that Kevin should be compensated and if so by whom?
3   How should the ASA deal with the agency?

In 1981 the ASA had a budget of £800 000 and 38 staff. Some people were not happy with their findings. Three nurses objected to an advertisement which appeared in the *Nursing Mirror* which showed a nurse being seduced under the heading 'Are you willing to be seduced?'. The nurses felt it showed women in a degrading light. The ASA found:

'Although the advertisement was not considered likely to cause grave or widespread offence, the Authority none the less deprecated the copy approach which they considered to be in bad taste and demeaning to the nursing profession.'

The ASA did not call for the withdrawal of the advertisement. It is much easier to prove that an advertisement is inaccurate than degrading to women. For this reason some people feel that the rules should be altered.

ADVANTAGES AND DISADVANTAGES OF ADVERTISING

Advantages

Informs public about the range of products on sale Without it how would consumers know what was available or good value?

Helps consumers make rational choices By providing information about products the consumer knows what is a good buy for them.

Advertising money helps to finance newspapers, radio and television ITV and Channel 4, commercial radio, local and national newspapers all depend upon advertising revenue. Without advertising there would not be the range of entertainment and news media.

Supports sporting events Most sporting events are sponsored by firms who want the advertising this gives them. Football players wear slogans on their shirts and the cups and trophies bear the names of their sponsors—Milk Cup, Canon League. Without advertising many sports would not take place at all.

Advertising increases sales This might keep firms in business and therefore keep jobs for the workers. Advertising also helps to increase profits. If increased sales mean companies can enjoy economies of scale it might even reduce prices.

Disadvantages

Could cause people to buy things they do not really want Weak minded people and children might find they are tempted into purchasing an item they did not want.

Advertising can spoil the environment Large posters can offend people who would rather look at the countryside.

Expensive and puts up prices In some industries millions of pounds are spent by a few firms competing for the same market.

Can cause dissatisfaction Advertising paints a perfect picture of the world, people begin to believe that this is how real life ought to be and become dissatisfied with their life.

Advertising creates 'media stereotypes' which could influence attitudes Many people complain that women are usually shown merely as sex objects in advertising. This builds up a stereotype image of women which could affect the way the next generation thinks of them.

Consumer Protection

In this country the consumer is protected by a number of laws which prevent the retailer taking advantage of him or selling faulty or dangerous goods.

The laws are divided into 2 types. **The civil laws** which gives the customer the right to take a trader to court if he has an individual grievance against the trader and the **criminal laws** which protects the general public from unsafe goods. The table opposite shows the main consumer laws.

Perhaps the most quoted is **The Sale of Goods Act** which gives the consumer far reaching rights when buying goods from a shop. In most cases if a good is not 'of merchantable quality' or fit for the purpose described or as described the trader will exchange the faulty good or give the customer back his money. If he does not the consumer would have to take him to court since he has not broken a criminal law and the customer has only civil law rights. Taking a trader to court has, however, become very much easier. For large amounts (over £5 000) it would still be necessary to seek the advice of a solicitor which may be very expensive (although there is a system of legal aid). For small amounts the case

Law	Goods/rights covered	Example	Enforcement
Sale of Goods Act 1893 and 1979	Trader must ensure: • goods of merchantable quality—fit for normal purpose • goods fit for any purpose made known to trader • goods must be as described	Handle should not fall off new kettle If you ask 'does this glue stick plastic' and are told yes then it should A sheet described as double should fit a 4' 6" bed	If goods are returned to seller then they must be replaced or money refunded. Consumer has rights under civil law therefore and would have to take trader to court if not satisfied
Consumer Safety Act 1978	Enables Secretary of State to require that certain goods are labelled with warnings, or to ban very dangerous goods	A child's toy that proves to be dangerous can be banned	It is a criminal offence to sell goods which do not comply with regulations
Food and Drug Act 1955	Food must be fit for human consumption and sold under hygienic conditions. Many specific regulations	Shop assistants must be able to wash their hands when serving fresh food	It is a criminal offence to sell goods which do not comply with regulations
Trade Descriptions Acts 1968/1972	Must not describe goods falsely	Turn back a clock on a car and say it has a low mileage	This is a criminal offence
Unsolicited Goods Act 1972	Trader cannot ask for payment for goods delivered but not ordered	Carbon paper sent to firms and then an invoice	This is a criminal offence. If goods are not collected within 6 months they become the property of the recipient—a gift
Weights and Measures Act 1963/1979	It is an offence not to mark weight or quantity on packaged groceries	Unmarked box of sweets	This is a criminal offence

would be dealt with by the **Small Claims Court**, which is a division of the County Court. For amounts of less than £500 this is usually done by **arbitration**, that is an informal discussion between customer and trader in front of an arbitrator appointed by the court. Costs are very low. Although cases involving larger amounts might be heard in a full court session the proceedings are explained to the consumer and they would not need a solicitor.

The other laws—those which affect the health and safety of us all—are criminal laws and are enforced for us by the local authority. **The Trading Standards Office** (in some local authorities known as the **Consumer Protection** or **Weights and Measures Department**) will make sure that retailers in a local area are not breaking **Trade Descriptions** and **Weights and Measures Acts**. This will involve regular inspections and following-up complaints. They are also responsible for enforcing some of the food laws such as correct labelling. Some local authorities have **Consumer Advice Centres** either as part of the town hall or even in high street shopping centres. Here consumers can receive help and advice on a whole range of shopping matters in some areas. The local authority may even run a mobile advice centre from a converted van. **The Environmental Health Department** will be responsible for all health aspects of food sales as well as the cleanliness of such places as hairdressing salons.

Consumers not lucky enough to have an advice centre can use the **Citizens Advice Bureaux**. These are independent advice centres and there are some 900 throughout the country. They will give advice on far more than just consumer affairs.

Many manufacturers and retailers belong to **Employers' Associations** as we saw in Chapter 6. Some of these have their own Codes of Practice. For example, Association of British Travel Agents (ABTA) have codes of practice covering overbooking, cancellations and package holidays. They operate a fund into which all members contribute so that if a company which is a member fails then the customer is compensated. Remember also that in Chapter 3 (public services) **consumer consultative councils** were also mentioned.

BUYING GOODS UNDER SPECIAL CIRCUMSTANCES

Most shops will refund money if they sell faulty goods, but what about secondhand goods and auctions? Here is a summary of your rights:

Secondhand goods Sale of Goods Act rights still apply but the right to compensation will depend upon the price paid and its description. You cannot expect a secondhand car to be perfect, but if it is sold as in good condition the purchaser would not expect the engine to drop out after 2 miles.

Auctions Unlike other traders an auctioneer can disclaim Sale of Goods Act responsibilities if there is a notice in the catalogue or in the sale room. A court might think that this is unreasonable but also might not. Most auctions have a preview and it is best to examine goods carefully.

Buying privately The Sale of Goods Act covers only traders not private individuals. A private person cannot lie to a potential buyer however, the item must be as described. If it is not then the purchaser could sue the seller for misrepresentation. For this reason when buying large items, like a motorbike, it is best to take a friend who can act as a witness.

Sales Goods bought in Sales must conform to the rules laid down in the Sale of Goods Act. A notice saying 'No refund on sale goods' is illegal.

ORGANISATIONS WHICH HELP THE CONSUMER

1 National Consumer Council

Established in 1975, an independent body, financed by the Government, to:

- persuade the Government to introduce policies to help the consumer
- influence businesses to meet the needs of consumers more efficiently
- induce public services to be responsive to the needs of the consumer and give better value for money

With a small staff of 30 the NCC carries out research and presents reports and publishes leaflets.

2 The Consumers' Association

Publishes *Which* magazine which contains reports on hundreds of household goods tested in laboratories so that consumers can make better choices.

3 The British Standards Institute

Government backed organisation which awards a kite mark to products which comply to the specifications laid down by the institute (see opposite). Products of a very wide range are covered by the standards and companies wishing to display the kite mark must allow the institute to sample and test their products.

Exercise

Your neighbour uses a glue to stick a broken handle back on to a china cup. The glue has been recommended by the owner of a do-it-yourself shop as being perfect for this job. The first time that this cup is used after the handle has been stuck on it falls off again.

BSI and labels

LABEL	NAME OF LABEL	WHAT DOES IT SHOW?	EXAMPLES OF WHERE IT CAN BE SEEN
BS 1970	BS 1970 is the number of the British Standard. This standard is for hot water bottles, describing the materials and construction.	Manufacturers' claim that this article meets the standard.	Knitting wool labels, white spirit bottles, manhole covers, lamp posts, plugs and sockets, car number plates.
BS 4040 BS 4040 BS 4040 BS 4040	Stars for petrol classification.	One of four grades of petrol.	Petrol pumps. Car owners' handbooks show or refer to the recommended star grade to use.
BS 857	Kitemark BS 857 is one of two standards, for safety glass, often seen on car and train windows.	BSI has checked the manufacturer's claim that the product complies in every way with the standard quoted.	Kitemarked consumer goods include pushchairs, fireguards, cots, climbers' helmets, pressure cookers, etc. Most Kitemarked goods are used in industry e.g. steel plate sheets.
(Safety Mark symbol)	Mark for safety standards. 'Safety Mark.'	A product has been checked to British Standard specifications for safety.	Domestic gas equipment (cookers, fires, boilers for central heating), electrical luminaires, floodlights etc.
BEAB-Mark of Safety PRODUCED TO BS 3456	Mark of the British Electrotechnical Approvals Board for household electrical equipment.	Samples of electrical appliances are tested on behalf of BEAB for compliance to the standard. BS 3456 covers electrical safety and includes the factor of durability as a safety feature.	On the majority of household electric goods: kettles, clocks, hair dryers etc. It is also used with BS 415 on televisions, stereo equipment etc.
(Double insulation symbol)	Double insulation mark.	An appliance has double insulation and/or reinforced insulation thoughout. There is no provision for earthing.	On some household electrical appliances e.g. shavers, hair dryers, vacuum cleaners and table lamps.
OAMA Mark	Symbol showing Oil Appliance Manufacturers' Association sign and the Kitemark. The Association and BSI together drew up BS 3300.	Paraffin heaters on which it is found meet the strict requirements of BS 3300. This means they are draught resistant, will not emit dangerous fumes and the flame will go out if the heater is accidentally knocked over.	Paraffin heaters (usually found on the inside panel).
PARAFFIN (wavy lines symbol) BS 2869C1	Paraffin symbol.	This fuel is class C1 fuel which gives efficiency and clean burning in an appliance. It is recommended for use in paraffin (flueless) heaters in the home.	Shops and distributors selling paraffin or kerosene.

PP571A/8110/20k/B

1   What are your neighbour's 'rights' under the **Sale of Goods Act?**
2   What additional rights does this act give her? For each give an example of where it would apply.
3   Your neighbour, acting on your advice, returns the glue to the shop and demands her money back. The owner of the shop refuses to give her back the money because she has opened the glue. Where could she go for additional advice and how could the law help her get back the money?

What would be your rights if you bought goods which were faulty:

a   at an auction
b   secondhand from a shop
c   in a sale
d   from a friend?

SUMMARY EXERCISE

1   Wholesalers buy goods from producers at a lower price than they charge the retailers they sell them to. Give 4 services provided by wholesalers in return for these higher prices.
2   Give 2 industries where there are no wholesalers. (In other words the producer has a distribution network and supplies retail outlets.)
3   The majority of goods are transported by road. Give 3 advantages of road over rail.
4   What is meant by **containerisation** with reference to transport?
5   Retail trade has changed over the last 25 years with small independent shops becoming less important and multiple chain stores more important. Give 2 reasons for this change.
6   Think of a country where there would be little or no advertising and explain why this is true.
7   Name 2 ways in which the consumer benefits from advertising.
8   Name 2 ways in which the consumer suffers from advertising.
9   In what ways does an organisation like the Consumers' Association help to protect the consumer?
10   What advantage is there for a tourist to book a holiday through a travel agency which is a member of ABTA?

ASSIGNMENT

1   *a*   Show the difference with examples, between **informative** and **persuasive** advertising.
    b   Why do firms advertise?
    c   Describe in detail 2 advantages and 2 disadvantages of advertising.

2   Explain how changes in 'costs' have influenced the forms of transport used to move goods internally in this country over the last 20 years. Do the costs looked at by the entrepreneur include social costs?

3   Some people argue that a wholesaler only serves to increase prices. Explain the services undertaken by the wholesaler and their importance to the small shopkeeper.

4   In a supermarket the shopper undertakes much of the work including weighing and packing fresh vegetables, pushing and unloading the trolley and reaching up to the high shelves. Given the truth of the statement above explain why supermarkets are growing in popularity. Are there some types of good which will never be sold in supermarkets? If so, give examples and explain why this is so.

13 The Individual and Money

Saving

CASE STUDY

Who saves most?

Profile 1

George and Hilary aged 30—one child. George is the only wage earner. He is a civil servant.

Monthly Budget	
Income:	£
Take-home pay	600.00
Child benefit	26.00
Interest (savings)	24.00
Total	650.00
Expenses:	£
Mortgage	90.00
Standing orders at bank (rates, insurance)	100.00
Cash payments (food, petrol)	250.00
Cheques (electricity, phone)	145.00
Total	585.00

Profile 2

Susan aged 20 lives at home, is unmarried and a hairdresser.

Weekly Budget	
Income:	£
Take-home pay	65.00
Expenses:	£
Rent to mum	15.00
Entertainment	10.00
Clothes	15.00
Food (mid-day)	6.00
Total	56.00

In each of these profiles the income is in excess of the expenditure. This means that both George and Hilary and Susan can save part of their incomes.

Exercise

1 How much can George and Hilary save per month?
2 What percentage of their total income would this saving represent for George and Hilary?
3 How much can Susan save per week?
4 What percentage of her total weekly income would this saving represent for Susan.

5 List 4 things George and Hilary might be saving up for.
6 Can you think of any other reason George and Hilary might have for saving?
7 List 4 things that Susan might be saving up for.
8 Can you think of any other reason Susan might have for saving?
9 If Hilary were to take a part-time job what might happen to her family's savings and expenses?

10 Susan decides that her life is dull and decides to take up horse riding. This costs £9 per week. How might an economist describe the opportunity cost of Susan saving £9 per week.

REASONS FOR SAVING

Saving is therefore that part of current income which is not spent on consumption. Individuals and companies (both in the private and public sectors) can and do save. In order to save, people or firms must give up some spending.

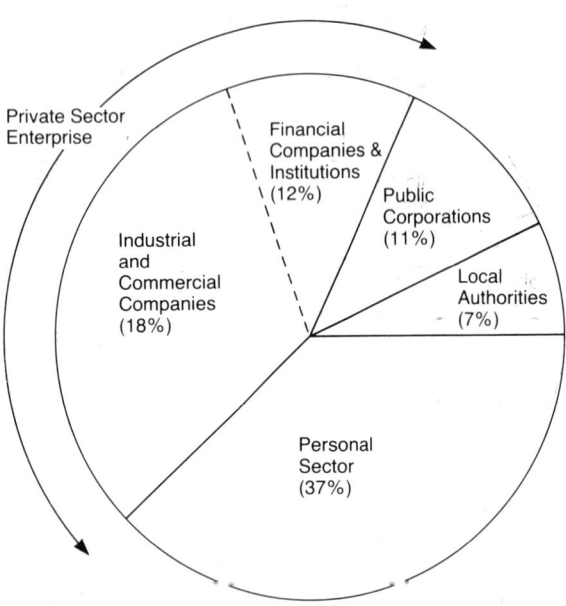

Total savings in 1982 amounted to some £54.3 thousand million. Central Government had no surplus, or savings, and was £3.4 thousand million in deficit.

Saving in the UK 1983, Financial Statistics, March 1983 HMSO

People save for many different reasons.

Luxury items   Families save up for those expensive items which they cannot buy out of their normal wage. For example, people save in order to buy a new car or take a foreign holiday.

Emergency funds   Most families like to have a sum of money available in case of an unexpected financial problem. For example, their car might suddenly develop trouble needing major repair

work. The wage earner might lose his or her job or, on a happier note, an elder daughter might decide to get married. Some financial experts feel that the average family ought to have about £2 500–£3 000 in such a fund which for most families would mean all of their savings.

Saving by mistake   A family with a high income might simply not spend all of their income. Saving does not take place intentionally but funds tend to build up. This could happen with a middle-aged couple, both in paid employment, whose children have grown up and left home. It would be a good opportunity to save for old age when income inevitably falls.

Companies save by not distributing all of their profits to the shareholders. This retained profit is a form of saving and can be used to finance large capital expenditure, such as a new plant, or to pay tax liabilities in the future or even to pay for the unexpected (contingency reserves).

People with high incomes will be able to save more than those with low incomes. A company making a high profit in any one year will be able to retain or save a larger amount than a company making a small profit. The size of income is therefore one of the most important factors in determining the level of saving in the society.

In Chapter 1 it was shown that income flows in a circle between producers and consumers, business and households. Wealth, created by business is paid to households as wages—the reward to human resources, rent—the reward to natural resources and profit—the reward to enterprise. Most of this income is spent by households on goods and services but as we now know not all of it since some is **saved**. Much of this saving takes place in financial institutions like banks. These financial institutions lend this saved part of national income to both households and businesses who need extra income for consumption or investment.

Government too is able to borrow from financial institutions and directly from households and spends such borrowed funds on the provision of public and merit goods. People who do not want to spend all of their share of income at the present time are able to have this spending power rerouted, via the financial institutions, to those who do want to use this spending power now. Of course, those who save can be paid for giving up this present consumption. They can receive **interest**—an agreed percentage of the sum saved every year is added to this amount saved if it takes place with an institution in a special type of account. Those who borrow must pay interest for the privilege of using someone else's spending power.

If unwanted cash were to be saved under the bed then the owner would not receive interest. Most people who save, however, do put the money in a financial institution and receive interest (see table below).

WHERE TO SAVE

The **rate of interest** was mentioned earlier as the reward for saving. The rate of interest is not the same for all institutions or for all forms of saving. It varies considerably even on the same day. A person could receive between 3% and $11\frac{1}{2}$% on the same day in the same institution for different forms of saving.

If a person wants to take out their savings from the institution (make a **withdrawal**) whenever they choose they will receive a lower rate of interest than if they are prepared to leave their savings for up to 5 years. This is because the institution wishes to lend these savings to

Where to save

	Interest	Interest paid	Tax	£ min	Withdrawal
Banks					
Deposit	5.5	$\frac{1}{2}$ yrly	Paid	1	7 days
Savings	7.5–8.5	$\frac{1}{2}$ yrly	Paid	10/month	7 days
Lump sum					
3 months	8.25	yrly	Paid	2–5 000	Fixed term
Building Society					
Deposit	7	$\frac{1}{2}$ yrly	Paid	—	Demand
Share	7.25	$\frac{1}{2}$ yrly	Paid	1	Demand
Subscription	8.25	$\frac{1}{2}$ yrly	Paid	100	1–5 yrs
Post Office					
National Savings Bank					
Ordinary a/c	3	yrly	1st 70 free	1	£100 on demand
Ordinary a/c (if kept 1 calendar yr from 1st Jan)	6	yrly	1st 70 free	500	£100 on demand
Investment a/c	11	yrly	To pay	1	1 month
Monthly income bond	11.5	monthly	To pay	2 000	6 months
National Savings					
Certificate 1–5 yrs	8.25	when cashed in	Tax free	25	
Index-linked savings certificates	RPI linked 10.2 monthly	when cashed in	Tax free	10	
SAYE-Indexed	RPI linked 10.2 monthly	when cashed in	Tax free	4/month	Penalty

Insurance Company
Endowment Assurance—Policy holder's life insured but lump sum paid at prearranged date or on death of policy holder. Benefit is tax free.

another person or business. Savings which are not likely to be withdrawn can be lent, but where a person might draw on their savings enough must be kept ready for such withdrawals.

Take the Trustee Savings Bank who offer 3 types of account:

Account	Interest*	£ min	Withdrawal
Savings	4%	5 pence	Demand
Investment	5½%	1	7 days
Term	8%	1 000	1–5 years

* All rates quoted are for February 1984. In this case interest on all 3 accounts is paid annually and is subject to income tax.

As can be seen from this example the opportunity cost of wanting to be able to withdraw savings on demand (whenever one wants) is a lost 1½% interest.

There are other factors at work however. The highest rate of interest offered at the TSB is only available for a saver who is not only prepared to leave savings alone for at least one year, but also has £1 000 in the account. This is true in general. The more the saver has to deposit in an institution the higher the rate of interest.

With some forms of National Savings (money lent to Government) there is a slight tax incentive. The interest or part of it is tax free. Some institutions are more convenient than others with a greater number of outlets or longer opening hours—the post office for example. Others such as the banks and building societies may promise a mortgage to savers who have had an account for a minimum period.

There are, therefore, many places to save your money. The following paragraphs highlight these places.

The Post Office   Many of you may have a **Post Office National Savings Account**. The ordinary account pays 3% and investment account 11% but the former allows up to £100 to be withdrawn on demand whereas the latter takes one month. These are both very popular probably because of the convenience of using the Post Office. There are 20 000 post offices all over the country. Nearly every village has one and they open on a Saturday and have longer hours than a bank. It is also possible to purchase **National Savings Certificates** at a post office. These are loans to the Government for 1–5 years. With the **non-index-linked National Savings Certificates** the purchaser pays for them in units of £10 (up to a maximum of £1 500). No interest is paid but after one year the holder can sell them back to the Post Office and receive the original purchase price plus 8¼% per year. They may be held for up to 5 years. **Index-Linked National Savings Certificates** were introduced in 1975 originally for the retired. Now everyone can buy them. They are essentially the same as ordinary saving certificates but carry no specific rate of interest. The purchase price is repaid and the amount of measured inflation (Retail Price Index) is added in addition to a bonus of 0.2% per month. **Premium Bonds** can also be purchased at the post office. These are similar to saving certificates but they can be held for ever. Bought in units of £5 up to a maximum of £19 000 they can be sold back to the Post Office at any time (taking 8 working days to gain repayment). The difference is that no interest is paid. Instead all of the interest which would have been paid to all of the small bond holders is added up and given to a few lucky bond holders each month in the form of a prize. The numbers of the prize winners are selected electronically and are designed to be completely fair with everybody having an equal chance of winning. **Save as you earn schemes** (SAYE) are also run. A person can save between £4 and £20 per month either by paying cash into a post office, by having the amount transferred from their bank account or some employers will take it directly from the workers pay packet. As with Index-Linked Savings Certificates this SAYE service offers the RPI plus 0.2% bonus monthly.

All Saving Certificate Interest is tax free as is the first £70 interest paid each year on National Savings Accounts.

Saving at a bank   Banks normally offer **deposit accounts** and **savings accounts**. However, the difference lies in the fact that the deposit account is for irregular deposits of £1 or more whereas the saving account is for regular additions to the account of £10 or more. People with large sums, such as £2 000 or more, can place the amount in an account for an agreed length of time (in excess of 3 months) and receive a higher rate of interest. Those banks which offer a mortgage guarantee account as previously described (see Chapter 10) have obvious attractions for the young married couple.

All bank interest is subject to income tax.

Saving at a building society   Building societies have become far more like banks. Most now offer their account holders cheque book facilities on some accounts, and a variety of banking type services as well as accounts which offer higher interest the longer funds are left untouched. They are excellent places for young people to save since they often give priority to account holders when granting mortgages.

Most accounts pay tax for the saver at 29p in the pound. If you are someone who does not pay tax, then this is lost and means lower interest than say the National Savings Bank Investment Account.

The Trustees Savings Bank   Already covered. These institutions are run on similar lines to a commercial bank although publically administered.

Life assurance   Looked at in detail later in this chapter.

Exercise

For each of the following suggest where they might best save giving reasons for each. Why might the institution offering the highest rate of interest not necessarily be the best place to save?

1 An elderly, retired couple who have recently sold a valuable house and bought a much smaller flat. They have a net gain of £25 000 but other than this have only a pension to live on.
2 A young school leaver who only takes home £40 after tax from a junior clerk's job. He pays his mother £10 a week for keep and spends most of the remainder on entertainment and clothes. He can save up to £10 per week.
3 A middle aged couple, both at work, children grown up, find they can save up to £100 a month with little trouble. They wish to save for their old age.
4 A new-born baby has many rich relatives who keep giving money to the baby for 'when he is older'.

Where should his parents save this money until he wants it?

Insurance

Insurance is a simple idea which developed towards the end of the 15th century to help traders reduce the risk of importing valuable cargoes from America and India. In those days ships were much more likely to be lost at sea and when this happened the merchant who owned the ship lost everything. On the other hand if the ship survived he stood to make a healthy profit. The merchants soon realised that bad luck could hit any of them but not all of them. If they put a percentage of the value of the ship into a common pool then those who were unlucky and lost a ship, could draw out their loss from the common fund. In this way all of the merchants were able to prosper. The idea was adapted to cover fire after the Great Fire of London in 1666 with the first fire insurance company founded in 1680.

The principle was the same. Those houses wishing to be insured against the risk of fire would pay a small sum known as **the premium** to people known as **underwriters**. This was put with all other premiums into a common fund. Those unlucky few whose house was burnt would be able to make a **claim** and receive the value of their house or repair from the common fund.

Life Assurance operates on the same lines but here people do not insure against dying since everyone dies. They are able to insure against dying before a certain date. This became popular during the 18th Century, although it was used before then. People are able to insure their own lives (or those of their wife or husband) but not anyone else's. Again a premium is paid each year calculated upon the age and health of the insured person. It is interesting that smokers have to pay higher premiums than non-smokers. If the insured person dies before the policy matures (agreed final date) their family benefit from a lump sum benefit or pension. Other policies called **endowment policies** are a way of saving as well as insuring a life. Here if the policy holder dies before a certain date their family receive a benefit but if they reach that date they receive a tax-free lump sum.

The end of the 18th Century saw the development of far more machines. Machines for moving people, railway engines, and for making goods more efficiently in factories. This increased the risk of accident. Special companies were established in 1850 to insure rail travellers. By 1889 it was possible to insure against burglary and soon after loss of valuables. In 1865 motor cars were beginning to be seen. They became very popular after World War I and in 1930 the Government made it a requirement of law for all motorists to have enough insurance to compensate any third party they might injure or kill on the roads. This is still a legal requirement. During this same period air travel was developing and in 1919 aviation insurance began.

Today it is possible to insure against most things where the likelihood of an event happening can be worked out. It is possible to insure against it raining on a holiday, at a wedding or fête, or for shopkeepers to insure their plate glass windows.

Some risks remain **uninsurable**. A shopkeeper cannot insure against a change of fashion which may make some of his stock difficult to sell.

TAKING OUT INSURANCE

CASE STUDY

John's Car

John is 21 and has been driving his father's car for 2 years. He has now bought his own small English car for £790. He knows that he must take out insurance. How can he do this? This is the procedure he should follow.

1 Obtain prospectus Any insurance company or broker will send a prospectus which lays down the details of the policies they offer. John discovers that he has 3 policies (exact cover given) to choose from:

a Third Party This would cover his legal costs and any compensation he would have to pay if he were to have an accident and injure or kill someone else.

b Third Party, Fire and Theft As above but would cover the cost of replacing his car if it were to be stolen or catch fire.

c Comprehensive As *b* above but protects car against accidental damage, medical expenses of occupants if car involved in a crash and the contents of the car against theft.

Obviously *a* is cheaper than *b*, which is cheaper than *c*.

2 Proposal form filled in John would now fill in a form called the **proposal form**. This is often part of the prospectus and is sent back to the broker or company asking them to calculate the cost of insurance.

3 Cover note John has decided on a company and is sent a **cover note** which gives him temporary insurance cover while the details are worked out.

4 The premium John is told how much it will cost for his chosen policy (third party, fire and theft). The premium will depend upon the type of

policy, type of car, age of driver, region of the country it is to be driven in and type of use it is to be given. For John, driving in London, for pleasure only will cost £160 per year. John decides to pay this over 3 months.

5 The policy After a few weeks John receives a full **Certificate of Insurance** and a detailed policy which sets out exactly what is covered.

This is how John insured his car. The procedure is the same for a motorbike. John would have to pay the first £50 of any claim as he is under 25. As he grows older the premium will fall and if he does not claim he will be given a discount over the next few years.

Exercise

Which of the following would be more expensive to insure to drive and why:

a A mini or a sports car?
b A man aged 21 or a man aged 31?
c A car in London or a car in the Isle of Wight?
d A car for pleasure use only or a car for business use?
e A male driver or female driver?

INSURANCE TERMS

Someone requiring insurance cover can approach either an insurance company or use an agent (might be a garage owner or bank manager) who put people in touch with the insurance companies (see diagram overleaf). **Friendly Societies** offer life and sickness insurance often operating through local agents who might collect the premium on a weekly door-to-door basis. A broker is a full-time insurance salesman, he does not work for any company or underwriter but is paid a commission for placing insurance work with a company or underwriter. He is able to give advice to the customer.

One well-known group of underwriters is Lloyds of London. You've probably heard of them. It dates back to, and takes its name from, a 17th century coffee house where insurance was undertaken. Lloyds is not a company and has no

shareholders. It is simply a society of underwriters or individuals who accept insurance risks in return for a premium. The public are not allowed to approach these 19 000 underwriters directly but do so through several hundred Lloyds brokers who can be found all over the country. Today the constitution of Lloyds is governed by Acts of Parliament and they have their own building.

SUMMARY OF INSURANCE COVER

There is a variety of insurance cover available. These include:

Household Can insure 'contents' or 'buildings' against loss or damage caused by such things as theft, flood, fire and even aircraft hitting it!
Motorist The **Road Traffic Act 1972** makes it illegal not to have third party cover.
Businesses Not only is it possible for a business to be covered against loss or damage due to theft, fire, flood etc, but they can also have special policies to cover plate glass windows, company vehicles etc. They can also insure themselves against **employers liability**; if an employer is careless and one of his workers hurts themselves it is the employer's fault (or liability) and businesses can insure against any compensation they

Insurance Terms

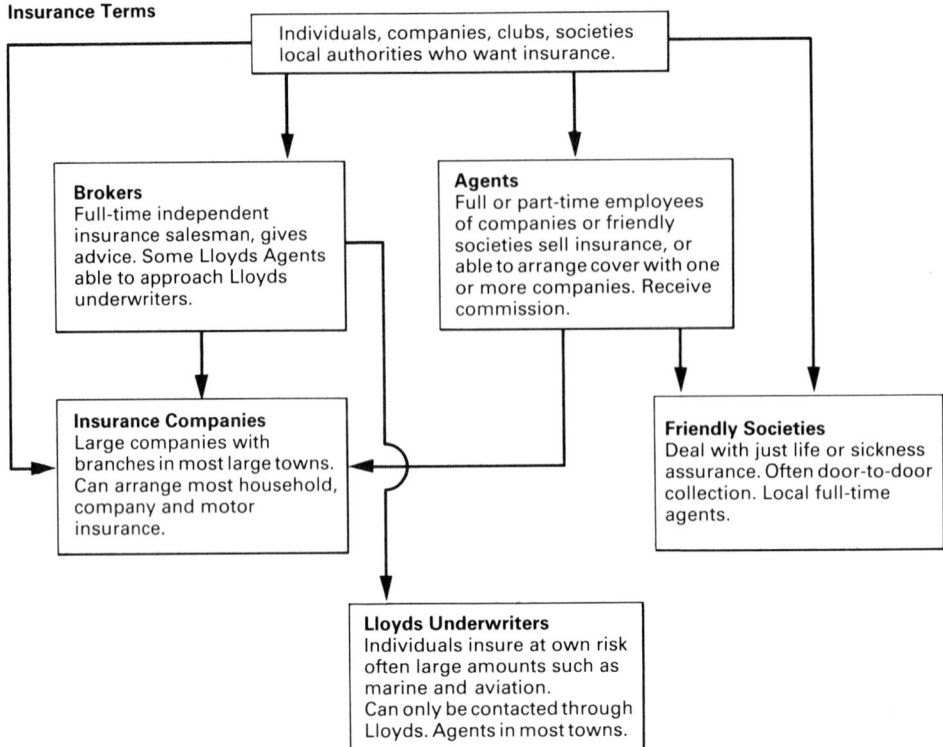

might need to pay. They can also insure against any claim from the general public who may be hurt due to the carelessness of the business.

Apart from these the **holidaymaker** can insure against loss or theft of baggage, cancellation of the holiday or medical expenses abroad. **Cyclists** can insure against theft, damage in an accident or third party liability. **Sportsmen** can insure against loss or damage to expensive equipment and against the compensation they might need to pay if they hurt someone. An **individual** can insure against any compensation they may have to pay due to their carelessness. This is called **personal liability insurance**.

INSURANCE COMPANIES AND INVESTMENT

Insurance companies take vast sums of money every year in the form of premiums. Much of this is not paid out at once. A small percentage (11%) is kept for paying claims and the rest is invested. The approximate distribution of insurance com-

pany funds looks something like this:

Stocks and shares in companies	34%
Mortgages and loans	29%
British Government (local and central) borrowing	26%
Money kept in reserve for claims	11%

Exercise

1 It is impossible to insure against a change in fashion. Why do you think this is so?
2 When 'fire insurance' was first offered, policy holders were given a special plate or 'fire mark' to attach to the outside of their house. Each insurance company ran its own fire brigade which would extinguish a fire in one of their insured homes. In 1833 a single brigade was formed in London which eventually passed into the control of the London County Council (now the GLC).

a Why do you think the early fire insurance companies ran their own fire brigades?
b Why do you think they formed one brigade in London in 1833?
c Why do we now consider a fire service a merit good and provide it through rates to all householders?

3 Why does the law make motorists take out third party cover?
4 Why do some car insurance policies cost more than others?
5 Why does a life insurance policy cost more for a smoker than a non-smoker?

Building Societies

Housing needs our special attention since it represents the largest single item in the expenditure of most families (16% in 1981) and is surely one good that we all need. In 1980 the Department of the Environment accepted that 64 000 people were homeless in England and Shelter, the national campaign for the homeless, estimate that this figure was closer to 70 000 for England and Wales in 1981. Clearly some needs are not being satisfied.

For those who have somewhere to live there are 3 main methods of acquiring a home:

- buy with the help of a loan (owner occupied housing—the occupier owns or is buying the house)
- rent from the local council (public rented housing)
- rent from a private landlord (private rented)

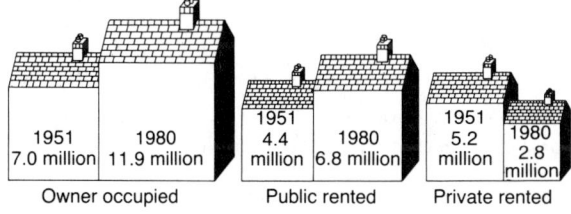

Source: Britain 1983, HMSO

Over half of all homes are owner occupied, the majority of these bought with the aid of a loan. Only 12% of homes are rented from private landlords and the figure is falling. In city centres this figure is far higher due to the higher concentration of young single people. **The 1980 Housing Act** gave those who rent from the local authorities certain rights which included the right to purchase the property they rented at a

discount if they had lived there for more than 3 years. This will obviously affect the number of publicly rented homes.

Most people who buy a home do so with the aid of a loan. This is because the price of a house usually represents a very high proportion of their expected working life's income.

Building Society Loans, 3rd Quarter, 1983

House Prices (%)

Price	All buyers
Under £15 000	19
£15 000–£19 999	17
£20 000–£24 999	18
£25 000–£29 999	15
£30 000–£39 999	17
£40 000–£49 000	7
Over £50 000	8

Income of Borrowers

Income pa	All buyers
Under £6 000	14
£6 000–£6 999	10
£7 000–£8 999	24
£9 000–£10 999	20
£11 000–£14 999	21
£15 000 & Over	12

In the third quarter of 1983 for the United Kingdom we see that the average house price was £27 509 but average income of borrowers only £10 079 (see table overleaf). To save up such a figure would take a life-time and where would a family live while this saving was taking place? About 80% of these loans come from special institutions called **building societies**.

Building societies developed in 1775 and were just what the name suggests. Working people would gather together to save up to build houses. As money accumulated land was purchased and houses constructed. When all of the members of a society had a home the society was closed having achieved its aim. In 1845 the first permanent building society was established where people could save any extra cash they had and receive a rate of interest and others could borrow in order to buy property. This is their role

Building Society Loans: Regional Figures, 3rd Quarter, 1983

Region	Number of loans (000s)	Percentage of UK total	Percentage of loans to first-time buyers	Percentage of loans on new houses	Average house price £	Average advance £	Average percentage advance	Average income of borrowers £
Northern	12	5	58	13	20 125	14 161	70	9 088
Yorks & Humber	22	10	52	10	21 912	14 929	68	8 849
East Midlands	19	8	50	16	22 944	15 649	68	9 174
East Anglia	9	4	47	16	25 385	16 835	66	9 045
Greater London	21	9	60	6	35 370	24 122	68	12 147
South East (excl GLC)	50	22	44	13	35 497	21 938	62	11 508
South West	22	10	47	14	28 660	18 178	63	9 454
West Midlands	22	9	50	12	24 527	16 561	68	9 424
North West	24	10	50	7	24 135	16 582	69	9 575
Wales	8	3	55	9	23 648	16 044	68	9 114
Scotland	19	8	58	14	24 130	17 535	73	10 234
Northern Ireland	5	2	70	25	21 885	15 934	73	9 351
United Kingdom	233	100	51	12	27 509	18 246	66	10 079

Source: The Building Societies Association and Department
of the Environment, BSA Bulletin No 37

today. They are non-profit-making organisations controlled by various Acts of Parliament
(for example the **Building Societies Act 1962**),
supervised by the Chief Registrar of Friendly
Societies, which attract savings on the one hand
and lend money to home buyers on the other.

There are approximately 37.7 million accounts
in some 227 building societies in the UK which
save a total of £68 123 million. These accounts
earn interest at a rate of roughly 9%. Borrowers,
roughly 5.6 million of them, borrow £56 696 million and repay the amount borrowed at an interest rate of roughly 13%. From 1 January 1987
Building Societies are able to offer banking services similar to those of the High Street Banks.

THE SIX MORTGAGE STEPS

There are 6 steps in taking a building society loan
to buy a house.

**Step 1 Agree size of loan with building
society** Building societies exist to help people
buy homes. It would be foolish for them to lend
so much to a person who could never afford to
repay the loan plus interest. For this reason they

apply a simple rule of thumb usually lending
up to 2½ times a person's income. Someone on
£10 000 a year could expect to borrow up to
£25 000. A couple can often borrow more—2½
times the larger income plus once times the
lower. The potential borrower could then add
this to his savings, deduct the cost of buying
(legal costs etc) and decide upon the price of
house he was looking for. Once the loan is
agreed in principle, a house must now be found.
The average is under double the income but this
includes second mortgages of older people.

Step 2 Find a house Finding a suitable house
can be made very easy by using an **estate agent**.
These companies specialise in putting potential
buyers in touch with potential sellers. They
charge a commission but only to the seller. They
will provide lists of suitable houses and arrange
visits. Once having found a suitable house the
buyer informs the building society.

Step 3 Survey/valuation The building society
will have the house checked by a surveyor. This
involves a valuation, that is an independent
assessment of the value of the property.
Although the purchaser pays for this (average

cost about £50, he does not see it and it is not a full structural survey. He might be well advised to ask for a full structural survey from a proper surveyor. This will cost a further £150.

Step 4 Offer of loan If all is in order the building society will offer a loan. Building societies do not give mortgages—the **mortgage** is a legal contract between the purchaser and the building society which the purchaser signs and gives to the building society. As a legal contract, once signed, it puts certain requirements upon the borrower (he must make the agreed repayments and insure the property etc). It does not state the rate of interest since with a building society loan this can vary. The loan can last for many years, the most usual being 25 years and over this time a person will repay the sum borrowed and the interest. (The interest on the first £30 000 of a loan qualifies for income tax relief and is calculated by the building society and never charged.)

Step 5 Legalities Although it is possible to undertake the legal paperwork oneself most people use a solicitor. The solicitors fees are about 1% of the cost of the house. For this the solicitor will check with the local authority on development which might affect the house, make sure there are no people renting the property, draw up the contract and check the mortgage deed, as well as many more important jobs.

Step 6 Exchange of contracts/completion At this stage both the buyer and seller sign a contract to sell. Once signed neither side can back out. The purchaser is asked to pay a deposit of 10% to be handed over to the seller's solicitor. Usually one month later the mortgage money is paid and the house becomes the purchaser's property—or at least he can move in and start repaying his loan!

All in all it is a very expensive business. Further costs also include **stamp duty**, a tax of half a per cent which is paid to the Government on house purchases over the value of £25 000, **land registry fees** and **moving fees** (removal charges or self-hire van).

SUMMARY EXERCISE

1 Give one reason why companies save part of their net profits (retained profits) and state why the shareholders might be pleased for this to happen even though it means lower dividends.

2 If an old age pensioner saved £10 per week in a box under her bed what would be the opportunity cost to her of such a method of saving and why might she be happy to accept this?

3 What might be the results to the economy if most people saved in the manner described in question **2**?

4 Financial institutions act like huge sponges. They soak up spare cash in one part of the economy and squeeze it out where it is needed. Name 3 such institutions about which you have learnt in this chapter.

5 What type of insurance could be considered a form of saving and why?

6 In what circumstances would **index-linked national savings certificates** prove a better form of saving than **ordinary national savings certificates**?

7 Since no interest is paid on **premium saving bonds** and the odds against winning are very high explain their popularity amongst small savers.

8 Some people feel that cyclists should be compelled by law to have third party insurance. Why do you think people think like this and what would premiums for such a policy be like—high or low?

9 Give an example of 2 types of people who would find it very difficult to borrow from a building society.

10 A man lives in a flat which is worth £50 000. He rents it at a monthly cost of £200 (just under 5% per annum of the capital value of the flat). He inherits £50 000 and is offered the flat to buy but refuses to do so claiming he is better off financially not buying the property. Do you agree with him? Explain your answer.

ASSIGNMENTS

1 People like to save some of their income. You may well save already. They like to save up for things or just 'for a rainy day'.

a List 4 different institutions where you could save and receive interest.
b For each institution you have listed give one advantage and one disadvantage of saving there.
c For each institution give an example of a group of people for whom you would suggest it would be a good place to save giving your reasons.

2 Suppose your father owned a small engineering firm on a local industrial estate. Explain fully 5 important forms of insurance you would expect him to have to protect his business interests.

3 You are thinking of getting married. How would you go about securing a mortgage to buy your first home? Be sure to mention *all* of the steps that would be needed including the calculations of how much you could borrow.

4 Insurance is expensive and with any luck you may never need it. Write a letter to a small shop owner, as if you were an insur-ance agent trying to sell him adequate insurance. Be sure to point out all the advantages he will gain from proper insurance.

5 'Principles of Insurance—What can you insure?'

'You can insure against losses which can be calculated and predicted but you cannot insure against things which are not measurable by past experience . . .

You must also have what is called an 'insurable interest', which means that you can only insure against something causing you or your dependents financial loss.'

Source BIA Insurance Today Series Pamphlet 8

a Give 2 losses, other than motor accidents, which you can insure against.
b Give an example of things you cannot insure against because the 'risks' cannot be calculated.
c In motor insurance what is understood by:

third party cover, and
fully comprehensive cover

d We are told that you must have 'an insurable interest' to insure something. With examples explain why you think this is so.

14 Government Income and Spending

Chapter 1 considered certain types of goods and services and concluded that 2 special types of goods and services, **public goods** and **merit goods**, would have to be provided by the state.

Public goods These were goods and services which when provided for *one* consumer actually satisfied the wants of *other* consumers. If defence is provided for one person it is also provided for most others. Such a service is almost impossible to sell in a normal way for who would be silly enough to pay for it? For this reason no entrepreneur could provide such a service as they would lose money.

Merit goods Other goods society considers so important and essential that people should have them when they need or deserve them—not only if they can afford to buy them. Services like the health service fall into this category. The state therefore provides a minimum level of health care for those who need it. This does not prevent entrepreneurs offering private sector health care and people who can afford it from buying it.

To this list we can now add a third—**transfer payments**.

Transfer payments In most developed countries people are not allowed to starve if their income falls below a level necessary to provide basic needs. People who cannot work because they are disabled, have small children or simply cannot find work are likely to fall into this position of not being able to provide basic needs. The Government therefore takes part of the income from those who can provide for their families needs and gives or transfers it to those who cannot. These payments are called **social security payments**.

Chapter 3 showed how, for various reasons, the Government becomes an entrepreneur taking over and running certain industries. The Government needs to have, therefore, an income and will obviously be undertaking a great deal of spending.

Each year the Government must plan how much it requires to take from the circular flow of income either by taxation or borrowing to meet its spending plans. Since a Government must seek the permission of Parliament and since the financial year runs from April to March these plans are usually presented to Parliament at the end of March in what is called **the budget**. Here is a summary of the 1984 budget proposals:

1984 Budget Proposals

Government Income:

Expenditure taxes	£49.4 bn
Income Tax	£43.6 bn
Nat Insurance	£21.4 bn
Other	£20.7 bn
Total	**£135.1 bn**

Government Spending:

Defence	£17.0 bn
Health	£15.4 bn
Social Security	£37.2 bn
Other	£72.7 bn
Total	**£142.3 bn**

Government Borrowing:

Sale of Govt Bonds	
National Savings	
Others	
Total	**£7.2 bn**

The Government plans to spend more than it will take out of the circular flow in taxation. The difference, £7.2 billion, is paid for by borrowing. Most of this is from British families either from National Savings (see Chapter 13) or the sale of bonds on the stock exchange.

Government Spending

The chief items of Government expenditure (local and central) are social security benefits, defence, health and education. The comparison between 1983/84 and 10 years earlier (see Fig 30) does show some major differences. The growth of social security benefits can of course be accounted for by the increase in unemployment. (2.4% in 1973—13% in 1983.)

Exercise

Study the differences between the pattern of Government expenditure in 1973 and 1983 as shown in Fig 30.

a Name 2 areas other than social security benefits which have an increased proportion of Government expenditure. Suggest reasons as to why this might be.
b Name 2 areas of Government expenditure which have a decreased proportion of total expenditure. Suggest reasons as to why this might be so.

How Public Spending is Paid for—1983/84 (£bn)

Income		Expenditure	
Central government taxation		Social security	34.4
Income tax	31.4	Defence	16.0
Value added tax	15.5	Health and personal social services	14.6
Oil duties	5.7	Education and science	12.6
Corporation tax	6.2	Scotland	6.4
Tobacco	3.7	Industry, energy, trade and employment	5.6
National insurance surcharge	1.7	Transport	4.3
Spirits, beer, wine and perry	3.9	Order and protective services	4.6
Petroleum revenue tax	5.2	Other environmental services	3.6
Supplementary petroleum duty	—	Northern Ireland	3.8
Vehicle excise duty	1.9	Housing	2.8
Taxes on capital	1.5	Wales	2.5
European Community duties	1.4	Overseas services	2.2
Other (including accruals)	3.3	Other public services	1.7
		Common services	1.0
Total	**81.5**	Agriculture, fisheries, food and forestry	1.7
		Government lending to nationalised	
National insurance, etc contributions	21.2	industries	1.1
Local authorities' rates	13.0	Arts and libraries	0.6
North Sea oil royalties etc	1.6	Local authority current expenditure not	
General government trading surplus and rent	3.3	allocated to programmes (England)	0.9
General government interest and dividend		Adjustments to programmes—	
receipts	2.3	PC market and overseas borrowing	−0.3
Adjustments		Special sales of assets	−0.8
Accruals	—	Contingency reserve	1.5
Public corporations' transactions	3.4	General allowance for shortfall	−1.2
Other†	−0.5	**Planning total**	**119.6**
		Revisions	−0.3
Total receipts	**125.9**	**Revised planning total**	**119.3**
Public sector borrowing requirement	**8.2**	Gross debt interest	14.8
Total receipts and borrowing	**134.1**	**Planning total plus gross debt interest**	**134.1**

Source: Economics Progress Report No 156, April 1983 Treasury, HMSO

The full picture is shown in this chart:

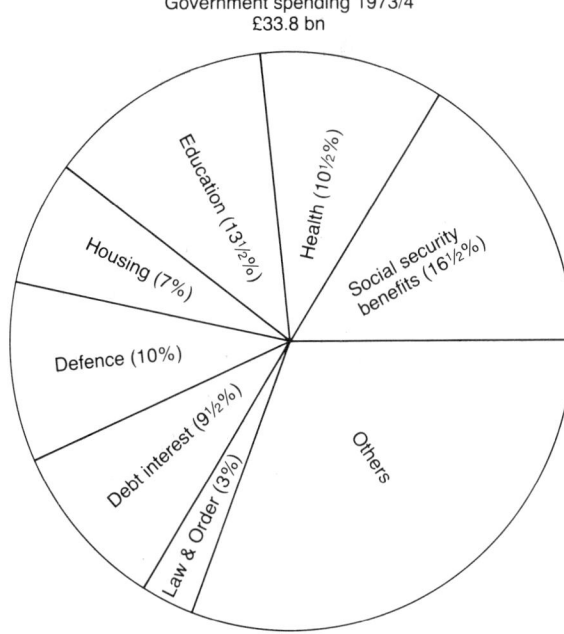

Government spending 1973/4
£33.8 bn

Government spending 1983/4 (forecast)
£134.1 bn

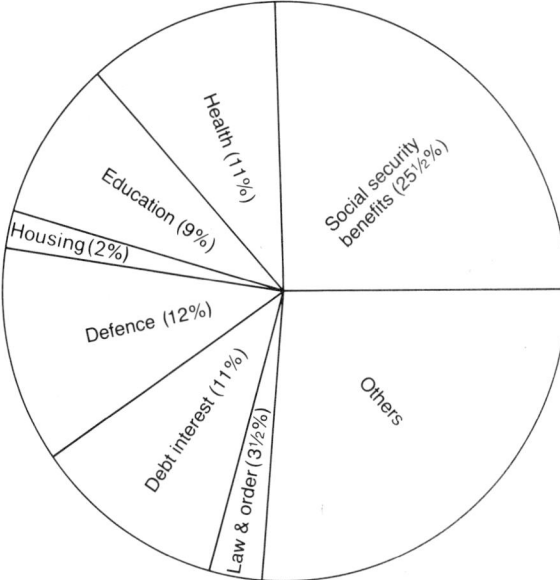

Fig 30 Comparison of selected items of Government spending 1973/4–1983/4. Source: Britain: An Official Handbook 1975, HMSO and Economic Progress Report No 156, April 1983, HMSO

The Welfare State

During the 20th Century Government has provided more goods and services for the population. These, we have seen, are called **merit goods** and are provided for people who need them. The National Health Service (1946) is a good example. State Education also comes under this heading. Alongside the provision of these goods and services has been the development of a comprehensive system of **transfer payments** or **benefits** which are paid to people at different times in their lives.

National Insurance is paid by all people in paid employment and by their employers. This is a percentage of income (between a lower and upper limit) and is currently 9% for the employee. This money is paid into the National Insurance Fund and people who have made sufficient contributions qualify for the following sorts of transfer payments when and if the need arises:

Retirement pensions Payable to women over 60 and men over 65. It is possible for an employer to provide own pension and contract out of state scheme thus paying lower contributions.

Sickness and invalidity benefit Sickness benefit lasts for 28 weeks after which an invalidity pension is paid.

Unemployment benefit Same rates as sickness benefits payable for one year of unemployment.

Widow's benefit Payable for first 26 weeks of widowhood, with additions for children. Then a widowed mother's allowance followed by widow's pension for women over 40. All would cease if the woman remarried or reached 60.

Maternity allowance Paid for 11 weeks prior to expected date of birth and for 6 weeks afterwards. A non-contributory £25 maternity grant is also paid.

Death grant A small sum of £30 is paid to a contributor's relatives to help with funeral arrangements.

Industrial injuries benefit Non-contributory but paid from the National Insurance Fund.

These are non-means tested, that is they are not dependent upon the size of a person's gross income. They are, with the exception of a maternity grant and industrial injuries benefit, paid to those who have satisfied the correct criteria with regard to National Insurance Contributions and are of course in need (ie to claim maternity allowance a woman has to be pregnant).

A number of non-contributory, means tested benefits also exist as a safety net for the welfare state. Families whose gross income falls below a prescribed level, 'the poverty line', are able to claim certain benefits:

Supplementary benefit Anyone over the age of 16 and under the retirement age who is not in full-time employment is entitled to claim supplementary benefit if their gross income falls below a certain level. As already mentioned it is not dependent upon contributions to the National Insurance fund but its size will depend upon a persons financial responsibilities, with additions for special needs.

Family income supplement (FIS) Anyone, married or single, who has at least one dependent child and whose gross income falls below a certain level can claim FIS. (This level was £82.50 for a married couple with one child in November 1982.) The amount paid is half of the difference between the benefit level and income level.

Health benefits Free prescriptions, dental treatment, milk and vitamins and fares to hospital are given to people on FIS or supplementary benefit. (Children, pregnant women and others also qualify for the first 2.)

Housing benefit People on supplementary benefit automatically qualify for rent and rates benefit (that is these are paid). Others on low income can receive a rent and rates rebate.

Educational benefits Free school meals (in some areas) and uniform grants and fares to school can be given to children of families on FIS or supplementary benefits. These are up to the local authority and the situation varies.

This list comprises the means tested allowances, that is they are paid to people whose gross income falls below a certain level. If their income were to rise above this level they would no longer qualify for certain benefits such as FIS, educational benefits and some housing benefits.

They could also become liable for income tax. This could result in a person being left with less income after a pay increase than before. This situation is known as the **poverty trap**.

Other benefits include a **non-contributory child benefit** which is given to a family for each child. This is paid through the Post Office and claimed through the DHSS. At the time of writing it stands at £6.50 per week (April 1984) per child.

The administration of both social security and supplementary benefits is undertaken by the Department of Health and Social Security (DHSS). Claims are usually made in writing on special forms and payment is made by a giro cheque or book of orders which can be cashed at a post office. Some benefits can be paid directly into a bank account.

Exercise

1 Read the case study opposite. Two suggestions are made to explain why so many benefits remain unclaimed. Think of 3 additional reasons.
2 Discuss with friends and produce a 5 point plan which you would put into practice if you were a Minister at the Department of Health and Social Security to try to reduce the number of benefits which are not claimed.
3 Name 2 public goods, other than defence, provided by central and local Government.
4 Some societies consider different goods and services to be merit goods. Name 2 goods and services provided in this country as merit goods other than the health service.
5 Name one means tested benefit paid to families for children and one non-means tested benefit paid to families for children.
6 What is the single largest item of Government expenditure in 1983/84. What type of expenditure is it?
7 Calculate what proportion of the average wage for manual workers in 1982 the FIS qualification level (one child) represented in that year.

CASE STUDY

Unclaimed benefits

Every year it is estimated that at least £750 million are not claimed by people who qualify for transfer payments. This might be for a variety of reasons. Perhaps some people are too proud to admit that they have a low income and cannot cope, others might be afraid to go and claim. Whatever the reason the problem is large. Groups like the Child Poverty Action Group and others are trying to publicise the benefits and help people to claim. Look at these facts:

- One out of every 5 unemployed people does not claim all they are entitled to.
- Only 4 out of every 100 pregnant women on low incomes claim the milk and vitamins to which they are entitled.
- One in 3 pensioners live below the poverty line because they do not claim supplementary benefit.

ASSIGNMENT

Find out the levels of as many of the transfer payments listed above as you can. (There should be at least one claimed on you!)

Central Government Taxes in the UK

Whilst Governments can borrow and sell services to the country (ie electricity) the major source of income for a Government to finance a programme of spending lies in **taxation**. National Insurance is a form of tax already considered. We will look in detail at the other major central Government taxes.

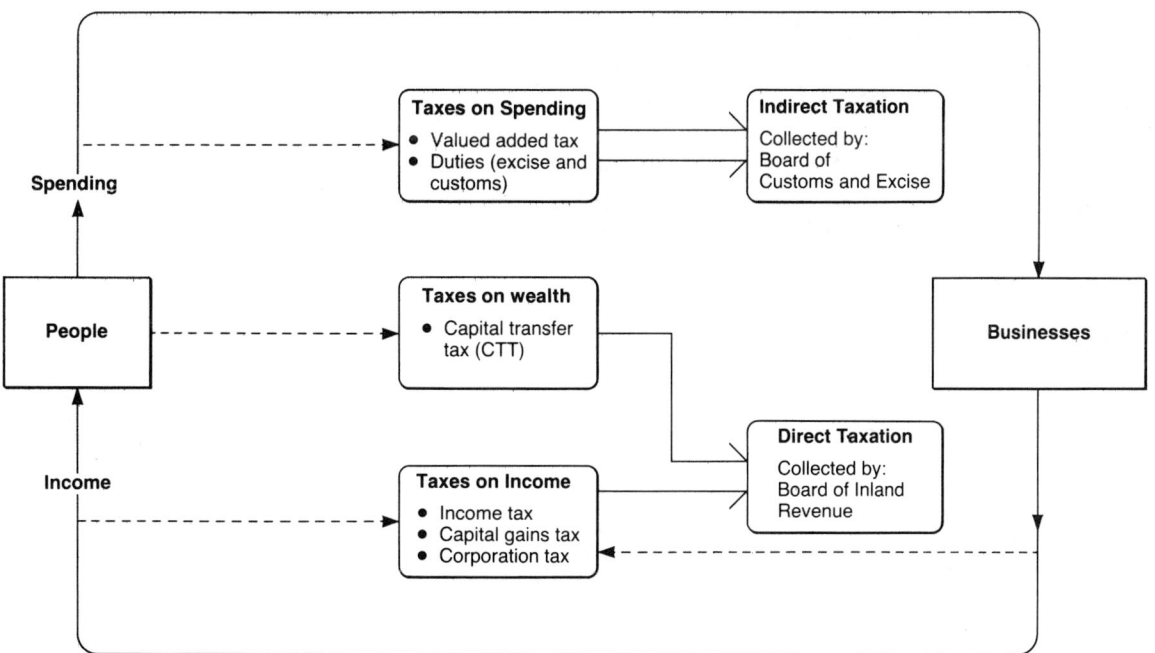

Central government taxes in the UK

There are 2 Government bodies responsible for collecting taxes. Taxes charged directly upon the country are collected by the **Board of Inland Revenue**. These include income tax, corporation tax and capital gains tax which are taxes on income and capital transfer tax which is a tax on wealth. Some taxes are charged indirectly, that is people pay the tax as they purchase goods and services. These indirect taxes are collected by the **Board of Customs and Excise** and include value added tax, customs and excise duties.

DIRECT TAXES

Income tax This is the most important tax levied. It accounts for about one quarter of all tax revenue. For most people it is charged at 30 pence in the pound but everyone is allowed a certain amount of income, tax free. This is their allowance and it is deducted from their gross income to calculate their taxable income. The allowances are, for most people:

£3 655   Higher Allowance (married man)
£2 335   Lower Allowance (single person or wife's earned income relief)

To this is added expenses incurred in earning the income (other than the cost of travelling to work) and allowances for a housekeeper and other expenses. The total is deducted from gross earnings to give taxable income. (These allowances minus the last figure are a person's tax code. The letter H or L is put at the end to signify the higher or lower allowance.)

Taxable income is then taxed as follows:

1986/87 Taxable Income Bands:

£1–£17 200 of taxable income	29% tax
£17 201–£20 200 of taxable income	40% tax
£20 201–£25 400 of taxable income	45% tax
£25 401–£33 300 of taxable income	50% tax
£33 301–£41 200 of taxable income	55% tax
£41 200 and over of taxable income	60% tax

Taking into account the tax free allowances Fig 31 shows how the average amount of gross income paid in tax increases as gross income increases. In this example a married man with only the higher tax free allowance of £3 155 has to earn over £25 000 per year to be losing 30% of his income in income tax. At £50 000 he still keeps over half of his income.

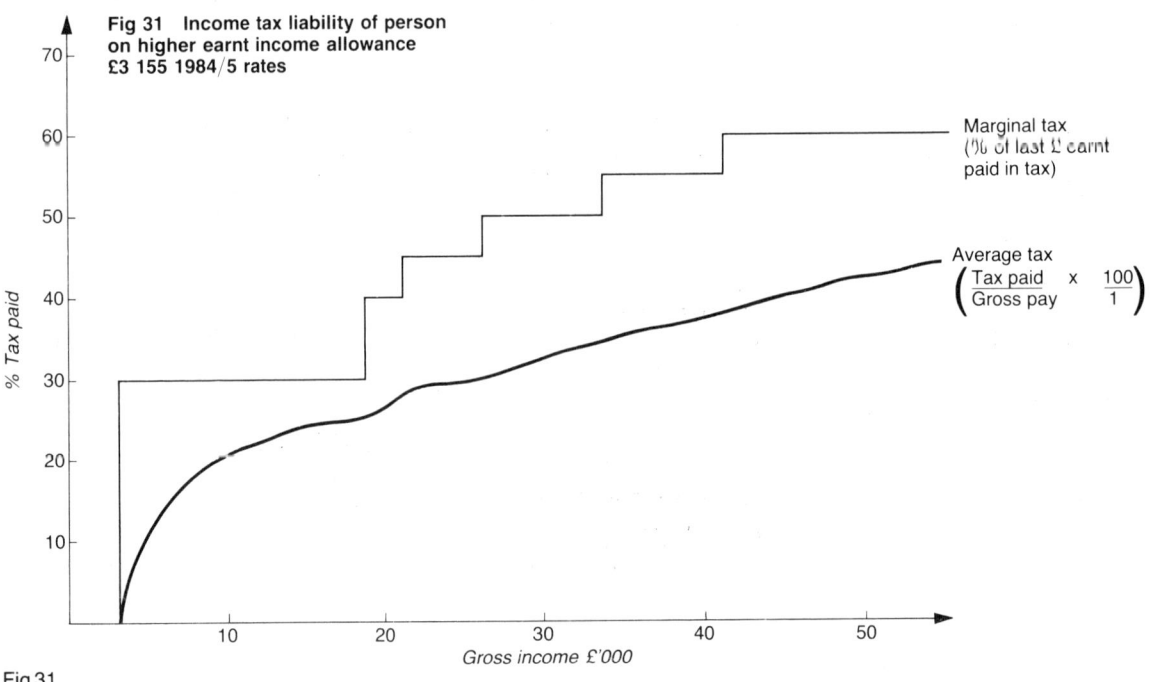

Fig 31   Income tax liability of person on higher earnt income allowance £3 155 1984/5 rates

Fig 31

People in full-time regular employment usually pay their tax as they earn it—PAYE. Under this system the tax a person is due to pay throughout the year is divided by 12 if they are paid monthly or 52 if they are paid weekly and simply deducted by the employer from their pay who then pays the Inland Revenue. In this way the tax payer does not face a large bill at the end of the financial year and the Government receives a steady income throughout the year.

Corporation Tax   Companies much like individuals are taxed upon their income or profits and this tax is called **corporation tax**. The rates charged were set in the 1984 budget at 50% for most companies with a reduced rate of 30% for small companies. The rates will be 45% for the year 1984/85, 40% 1985/86 and 35% 1986/87 for large companies.

Companies do not have tax free allowances like individuals but can deduct expenses incurred in earning those profits and sums set aside to replace the capital of the firm (depreciation allowances). There are also allowances for increases in stock and for investment in the assisted areas.

Capital Gains Tax   In Chapter 2 it was demonstrated how through clever anticipation a person or company could buy and sell stocks and shares and make a **capital gain**. Such gains are subject to 30% tax. Individuals are allowed the first £6 300 of gains tax free and private houses are exempt. Both individuals and companies can offset capital losses (selling an asset at a lower price than the purchase price) against capital gains.

Capital Transfer Tax   This is a tax on wealth, or rather the accumulated wealth of a family. Originally such taxes were only imposed when a person died. Since it was possible for people to give away their wealth before they died only a few who died young ever paid it. It became known as the 'unfortunate tax' rather than the proper title—**estate duty**. In 1974/75 **capital transfer tax** was introduced. This taxed a person on their lifetime gifts. In 1986 it was replaced by **Inheritance Tax**. Now, lifetime gifts are exempt from tax up to 7 years before death but,

on death the value of an estate is taxed as follows:

Value of Estate	Tax Rate
£'000	%
0–71	nil
71–95	30
95–129	35
129–164	40
164–206	45
206–257	50
257–317	55
over 317	60

Gifts in the years before death are subject to the following taper:

Years between gift and death	% of full charge at death rates
0–3	100
3–4	80
4–5	60
5–6	40
6–7	20
over 7	nil

There is no tax when an estate is left to a husband or wife.

INDIRECT TAXES

Value Added Tax   This is a tax on spending and is levied on most goods and services at a standard rate of 15%. You might well have received a bill in a restaurant for £10 and seen 'plus 15% VAT £11.50'. That extra £1.50 is a tax and goes to the Government. VAT is an important source of revenue. A few items such as basic food, children's clothing and educational services are exempt.

The name comes from the manner in which it is collected. At each stage of production value is added. A carpenter might buy wood costing £50 and produce furniture which sells at £250. He has added £200 to the value. He would have to pay £30 VAT (15% of £200). He can pass this on to the furniture retailer by charging £280. He can also claim back that part of the £50 he paid for the wood which was VAT. The retailer might add a further £100 to the value and thus pay £15 VAT but would charge £395. In this way the full tax is passed on to the consumer.

Customs Duties As members of the EEC it was explained in Chapter 9 that goods imported into this country face the **common external tariff**. The importer will add all or part of this to the price he charges. Such taxes are not imposed to raise revenue but to prevent or discourage imported goods from non-EEC countries.

Excise Duties Certain goods, whether they are imported or manufactured in this country, face an additional tax to VAT. These goods include beer, wine, spirits, tobacco, petrol and others. They are known as excise duties. Here is a typical example:

Where Your Petrol Money Goes (12 March 1984)

Supplier	74.6p
Garage	7.5p
Duty	74.1p
VAT	23.4p
Total per gallon	179.6p
Total tax paid	97.5p (54.2%)

In addition there are special specific expenditure taxes in the form of licences. For example, one is required by law to have a dog licence if you own a dog. More seriously, television and road fund licences (for cars) are again annual and raise a good deal of revenue. Legal documents often have a stamp duty in particular when selling a house of over £25 000 value.

Exercise

Assume 1984/85 tax rates throughout.

1 Calculate the total income tax of a single person with a gross income of £4 005.
2 In the above example how much would this person pay per month under PAYE.
3 If a speculator on the Stock Exchange made a £10 000 capital gain on one deal but a £3 400 capital loss on a second, what would be his capital gains tax liability if these were the only 2 deals he undertook in a year?
4 Income tax increases as a proportion of gross income, as gross income increases. That is to say, the more a person earns, the greater proportion of income is lost in tax. Is the same true of VAT? Explain your answer.
5 Petrol, beer and cigarettes all have high revenue excise duties on them. (A large % tax designed to raise money for the Government.) Why do you think the Government chose to tax the drinker, smoker and motorist so heavily?

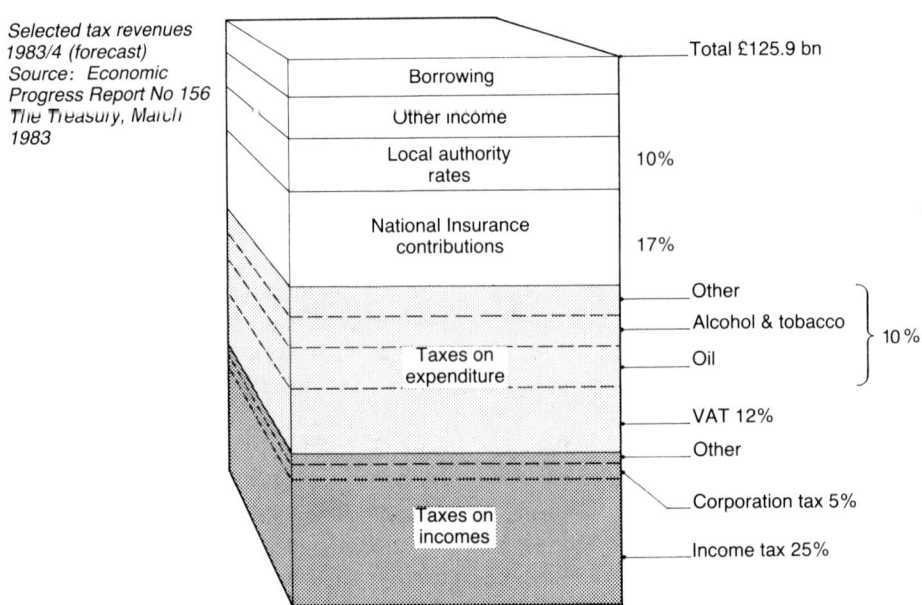

Selected tax revenues 1983/4 (forecast) Source: Economic Progress Report No 156 The Treasury, March 1983

Selected tax revenues (forecasts) Source: Economic Progress Report no 156, The Treasury, March 1983, HMSO

THE BURDEN OF TAXATION

Income tax takes a larger proportion of a person's income the higher that income is.

Exercise

Look at Fig 31. What % of gross income would be taken in income tax if the man earned:

a £10 000
b £20 000
c £30 000
d £40 000
e £50 000 per annum?

Such a tax is called a **progressive tax**. It ensures that high income earners contribute more to the provision of Government goods and services than low income earners. With the system of tax free allowances some income earners pay no income tax at all.

The opposite is a **regressive tax**. Look at the following example:

Two men are drinking in a pub. Both buy a pint of beer. Suppose that the excise duty is 50p. One of the men is a pop star who earns £20 000 a week. The second is unemployed and is given £25 a week. Both pay the same tax on the beer. For the pop star this represents a mere 1/40 000 th of his weekly income but for the unemployed lad the tax represents 1/50th of his weekly income.

Excise duties are regressive. They take a larger proportion of a low wage earner's income than a high wage earner's income.

It would be possible to devise a tax which took the same proportion of everyone's income. Income tax, with no tax free allowances, set at a constant 25% for example would do this. Such a tax would be known as a **proportional tax**. This can be shown diagramatically (below left).

Local Government Spending

Local Governments are responsible for providing many services for the local community. Central Government often requires through law that local Governments provide minimum services for their residents.

Education is the largest single item of expenditure. **Social services** is another and includes the provision of social workers and residential care facilities for children and the elderly. **Environmental services** deal with refuse collection, parks and housing. **Roads**, minor roads not trunk roads and motorways need to be maintained. The **police** are also on the spending list. **Local** authorities can also give **subsidies** to organisations, clubs and societies as well as local industry. **Grants** are given to students and **rebates** to housing tenants on low incomes. Local authorities **borrow** to build large projects like shopping centres and housing estates and have to pay back the interest on funds thus borrowed. To organise all of this they have to employ many officials and have offices. All the **administration** involved also needs to be paid for.

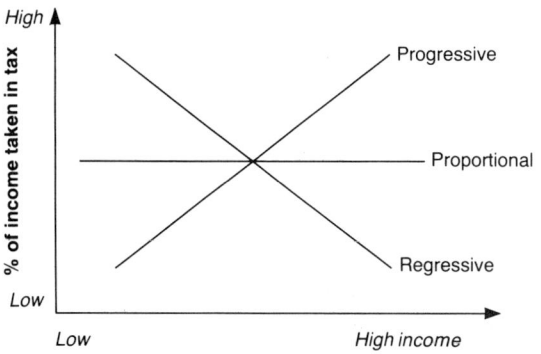

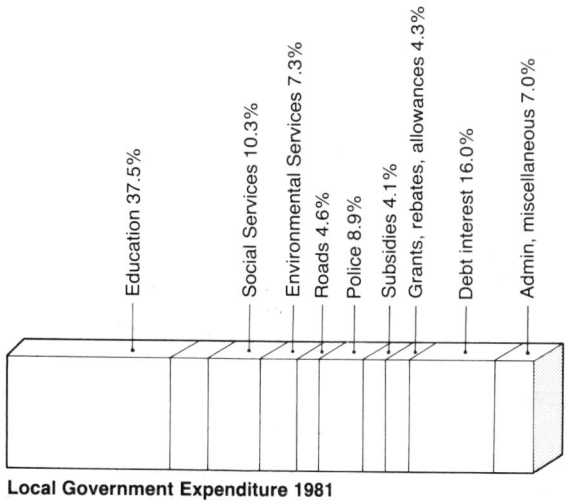

Local Government Expenditure 1981

Education 37.5%
Social Services 10.3%
Environmental Services 7.3%
Roads 4.6%
Police 8.9%
Subsidies 4.1%
Grants, rebates, allowances 4.3%
Debt interest 16.0%
Admin, miscellaneous 7.0%

We have a 2-tier system of local Government in this country, that is the major services are provided by a County Council and more local needs satisfied by a District Council. In some areas even smaller Parish Councils look after services such as bus shelters and allotments.

In the major cities where people are much more concentrated a smaller area will contain enough people to make such services as education worth providing. In this case the Metropolitan County provides mainly overall planning functions, police and fire services leaving education, libraries etc to smaller Metropolitan Districts.

County Councils	Education
	Large-scale planning
	Roads
	Police
	Fire services
	Libraries
	Museums and art galleries
	Social services
	Consumer protection
	Waste disposal
	Pollution control
	Old people's welfare
	Youth employment
District Councils	Planning applications
	Housing
	Refuse collections
	Parks, sports and leisure facilities
	Local museums
Parish Councils	Parish halls
	Bus shelters
	Playing fields
	Footpaths and allotments

Local Authority Income

Local authorities have 3 main sources of finance:

Central Government Grants Since much of the work of local authorities is as a result of central Government legislation it seems only fair that some of the money comes from central Government taxation.

Fees and Charges Many of the services provided by local Government, although subsidised, have a fee or charge which is paid by the local citizens. Car parking, swimming pool entrance, rent of property (school lettings etc) and of course council house rent.

Rates Local authorities are allowed to charge their own tax called **rates**. This is a property tax.

In 1981 local Government income was split into these percentage portions: 51.4% from central Government grants; 34.4% from rates; 11% from rents, 11% for interest and finally 0.8% on miscellaneous income. This meant that over half of local authority revenue came from central Government grants and a little over one third from the rates.

RATES

The rates are a property tax administered and collected by the local authority.

Each property in an area is given a **rateable value**. This includes domestic housing, commercial and industrial property, but not agricultural land. A council will be able to calculate the **total rateable value** of all property in the county:

Example **Rateable values of properties in Essex, April 83**

	£m	% of total
Domestic	137.4	58
Commercial	45.6	19
Industrial	24.4	10
Other	31.0	13
Total	**238.4**	

The rateable value of a house will depend upon its size and facilities. The larger the house the higher its rateable value. Valuation is undertaken by the local valuation officer (inland revenue) who will set a new rateable value upon a property if it is extended or improved.

The local authority will know the size of central Government grants and be able to decide upon a scale of charges for services and thus calculate income from fees and charges. The central Government now has the authority to give each county a target for total spending. The council can calculate therefore how much it must raise through the rates if it is to keep within the Government target.

The Council would now know how much it needs to raise through rates and the total rateable value of all property in the county. It is possible to discover therefore how much per pound of rateable value property owners need to pay:

$$\frac{\text{Total revenue needed from rates}}{\text{Total rateable value}} = \text{Rate poundage}$$

If, for example, the total rateable value were £250 m and a county needed £375 m from the rates then:

$$\frac{£375 \, m}{250 \, m} = £1.50$$

In the above case if property owners were charged £1.50 for every £1's worth of rateable value of their property the county would raise the desired £375 m.

The rates are paid by the individuals using the property therefore, even people who rent property will pay rates.

CASE STUDY

Control of Local Authority Spending

Essex County Council in 1984/85 estimated the total expenditure needed to provide services in the County to be £623 m which would have required a rate poundage of £1.38. This spending, however, was in excess of the Government's 'target' for the County. The Government therefore reduced the proposed grants to the County by £7.2 million. Rather than cut their spending the County increased the rate poundage to £1.41.

This is how it was calculated:

Essex County Council Budget 1984/85

	£m	£m
Total planned spending		*623*

Revenue Sources:

Government grants		
Block	140	
Specific	55	
Fees & Charges	83	
Use of Reserves	13	
Total other than rates	291	

Total required from rates ⟶ 332

Total rateable value of property in Essex £238.4 m

Estimated income from 1p county rate £2.365 m

Rate poundage $\dfrac{£332}{2.365} = 140.38$

Rate poundage charged = 141.00

(*Note* The rate poundage is calculated here by dividing by how much a 1p county rate will raise as this is slightly lower than the £2.384 due to people who will not pay and empty property.)

The Government block grant is reassessed during the year and the actual level of penalty altered depending upon the level of overspending.

To prevent local Governments from raising their rates, in order to exceed the Government set 'targets', legislation is currently being put through Parliament which will allow the Government to stop such rate increases.

Some people feel that rates are unfair since they are a tax upon property and not income or expenditure. Such a tax does not take into account the use a property owner makes of local authority services. Clearly a childless couple are contributing a large amount of tax to pay for the education of other people's children.

CASE STUDY

Unequal neighbours

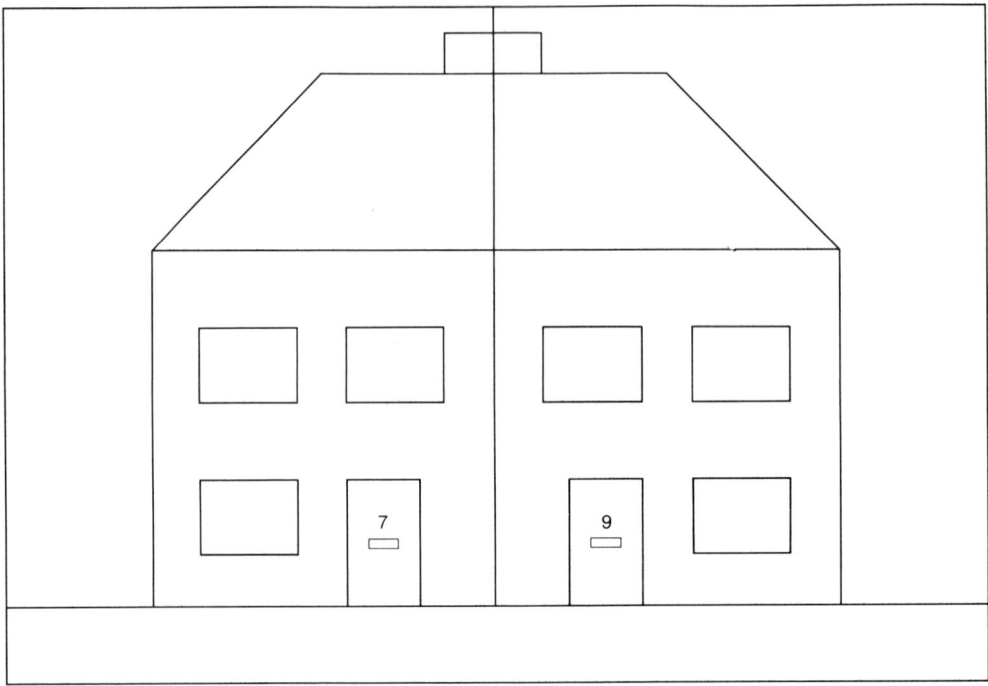

Number 7 Beech Grove		**Number 9 Beech Grove**	
Rateable value	£280	Rateable value	£280
Rate poundage	138.9p	Rate poundage	138.9p
Total rates	£388.92	Total rates	£388.92
Weekly rate bill	£7.46	Weekly rate bill	£7.46

Profile: Mr & Mrs Green:
Both retired, total income: £6 000 in pensions per year. They have some money saved which brings a further £500 per year in interest.

Profile: Mr & Mrs Brown:
Both at work. Mr Brown earns £12 000 and Mrs Brown £7 500 per year. They have 2 daughters who live at home: Marion is at school and Louise is a bank clerk and earns £4 000 per year.

Exercise

Calculate the following:

1 What percentage of their total (gross) income do the rates represent for Mr and Mrs Green? (rates ÷ gross income × 100. You will need a calculator.)

2 What percentage of their total gross income do the rates represent for the Brown family?

3 Why might Mr and Mrs Green feel that the rates system is unfair to them if they have no children?

4 If the rates were scrapped and a local income tax introduced at 4p in the pound of gross income, calculate the new local income tax paid by each family.

5 Why might the rates be higher in one part of the country than another?

This case exercise shows that rates are regressive, they formed a higher percentage of the Green's income (a low income family) than the Brown's (a higher income family). Some people criticise the rates for other reasons. Since home improvements can increase the rates this might stop people from improving their property. Question **5** asks why one area might have higher rates than another. This could be because in poor areas there is a greater need for social services and more people who qualify for rate rebate which would tend to raise the level of rates in a poor area. Our question **4** suggests an alternative. A local income tax could provide a solution. It is progressive which means the people who could afford to pay higher taxes would pay. In our example the Green's would face a 36% reduction in local taxes but the Brown's a 142% increase. Since 52% of local Government spending is financed from central Government some would argue that rates ought to be abolished anyway. The system of grants can help to even out the standard and costs of services since people on very low income receive a rate rebate.

The new legislation will give central Government even more control over local Government spending and the level of rates.

Local authorities work to the same 'financial year' as central Government and business, April–March. For this reason rates are set in the spring of each year. A rate payer can elect to pay the rates in one lump sum, 2 equal halves (April and October) or in monthly instalments (10 or 12) directly debited from a bank account. (There is often a small discount for people who pay in a lump sum.)

SUMMARY EXERCISES

1 In 1377 the King introduced a poll tax. This simply meant that everybody over the age of 14 had to pay 4 old pence (1½p) to help fight the war against France. Is a poll tax regressive or progressive?
2 In 1837 a horse tax was still in existence. A person was allowed one tax free horse if it was necessary for their job but after that the tax was:

1 horse: £1 8 shillings 9d
10 horses: £3 3 shillings 6d
20 horses: £3 6 shillings 0d.

Is this a progressive or regressive tax? To which modern expenditure tax is the horse tax equivalent?
3 Name one group of people who might like to see the rates system of financing local Government replaced by a local income tax.

4 Name 3 regressive taxes other than rates. What have they in common?
5 The Government aims to reduce corporation tax from 50% to 35%. How might this help to reduce unemployment?
6 Capital transfer tax raises very little revenue since it is very expensive to collect. Why was it originally imposed?
7 Child benefit replaced tax free allowances. The benefit is paid through the Post Office to mothers—the tax free allowance did increase the take home pay of fathers who paid tax. Give 2 reasons that might have been given for the change.
8 The current rate of unemployment benefit for a married man with one child is £43.90 per week (April 1984). Some people believe that this ought to be reduced in order to reduce unemployment. Explain why a reduction in unemployment benefit might reduce unemployment and state why you consider the suggestion above would or would not work.
9 If the national insurance scheme, the national health service and state education were to be abolished and replaced by private insurance, private health schemes and private education; name one group of people who would be financially better off.
10 Name one group of people who would suffer in the situation described in question **9**.

ASSIGNMENT

1 *a* The Government often produces goods and services for the public. Give detailed examples of 4 such Government produced goods and services. In each case explain the type of business organisation and suggest 2 reasons as to why the Government produces it.
b Why do some goods, public goods, have to be produced by the Government?

2 *a* What do you understand by the term **the national insurance scheme**?
b How would you, if in paid employment, make contributions to the national insurance scheme?

c Give 2 examples of benefits to which you might at some stage in your life be able to claim from the national insurance scheme—and describe fully in what circumstances you would have to be, how you would claim and how you would expect to be paid.

3 If you were to become unemployed after working for about 10 years:

a What benefits would you be entitled to and how would you claim them?
b What help would you expect to be given and from whom in finding a new job?

15 The Special Study

Helpful Hints

Many external examination courses require candidates to undertake a special study—to look at one area of economics in detail and to discover some economics for themselves. Before listing some suggestions for topics to look at here are a few do's and don'ts.

DO:

- Choose a topic or area of study where you are sure that you can find out some information. It is best to choose an area where a friend or relative can help. Have a *contact*.
- Choose a topic in which you have a genuine *interest*.
- Choose a topic that is *manageable*.
- Know the *timetable*. With most boards failure to hand in a project on the correct date is the same as not arriving for the exam.

DON'T:

- Choose a topic on the syllabus. Whereas to conduct a local shopping survey and write up the results is fine, to simply copy out notes on different types of shops from this or any other text is a waste of time. Try to undertake some *original research*. Ask people questions and record the results.
- Write to a firm for help and simply stick the pretty pictures they send back in a folder and call it a special study. Many firms and organisations will send you lots of glossy literature if you write to them. To use it you must read it and come to some conclusions of your own and write these up.
- Leave the work to the last minute. You may have several pieces of course work to complete in your fifth year. You can't write them all during the Easter vacation!

Suggested Titles

A special study can take 2 forms:

1 A diary of economic events Here the idea is to follow the progress of an economic event in the newspapers or television, to trace the story as it unfolds and to write it down as a diary. At the end of the period, which may be a few weeks or months, you should reflect upon the story using the economics you have learnt. For example, the story used in Chapter 8 about the Nissan car plant is ideal. It was used to illustrate the way in which Government grants can and do influence the choice of industrial locations. Much more came from the story which was not included in the book. For example, one of the main reasons Nissan chose Washington New Town was their excellent industrial relations record, an agreement that there would be only one trade union in the new plant and that Nissan could choose which union! It is often a good idea to watch for a story to be reported on the television and then to buy several newspapers the following day.

Here are some successful diaries some students have kept:

a An industrial dispute (other than wages). The closure of a plant or firm and the reaction of the workers. Why is the plant to be closed? How do the trade unions react?

b A wage dispute. Try to keep records of the offer, the claim, negotiation, industrial action etc. What is the result? Why was a particular settlement reached?

c A take-over bid. Follow the bid and campaign of one company to take over another.

d Unemployment figures. Follow and record the monthly unemployment figures and give reasons for changes/trend.

e A commodity price or share prices followed for a period of time to trace movements in price and offer suggestions for movements.

f The balance of payments' figures, recorded for a period of time and explanations for trend recorded.

g The formation of the budget. Every year the Chancellor is given advice from the CBI and TUC as to what ought to be in the budget. Then when it is made public it is possible to compare what is proposed to what was suggested and record and analyse reactions. (Could be local council budget.)

h Following the possible siting of a new firm in an area like the Nissan factory. If this were to be local then it is by far easier to find out the true facts.

i Following an economic event or proposal and explaining the arguments for and against. For example, the proposal of the GLC to ban night time movement of heavy lorries in London. Or the EEC economic summit meetings in which Britain is trying to reduce budget contributions.

j An economic crisis such as the oil crisis or the 3 day week.

Remember the diary should follow an event preferably to its conclusion and you ought to explain, comment on and analyse the events in the light of your course. Local topics are always preferable and an inside contact makes all the difference.

2 The project Everyone has written at least one project in their lives and we all probably have a different idea as to what it should contain. A project at this level ought to ask a question about something which is close to you or interests you and obviously has some economic basis. One year a student whose brother had a part-time job in a garage working the petrol pumps asked the question; 'Why does 4 star petrol vary in price so much in a small area?' His inside information proved invaluable and he learnt much about pricing.

Here are some more successful projects written by students:

a Local employment—what are job prospects in a local area and why are they as they are?

b Local property prices—what affects the price of local property, the accommodation or location?

c Local shopping survey—where is it cheaper to shop, a supermarket, market or local small shop taking into account all costs?

d A local firm—pricing policy. Why do they charge certain prices? *or* location decision— why did they choose your locality. Was it a good choice? Why have local firms remained small/grown large?

e Finances of local council—why were certain cuts made, how will these effect you and your family?

f Transport—is it cheaper to rent/buy a car or to use public transport taking into account all costs?

g Population trends in the local area—what are these trends, is your population growing or declining, ageing or becoming younger, what are the implications for the provision of local services?

h Housing—in your area is it cheaper to rent or buy a house?

i Saving—where do your friends save, where would it be best for them to save?

j Does a home freezer really save money?

k How much insurance ought a newly married couple to have, how much should this cost, does it pay to shop around?

l Why has my favourite football team started advertising?

m Why did a local bus route stop?

Whichever you decide to do it should show you have found the information for yourself. This might be through a simple questionnaire or letters sent to firms, the council etc. You will find your local reference library a wonderful source of information and help. Many of the statistics in this book have been located by the staff of a local reference library. Cutting out pictures is of no great use but compiling your own graphs and tables can help to illustrate a project. Plan your work, write in complete sentences and keep a record of all that you do. Always ask if you have problems. A teacher is allowed to help you find information but is not allowed to write the project for you.

If you approach your work in this fashion you

will find out the answers to your questions, and probably be better informed on a topic than your family and teacher! At least 2 student projects helped with this book—I hope you are able to teach your teacher something! Good luck.